WORKING GIRLS

'There are only three ages for women in Hollywood: babe, district attorney and *Driving Miss Daisy*.'

Elise Eliot (Goldie Hawn) in *The First Wives Club*

How has the 'new Hollywood' responded to the 'new woman'? *Working Girls* investigates contemporary cinema's ambivalent and complex relationship with gender and sexual identities in the wake of feminism.

Tasker addresses the versions of the working woman offered by contemporary Hollywood: 'spunky' heroines of action movies such as *True Lies* and *The Long Kiss Goodnight*; female cops and FBI agents, in *The Silence of the Lambs*, *Blue Steel* and *Copycat*, the singer as movie-star, as typified by Barbra Streisand and Whitney Houston, and sharp-shooting cowgirls in 'new Westerns' such as *Bad Girls* and *The Quick and the Dead*. She also discusses the increasing prominence of women as producers and directors as well as stars and performers.

In investigating Hollywood's depictions of 'working girls', Yvonne Tasker suggests that popular cinema makes a ready equation between working women and sexual performance, from the figure of the prostitute in films such as *Klute* and *Pretty Woman*, to modern *femmes fatales* such as Linda Fiorentino in *The Last Seduction* and Demi Moore in *Disclosure*.

Yvonne Tasker is Senior Lecturer in Film and Cultural Studies at the University of Sunderland. She is the author of *Spectacular Bodies*.

WORKING GIRLS

Gender and sexuality in popular cinema

Yvonne Tasker

Routledge
Taylor & Francis Group

LONDON AND NEW YORK

First published 1998
by Routledge
2 Park Square, Milton Park, Abingdon, Oxon OX14 4RN

Simultaneously published in the USA and Canada
by Routledge
270 Madison Avenue, New York, NY 10016

Routledge is an imprint of the Taylor & Francis Group

© 1998 Yvonne Tasker

Reprinted 2000, 2002 (twice), 2004, 2005

Typeset in Galliard by
M Rules
Printed and bound in Great Britain by
Biddles Ltd, King's Lynn, Norfolk

British Library Cataloguing in Publication Data
A catalogue record for this book is available from the British Library

Library of Congress Cataloguing-in-Publication Data
Tasker, Yvonne
Working girls: Gender and sexuality in popular cinema/Yvonne Tasker
Filmography
Includes bibliographical references and index
1. Women in motion pictures.
2. Women in the motion picture industry. I. Title.

PN1995.9.W6T36 1998
791.43′652042—dc21   97-38918
ISBN 0–415–14004–8 (hbk)
ISBN 0–415–14005–6 (pbk)

IN MEMORY OF JOHN JOSEPH HALL

CONTENTS

ACKNOWLEDGEMENTS

Thanks to Rebecca Barden (once again) at Routledge for her patience and encouragement throughout this project. *Working Girls* was written across different parts of the country, whilst working in several different institutions: I would therefore like to thank colleagues and students at Goldsmiths College, Chichester Institute, Sunderland University and, particularly, those who attended the Birkbeck Diploma Class in 1993/94, and to Mary Wood for offering me the opportunity to run a course on contemporary cinema. Versions of this material have been presented as talks over the last few years. Thanks to all who have listened and contributed on these occasions, including all my Finnish friends. Sessions at the Edinburgh Film House always leave me with more than I bring, not least since Shiona Wood's enthusiasm for the cinema is so infectious. Many thanks to Patricia Pisters of Amsterdam University and to the 'Projektor' team and all the delegates at the Film[subject]theory conference.

Thanks are due to all the friends who have helped and encouraged me in writing this book and in helping me move on (and endlessly move house) including Helen De Witt, Richard Dyer, Leslie Felperin, Mel Gibson, Mike Hammond, Val Hill, Stephen Maddison, Jill Marshall, Andy Medhurst, Margaret Montgomerie, Saija Nissinen, Mike Ribbans, Bob Tasker, Estella Tincknell and Tamar Yellin. I'm also grateful to Beverley Skeggs for sharing her forthcoming work.

Finally, special thanks are due to my good friends Michele Scott and Sarah Kember, and to Rachel Hall.

The author and publisher would like to thank the following for permission to use photographs: pages 1 and 161, Touchstone; pages 7, 115 and 177, Warner Bros; page 19, Twentieth Century Fox; page 89, Monarchy Enterprises; page 137, Monarchy Enterprises, C.V. and Le Studio Canal; page 195, MGM/UA; page 205, ITC. All photographs courtesy of Kobal.

INTRODUCTION
Bad girls and working girls in the 'new Hollywood'

Angela Bassett as Tina Turner in *What's Love Got To Do With It*

Hosting the 1996 Academy Awards ceremony, Whoopi Goldberg cracked jokes about the range of roles available to women in the films produced through the preceding year: Paul Verhoeven's critically berated *Showgirls* ('I haven't seen that many poles mistreated since World War II'), Sharon Stone as gangster wife (and former prostitute) in Martin Scorsese's *Casino* (nominated), Elisabeth Shue as a prostitute in Mike Figgis' *Leaving Las Vegas* (nominated) and Mira Sorvino who won Best Supporting Actress for her role as a prostitute in Woody Allen's *Mighty Aphrodite*.[1] There is no little irony in the fact that Susan Sarandon took the Best Actress award for 1996 with her role as a nun, another indicative archetype, in *Dead Man Walking* (Tim Robbins). This was doubly ironic, perhaps, since one of Whoopi Goldberg's biggest hits of recent years was as Deloris Van Cartier, a Las Vegas lounge singer who masquerades as a nun in her flight from mobster boyfriend, Vince LaRocca (Harvey Keitel), in *Sister Act* (1992). The enthusiasm with which popular culture recycles these limitations as comedy is evident in *The First Wives Club* in which Elise Eliot (Goldie Hawn) explains to her plastic surgeon that 'there are only three ages for women in Hollywood: babe, district attorney and Driving Miss Daisy'. Goldberg's ironic barbs may serve to alert us to some immediate propositions about the status of women in contemporary American films. First, that the foregrounding of sexuality as exchange remains as central as it has ever been in the popular cinema's representation of women, with the figure of the female prostitute (whether romanticised or situated as abject) functioning in an archetypal fashion as both symbol and symptom of a gendered, classed and raced hierarchy. Further, that the prostitute is an overdetermined space within Hollywood representations. She exceeds her various incarnations of 'tart with a heart', streetwalker, flapper and so on, in the process acquiring a significance that extends beyond a literal sexual/economic exchange. The prostitute's work involves the sale of sex for cash. Across a variety of popular genres, Hollywood representation is characterised by an insistent equation between working women, women's work and some form of sexual(ised) performance. Thus the caricature or the stereotype of the prostitute, whose physical labour is manifestly bound up with sex, signifies only one point on a continuum which extends across legal thrillers and crime movies into the paranoid scenarios of office politics. The equation which popular cinema/popular culture has forged between women's work and sexual display or performance functions here as a starting point for a broader analysis of gender, class and 'race' in the contemporary cinema.

The Academy Award nominations mentioned at the beginning of this chapter do not simply indicate the persistence of various stereotypes, but also underline the extent to which they have produced some powerful and critically acclaimed performances. However, the popular cinema's constant framing of women in terms of sexuality is in turn re-framed and modified by discourses of 'race'. Whilst for white performers these stereotypes can produce major roles, such opportunities are rarer for Black women, already operating in relation to stereotypical constructions of sexuality. Ed Guerrero writes that the Hollywood cinema has depicted black sexuality 'in the most distorted and perverse terms and images', pointing as an example to 'the Black woman's routine construction as the sign of the whore' (Diawara 1993: 238). Karen Alexander writes of the relentless marginalisation of black women in Hollywood cinema in terms of both the failure to provide roles for black women stars and 'the all-pervasive bit-parts for black women as hookers' (Gledhill 1990: 52). It is in both the marginality (the bit-part) as well as the role (of prostitute) itself that the stereotypical inscription of black women in Hollywood cinema has thus been constituted. Cathy Tyson's performance as Simone in the British-made film *Mona Lisa* (1986) functions as a rare occasion when a black performer cast in the role of prostitute is able to come centre stage. The film also underlines the ambivalence of such characterisations. Whilst Tyson earned praise for her charismatic performance, her character is located within a narrative in which she signifies enigma for a white male protagonist.[2] In such a context, Alexander wonders whether 'the price of stardom in Hollywood for the black female is still too high' (Gledhill 1990: 53). The power of the performer is to bring out the complexity of a role. The power of the star lies in their ability to cut across stereotypes, since audiences already understand them in terms of their star image as much as in terms of the particular role. The opening sequence of *Fatal Beauty* (1987), for example, has undercover cop Rita Rizzoli (Whoopi Goldberg) disguised as a prostitute. As discussed in chapter four, female cops are frequently dispatched to the streets dressed as prostitutes: a reminder that they are, after all, still working girls. The device serves to demonstrate the sexism of the police (part of the narrative almost inevitably revolves around the difficulties of women's inclusion into a male space) whilst confirming that women's work is always already a kind of sexual performance. Goldberg acts her way out of this scenario through her running monologue, and through her performance which sends up not only the conventions of the crime movie but the problematic framing of female cop as prostitute. Goldberg has been the subject of controversy, criticised for the image she presents as a black woman in Hollywood and for the roles she plays. She, in turn, has talked about the problems of being too selective when a limited amount of work is offered. Within the peculiarities of the 'star system', Goldberg remains a star *despite* many of the films she has worked in, partly (but not only) through the work of performance.[3]

If the 1996 Academy Awards ceremony provides one reference point for this book, another historical marker is Jane Fonda's performance as call-girl Bree Daniel in *Klute* (Alan Pakula, 1971) for which she won Best Actress. The film mobilises the conventions of *film noir*, involving a complex investigative structure centred around woman as enigma. It may come as no surprise that the attempt to characterise an independent, working woman heroine in the early 1970s, and perhaps to refuse the *femme fatale* associated with *noir*, produces her as a prostitute (however 'high' class). Indifferent to her clients, Bree nonetheless takes pleasure and comfort in the ability she has to manipulate them. Symptomatically situated off the street, conducting her business by phone, *Klute*'s call-girl is herself a would-be actress, constructing the prostitute as aspirational, frustrated career-girl.[4] 'New *film noir*', movies which hark back to the visual style and/or the plots of the 1940s and early 1950s, has retained and redefined the *femme fatale*, herself a long-time figure of fascination for feminist film criticism. The relocation of the sexually attractive but ultimately threatening woman in the context of the workplace, as in recent films such as *Presumed Innocent* (1990), *Disclosure* (1994) or *The Last Seduction* (1993), produces a distinct inflection of the archetype, literalising/embodying the threat of male redundancy whilst retaining the association between working women and sexuality.

The prostitute, unlike the *femme fatale*, has not particularly preoccupied feminist film criticism. If the former is less redolent with transgressive connotations than the latter, both are key figures in the cinematic articulation of gendered identities in relation to constructions of independence, self-reliance and sexuality. In the concern to explore the conflation of women's bodies, sexuality and work, 'prostitution' functions as a repeated point of reference through this book. This is not only in the generalised terms of a notion of sexual exchange and exploitation, but to the extent that the role makes explicit that 'femininity' – and the prostitute's distance from it – is a raced and a classed concept. Both explaining and containing women's location in the public space of the street, prostitution provides a way of figuring class as labour for women within a cinema wary of invoking class explicitly. 'In the literature of modernity', notes Giuliana Bruno, 'the most significant female figure inhabiting the arcade is the whore. Still today, we find prostitution identified as the female version of *flânerie*: a male loiterer is a *flâneur*; the female version is a "streetwalker"' (1995: 156). The role of prostitute/'streetwalker' allows female characters not only to inhabit urban space but to flaunt it (shouting, hailing passers-by) and, perhaps, to exhibit the 'toughness' through which working-class masculinities are regularly symbolised (though just as often to be inscribed as victim/corpse). Here then the visibility of the prostitute is about status: she asserts herself within spaces from which other women are excluded, while at the same time her visibility suggests the lack of any other place to go. In Hollywood representation the female prostitute stands as equivalent to the male boxer. Both exist within a corrupt(ing) world in which they have only marginal control over their lives, with little but their physical labour to sell. Both are suffused with a certain romanticism, seemingly measured in direct relation to the damage that their work does to them and their ability to resist it. In *Mighty Aphrodite* Woody Allen renders this sentimental view comic when his character, Lenny, attempts to reform Mira Sorvino's prostitute and to pair her off with a boxer who wants to settle down on a farm.

In her analysis of Dorothy Arzner's *Working Girls* (1931), Judith Mayne notes the ambiguity of the phrase which provides the title for this book, adding that Arzner's film itself plays on 'the double meaning of "working girl", in its innocent literal sense and in its acquired sense that women who worked outside the home were morally suspect'. Ultimately, Mayne adds, 'the term "working girl" became a code for "prostitute", a suggestive elision which typifies Hollywood and indeed wider cultural representations (Mayne 1994: 95). The phrase 'working girls' provides a starting point for this investigation of gender and sexualities in contemporary popular American cinema. This is not to identify 'Hollywood' as bad object, simply as a purveyor of stereotypes, but to consider the complexities that emerge from the intersection of these terms: women, work and sexuality. 'I'm a working girl – I gotta move. I gotta do something,' concludes Whitney Houston in an interview, here using the phrase in quite another (reappropriated) sense.[5] However limiting or exploitative, the phrase 'working girls' succeeds in putting together the two terms of women and work, by implication mutually exclusive, in some awkward union. By insistently speaking this in terms of sexuality, the contemporary cinema retains both senses of the phrase identified by Mayne, such that the representation of working women almost inevitably involves an invocation of sexuality/sexual performance. None more so perhaps than the female star, already defined in terms of the body and performance.

The female performer and the star body are repeatedly framed within an opposition between glamour and beauty, the body as spectacle, and performance, the work of the actor.[6] For performers perceived largely in terms of both their physical appearance and their 'strength', transgressive or 'bad girl' roles which can offer greater possibilities, may seem more tempting than passive stereotypes. In an interview to promote *Casino*, Sharon Stone observed:

> Bad girls are more fun to play because the boundaries are so much broader. And this was a great role because the character wasn't a cliché. She couldn't be stereotypically written because she was based on someone. Before this I've been cast in quite superficial roles. Here I got to play a character with a greater range and experience.[7]

Realism (a character based on an individual), clichés, stereotypes, experience: though Stone appeals to a sense of authenticity here, many of her famous roles have been 'bad girls' in any case. These comments make sense primarily in terms of Stone's star image and in terms of an opposition between physical beauty and acting talent. Such interviews ask audiences to rethink the peculiar combination of sex and old-style Hollywood glamour that has defined her image (accrued through her performances in such movies as *Basic Instinct* (1992), *Sliver* (1993) and *The Specialist* (1994)) in terms of her work as an actor. Here Stone presents herself as bridging the opposition of sex and acting through the performance of a complex bad girl role (she followed up with a remake of *Diabolique* and a challenging role as a death row inmate in *Last Dance*, both 1996). A publicity image (opposite) for *Klute* involves

6

The work of performance: publicity still for *Klute* showing Jane Fonda 'researching and working on the streets of New York City'

a similar juxtaposition of stereotype and star. The text that accompanies the image of Jane Fonda (seen in costume but relaxed, 'herself') foregrounds the investigative work of the actor:

> Researching and working on the streets of New York City: Jane Fonda plays a high-class call-girl in *Klute* . . . Miss Fonda spent several evenings with a prostitute in pick-up bars where she was able to observe the girls, their pimps and their customers.

Fonda's association with radical politics, her growing reputation as a performer and the work of investigation (researching the role) are evoked here, working to contextualise the role of call-girl, and indeed the work of that other investigator within the film, Donald Sutherland as John Klute.[8]

If an opposition between star bodies and star performances pervades the discourses surrounding the Hollywood cinema, Demi Moore is currently aligned firmly with the former. Her reputed $12.5 million fee for *Striptease* (1996) was the subject of media comment, simultaneously making her the highest paid female star of the day and foregrounding the extent to which the success of the female star is frequently linked to a physical performance of sexuality. Demi Moore's body, which is central to many of her films (as object of exchange in *Indecent Proposal* (1993), for example), is already framed by various controversial images, such as the *Vanity Fair* cover in which she posed naked whilst pregnant, the pin-ups she posed for in drag in *Arena* or the image of her with shaved head and muscles for her role as a Navy SEAL in *G.I. Jane*. In *Striptease*, her role as a stripper is unusual precisely to the extent that it casts a star body in a part more familiar to moviegoers as the figure in the background. How many crime movies have featured a scene in which the hero goes into a striptease bar, films in which 'dispensable' women strut their stuff in the background or wind up dead like Halle Berry's Cory in *The Last Boy Scout* (1991)? By placing a stripper at the centre of its narrative, *Striptease* also functions as a commentary on the very aspect of the film that caused the most publicity. Judith Mayne notes, in a different context, that while 'it is important to recognise how thoroughly the history of Hollywood cinema has been shaped by patriarchal assumptions and sexist practices . . . it is equally important to recognize that those assumptions and practices are not absolute' (1994: 45). While Lizzie Francke's book *Script Girls* demonstrates that women have long had an unacknowledged role in the American film industry, the increased visibility of women in Hollywood in the 1990s, working not only in performance but in writing, producing and directing, is an interesting development. Both Sharon Stone and Demi Moore, like other stars (male and female) have produced their own movies, for example. The question of how to evaluate the significance of this development is related to that of how to evaluate the role of the performer. Cultural studies and film studies have rightly questioned critical approaches based on a simple understanding of authorship, looking to the meaning generation activity in which audiences engage, emphasising the provisional, context-bound nature of meaning production. Yet, as Andy Medhurst rhetorically asks in his comments on Noël Coward's screenplay for *Brief Encounter*, 'is it always a good idea to slaughter the Author?' (1991: 206). The fact of black, female, lesbian and gay film-makers, working within popular, independent and alternative production, as well as the involvement of stars in production, has resulted in different kinds of stories being told. By understanding women in Hollywood as *performers* and *producers* as well as the *product*, this book aims to open up aspects of both the restrictions and resistance to gendered representation currently at work in Hollywood fictions.

New Hollywood

The front cover of Jim Hillier's 1992 book *The New Hollywood* shows a still of Linda Hamilton as Sarah Connor in *Terminator 2* (1991), complete with shades, cigarette, muscles and a semi-automatic weapon. On the back is a still of Spike Lee as Mookie in his own film *Do the Right Thing* (1989). Both movies were independently produced, though they are rather different in both budget and tone. So the 'new Hollywood' is framed here by 'images' of a white woman with a gun and a black man who works on both sides of the camera. Hillier's book is largely devoted to an account of film-makers in the contemporary industry, his stated intention is to 'explore the ways in which the changing economic structures have affected the day-to-day experience of the people who make the products on which the industry depends' (1992: 4). This experience is contextualised within a compact and highly suggestive history of the transformation of the industry in the post-war period. Hillier's account of the 'new Hollywood' foregrounds the spaces opened up for independent production at a variety of levels including exploitation movies. This is in turn set alongside the impact of television as a training ground and as a site of production, and the new levels of involvement of black-American and women film-makers in the industry, concerns already suggested by the dust-jacket images.

The concept of 'new Hollywood' operates as a structuring framework for this book, posing as it does a distinct set of questions to do with the historical development of popular cinema, in relation to other media and in terms of the specificities of the contemporary film industry. Put simply, this framework involves posing the following question: what significance might an emerging distinction between *classical* and *post-classical* cinema have for an account of gender, sexualities and 'race' in the contemporary Hollywood cinema? The extent to which the industry has changed, and the ways in which it is has stayed the same, generate a series of possible areas of exploration. Are the critical methods and models developed in relation to the 'classic' period appropriate to the 'new Hollywood'? Or is it the case that the interaction between film studies and cultural studies is operating to ask new questions of both classical and 'new Hollywood' (and indeed early cinema)? How have changing patterns of censorship and regulation, production and exhibition impacted on gendered representation? How has popular cinema responded to concerns about the politics of representation expressed in the public arena? Has the advent of the blockbuster and the increased significance of marketing in contemporary production had consequences relevant to an analysis of gender? What is the significance of an interaction (commercial and aesthetic) between the film industry and more recent forms of media such as music video? What impact, if any, have changing patterns of employment in (and outside) the film and television industries had? What is the significance of the increased numbers of women involved in film production, for example, or of the marketing of film directors as personalities? This book is not intended to address all of the many questions that the changes which have taken place in the industry pose for an analysis of contemporary representation. None the less such questions provide a framework within which to consider the work of movies of the 1980s and 1990s and the ways in which it might be distinct.

Phrases such as the 'new Hollywood' or 'post-classical cinema' signpost shifts in both the development and conceptualisation of the popular American cinema. In brief, the term 'new Hollywood' designates two distinctive dimensions of the post-war American scene. First, the economic and organisational changes in the film industry, ostensibly triggered by the Supreme Court decision on Paramount in 1948 that required divorcement, but necessitated in any case by a post-war slump in sales against a background of fragmenting audiences and the development and widespread popularity of television. Second, the emergence of an American 'arthouse' cinema or style facilitated by new technologies, an expanding independent sector and the influence of European 'art' cinema and its 'disorienting', non-classical techniques. The late 1960s and 1970s saw the production of films characterised by nihilist or 'alternative' politics, 'incoherent' narratives, ambiguous, questioning heroes and a collapse or erosion of classical style.[9] Not all critics accept the terminology of 'new Hollywood', arguing that as much as elements of the industry, and film form itself, have changed, such changes are part of an inevitable evolution rather than a dramatic shift. The intervention by Bordwell, Staiger and Thompson has become a reference point here, with the authors' contention that the whole economic, technological and aesthetic changes said to characterise the 'new Hollywood' are best understood in terms of the flexible framework of classical norms. They insist on both the complexity and the persistence of the framework provided by classic Hollywood in terms of narrative and production management. In response to those who have argued for a distinctive aesthetic in the American cinema of the 1970s, they point to the way in which classic Hollywood has, throughout its history, typically engaged in a 'process of stylistic assimilation' (1985: 373). In different terms, pointing to the medium itself ('unique in its facility to replay and repeat its own exact form') Anne Freidberg also cautions against reading the contemporary cinema's characteristic recycling of genres from the past as new. 'From its beginning', she argues, 'the cinema has rejuvenated and replayed its own genres and narratives' (1993: 174–5).

In addition to reworking its genres and narratives the Hollywood cinema has, as Bordwell, Staiger and Thompson suggest, always responded to, fed off and appropriated the forms around it: from variety and vaudeville to theatre, music, ballet, sports, news stories and 'hot' topics of the day. Elsewhere I have suggested that the distinctiveness of the 'new Hollywood can be best understood in terms of its location within a transformed media context (Tasker 1996). Within what Jim Collins terms the 'media-saturated landscape of contemporary American culture', a landscape defined by intertextuality, the cinema (mainstream and independent) is currently informed by and responds to new and developing media and technologies, such as television, video, the music industry and music video, electronic games, comics and advertising (*Collins et al.* 1993: 243). Genres developed in the classical cinema as a response to the need to rationalise production. They have developed since in relation to the changing demands of the industry, technologies of production, distribution and consumption. Generic hybrids such as the action/romance/musical *The Bodyguard* (1992), for example, are designed to appeal to a range of audiences and capitalise on different markets. Drawing on both the musical and the music video, the movie features a hugely successful soundtrack with a reworking of Dolly Parton's 'I Will Always Love You' and two Oscar-nominated songs, 'I Have Nothing' and 'Run to You'. The film's strong musical components framed Whitney Houston's performance in her film début, while Kevin Costner's associations with action movies and (to a lesser extent) with the romance genre are also exploited. Judith Mayne (1993: 142–56) suggests in relation to *Ghost* and *Field of Dreams* that genre mixing may serve a particular function in movies that centrally involve fantasies about 'race' and difference. In this context the genre mixing within *The Bodyguard* might be understood not only in terms of industrial imperatives, but in terms of its muted articulation of an inter-racial relationship. As I argue in chapter eight, music plays a central role within the movie in articulating a set of differences (to do with 'race', gender and culture) that the film itself refuses to explicitly address. A more general point to be made here is that developments such as genre hybrids may serve *economic* concerns, within an industry defined by commercial links across different forms of production, whilst simultaneously functioning as complex cultural forms. They are not, that is, reducible to the economic formulae that give rise to them and in terms of which they are often discussed.

Changing patterns of censorship and regulation, leading up to and since the adoption of a rating system in 1968 in the US, have been shaped by different forces and have in turn produced different effects within the post-classical cinema. It is not that the effective end of the Hays Code coincident on the Supreme Court's 1948 Paramount decision meant an end to censorship of course, but that a re-formulation of what could be said and shown within the mainstream followed from that demise. Richard Randell argues that following a variety of precedents that came after the 1952 case which admitted movies to the First Amendment, obscenity quickly became the area in which censorship was legally permitted. Thus, while the popular cinema continued to avoid political controversy, high-profile censorship cases centred on the equally nebulous concepts or categories of 'obscenity' and 'art' (Balio 1976). Thomas Schatz describes an '"American film renaissance" of sorts' in the late 1960s and early 1970s, linked to a growing youth audience and a climate in which 'filmmakers were experimenting with more politically subversive, sexually explicit, and/or graphically violent material'. At the same time, a 'new' group of male film-makers received publicity and contributed to the emerging sense of an American art cinema. Thus:

> the industry saw a period of widespread and unprecedented innovation, due largely to a new 'generation' of Hollywood film-makers like Robert Altman, Arthur Penn, Mike Nichols, and Bob Rafelson, who were turning out films that had as much in common with the European art cinema as with classical Hollywood.
>
> (Schatz in Collins *et al*. 1993: 14)

In turn, as Mandy Merck has written, the Hollywood cinema shares with the European art film an interest in the eroticised portrayal of the female body. In America of the immediate post-war period Merck points out 'the French cinema, for instance, found a defense from censorship on the grounds of the "adult" and "realistic" nature of art'. Creative and commercial imperatives worked to produce, by the mid-1960s to the mid-1970s, 'an explicitly erotic form: the soft-core art film' (Brunsdon 1987: 166–7). The (re)inscription of female (and indeed, male) bodies in the post-classical cinema has been in different terms than the classical cinema, though this itself has operated in terms of the division of the market into blockbuster, arthouse and other categories. The exploration of 'new *film noir*' in Chapter six indicates that the equation of an explicit portrayal of sexual matters (typically touching on taboo topics) with the connotations of 'art' frames the contemporary *femme fatale*, post the Production Code and post-feminism.

The innovative American cinema of the 1970s produced what Charlotte Brunsdon describes as 'a cycle of films . . . which bear the traces of feminist struggles elsewhere, even if it is only in the attempt to capitalise on a discernible new audience: the modern women' (1987: 119). Brunsdon's collection of essays *Films for Women* brings out the extent to which movies of the 1970s and early 1980s, such as *Girlfriends* (1978), *Julia* (1977), *Mahogany* (1975), *Gloria* (1980) or *Lianna* (1982), have proved problematic for film and cultural critics, operating as they do within a commercial cinema (studio or independent) informed by feminist ideas, and in the case of *Mahogany*, black political discourses. As Richard Dyer writes of the latter, the strategy of appealing to 'more than one audience looks like box-office sense' but involves the film drawing on 'values and sensibilities that can only tortuously be reconciled' (Brunsdon 1987: 132). Where commercial movies seek to package and commodify marginalised groups and experiences it is, for Dyer, both a territorial claim and a recognition of sorts. The contemporary articulation of 'strong women' in terms of an aggressive sexuality involves a particular kind of objectification and display, one that also picks up on mainstream 'post-feminist' discourses. In her discussion of *Lianna*, Mandy Merck suggests that 'if lesbianism hadn't already existed, art cinema might have invented it' (Brunsdon 1987: 166). For her, the film's use of lesbianism represents an intersection of sorts of the political concerns of American independent cinema and the erotic economy of the art cinema. In an analogous fashion the 'designer dykes' of *Basic Instinct* or *Bound* (1996) bring together an arty *noir* style in a simultaneous articulation and exploitation of lesbian desire. Like *Desert Hearts* (1985) some years later, questions concerning the extent to which movies such as *Lianna*, which clearly show lesbian characters, can be read as lesbian films pose anew the terms of an awkward appropriation. In framing the lesbian imagery deployed in contemporary media from 'new Hollywood' movies to popular music and television, we can point not only to the mainstream cinema's appropriation of the techniques of European art cinema or heterosexual pornography, but of the existence of different kinds of mainstream, narrative movies made by lesbians, with *Thin Ice* (1995) and *Go Fish* (1994) two recent examples, or even Donna Deitch's reappropriation of the terms of the Hollywood romance in *Desert Hearts*.[10]

Randell's account of the development of post-war discourses around censorship indicates the consolidation of distinctions between private and public consumption – distinctions which have in the intervening period become, if anything, more controversial with the availability of technologies of production and distribution such as home video playback, camcorders, pay-per-view and the Internet (Balio 1976). The near-future scenario portrayed in Kathryn Bigelow's *Strange Days* (set on New Year's Eve, 1999) feeds off the uncertainties surrounding new technologies and the possibility of not only 'recording' experiences but producing them as commodities.

Of all the factors that have transformed the post-war film industry in America, the success of television as a domestic medium in the 1950s, and the more recent proliferation of cable channels, is the most obvious in its impact. Critics agree that the industry moved fairly rapidly from competition to co-operation with the new media (Balio 1990; Hillier 1992). Television's function as a major channel for the transmission of films has been heightened via the allied technology of home video. Both networks and cable channels have also done much to facilitate production, as has Channel 4 in the United Kingdom. Though the significance of television as an outlet for feature films far from exhausts the significance of the medium, it continues to be regarded as the low-culture arm of the entertainment business, despite the occasional product which is hailed as exceptional. Interesting for its industrial patterns of ownership and for its potential influence, but not in terms of the texts that it produces, television is perhaps too transient for a critical practice (film studies) concerned with detail and still, implicitly, with value enshrined in the great work. As Jim Hillier observes, whilst 'many writers and directors (and others) are employed in television as well as film at some point in their careers, their television work often remains, if not hidden, at least not much spoken about' (1992: 99).

As a training ground and outlet for women involved in production and performance, television has, perhaps ironically, given its advertiser-led conservatism, opened up the industry to new forms and new voices. Director Penny Marshall, who moved from television performer (as Laverne in the comedy series *Laverne and Shirley*, which ran from 1976 to 1983) to television director to film director, is not alone in having her first experience of directing within television.[11] The medium has also provided opportunities for comics who, as Frank Krutnik notes, are marginalised within the film industry such as Roseanne Barr, for example (Karnick and Jenkins 1995). Citing Tracy Chapman, Alice Walker and Oprah Winfrey as examples, Karen Alexander contrasts the limited place for the black female star in Hollywood cinema with the women who have 'found a place in media over which she can win greater control: in music, in writing, in television even' (Gledhill 1990: 54). Oprah Winfrey's pre-eminence in her role as talkshow host is only one part of her involvement in and across media. She functioned as both executive producer for and performer in the 1989 television production of *The Women of Brewster Place*, for example.[12] In turn, music video, which has itself provided opportunities for creative work, has also brought a mainstream visibility for black women performers such as Janet Jackson. Music video has developed and deployed rapid editing techniques which appropriate and juxtapose images from diverse sources. It has also both showcased and framed the star personas of such performers as Madonna, who has attracted attention for her use of challenging imagery around the terms of sexuality, race and identity. Music video, like advertising on which it draws, has lent itself to the development of visual images of powerful women that imply a narrative context whilst not necessarily 'needing', as the Hollywood cinema so often does, to explain away their presence. In turn, the images and visual style deployed in music video has fed into the mainstream cinema itself.

The process whereby small-screen formats feed into cinema production is also evident in the crime genre, for example. Though high profile films such as *The Silence of the Lambs* (1991) and *Copycat* (1995) with big name stars in lead roles signal a shift in the cinematic portrayal of female investigators, this has very much been in the wake of television, with such police/investigative series as *Charlie's Angels* in the 1970s, *Cagney and Lacey* in the 1980s and *The X Files* in the 1990s, offering distinctive formulations of the role.[13] In turn, of course, television movies reflect cinema successes. Based on 'actual events', as is so often the case with TV movies, the CBS production *In the Company of Darkness* (1993) casts Helen Hunt as an undercover cop whose investigation of a murder case involves her in an exploration of her own past. Directed by David Anspaugh, who has worked as producer and director on both *Hill Street Blues* and *Miami Vice*, the film owes its opening sequence fairly directly to Kathryn Bigelow's *Blue Steel*, but operates within the combination of docu-drama, crime story and melodrama so distinctive to the television film. Laurie Schulze has argued that the made-for-television movie represents a distinct and interesting form with its own aesthetic and its own star system. She regards the generic location of the made-for-television movie in melodrama as contributing to a dismissive critical reception for the form, despite the range of social issues with which the TV movie deals. In their analysis of *The Women of Brewster Place*, Jacqueline Bobo and Ellen Seiter (1991) also argue that

14

a reluctance to engage with television at all, and particularly melodramatic forms, has resulted in the neglect of work that would repay analysis in its own terms and could serve to contextualise the more usual objects of feminist film studies.

Critics of the television movie, argues Schulze, have focused on the way in which the personalised and family-based stories 'de-politicise' the issues described and narrativised. Whilst Schulze agrees that the TV movie tends to offer family-based solutions for the 'problems' that it outlines, she also draws attention to the space opened up for female stars (and audiences) through its often melodramatic address. Thus 'TV movies are one of the few prime-time programming forms that permit a woman's story to be the story being told' (Balio 1990: 368). *Buffalo Girls* (1995), the epic CBS production discussed in Chapter two, stars Anjelica Huston as Calamity Jane and Melanie Griffith as her friend Dora. The television format allows the story to produce a version of the 'Wild West' through a focus on these two women's stories and their friendship.[14] And while Schulze acknowledges that the narrative form of the television movie tends to situate the ideological issues it opens up within a traditional version of the family, she also contends that:

> In its search for ratings through the controversial, the TV movie frequently brings the socially marginalized – women, people of color, gays and lesbians, the working class, the homeless and unemployed, the victims – onto popular terrain. Despite critical charges that it does so only to domesticate or depoliticize social issues or emerging ideologies, the TV movie may very well, for some audiences, make a space for progressive or even radical perceptions of the conflicts and fault-lines in American culture.
>
> (Balio 1990: 371)

For Schulze, critics of the form 'seem to underestimate both the essential contradictoriness of the TV movie and the audience's role in actively making meanings and pleasures from popular texts' (ibid.:371–2). Just as the family may typically offer a solution in the television movie, it is also typically defined as a problem to be negotiated in relation to issues of sexuality, for example. While network television has developed the made-for-television movie as a distinct form, Jim Hillier identifies a changing attitude on the part of directors towards movies made for cable, increasingly perceived as 'an opportunity to work on more offbeat material'. Cable companies will, he suggests, take on projects 'considered too uncommercial and, in some cases, too controversial, for features' in part because they 'are anxious to attract well-known names'. *The Last Seduction*, which was made for cable, subsequently achieved a theatrical release and international success, whilst Tamra Davis' *Guncrazy* (1992) was made for cinema but was first shown on cable TV. In the case of HBO, Hillier notes that the company 'actually wants to take risks, since its product differentiation is precisely to be different from studio projects' (1992: 118–99). This type of division of the territory, through which cinema (itself divided into different sectors), network and cable television are associated primarily with different kinds of output, is a characteristic of the contemporary situation.

The high profile NBC production, *Serving in Silence: The Margarethe Cammermeyer Story* (1994), for which Glenn Close won an Emmy in the title role, is an interesting example. Close executive-produced with Barbra Streisand, a factor which aided publicity for the project and gave it further potential within the video rental market. Constrained to some extent by its explicit basis on a particular individual and actual events, the film tells the story of a colonel who sues the military after being discharged on the basis of her sexuality. The script involves the rehearsal of statistics and arguments about 'issues' (both acceptance of homosexuality in the army and in a wider sense) which characterises the television movie. As the closing credits come up we are given an update on both Cammermeyer and her battle to change the law. This use of text and dialogue to air issues ties the television movie to the documentary or the docu-drama, associated primarily with television, and in turn provides a mark of distinction from the theatrical feature. The soundtrack over the closing images is of Cammermeyer's speech to a gay pride rally, anchored initially by the image of her father watching on television at home and then generalising outwards as an address to 'you' (i.e. to heterosexuals). At other points, the movie engineers encounters in which Cammermeyer (Close) and her partner Diane (Judy Davis) talk issues and anxieties over with Cammermeyer's four sons. In such instances the story of Cammermeyer's awareness of her lesbianism and her developing relationship with Diane is repeatedly framed (and explained) within the family and an insistence on her normality, an insistence that is presumably directed at heterosexual viewers. This framing suggests the kind of contradictory address Schulze identifies in the television movie more broadly, both admitting groups marginalised elsewhere whilst simultaneously addressing a conventional notion of the social norm. The fact that Jonathan Demme's big-screen success *Philadelphia* (1993) also mobilised this address in tackling discrimination (complete with footage of the supportive family), indicates that the strategy is not only associated with the small screen. Watching *Serving in Silence*, it is the contradictory desire to tell a 'controversial' story and to retain a 'mainstream' address that is striking; both the warmth and complexity of the love relationship that develops between the two women, and the fact that they share only one kiss at the close of the film. It is an exploration of a lesbian relationship framed within the institution of the family. With its concern for the family, its focus on a disciplined and conservative woman who is pictured in terms of tradition (as an American soldier, good mother and so on), the movie is far removed from the trendiness of Queer Cinema. Yet it produces meaning within a context that precisely contains a diversity of representations. Its use of cinema stars within a small-screen format, indeed the use of star power to get the story told at all, indicates something of the relationship between the two media and the specificities of both small screen and big screen which in turn contextualises the 'new Hollywood' cinema.

Cultural studies has developed critical approaches to popular media which acknowledge how provisional meaning is, how it is produced and reproduced across a variety of contexts. Cultural criticism that aims to produce a political evaluation of popular culture tends, as Richard Dyer has observed, to end up nowhere definite, describing popular phenomenon as having both oppositional and hegemonic potential. For Dyer, this is not necessarily a failure of cultural studies, but an indication of the fundamental ambivalence of cultural products.[15] In relation to the stereotype of the gay man as 'sad young man' Dyer argues that 'stereotypes can be both a complex and a formative mode of representation':

> We are accustomed to thinking of them as simple, repetitive, boring and prejudiced group images which, should they supposedly be about ourselves we angrily reject. We mistake their simplicity of formal means (a few broadly drawn, instantly identifiable signs endlessly repeated) and evident ideological purpose (to keep/put out-groups in their place) for a simplicity of connotation and actual ideological effect. What interests me in looking here at the gay man as sad young man is the way a stereotype can be complex, varied, intense and contradictory, an image of otherness in which it is still possible to find oneself.
>
> (Dyer 1993: 73–4)

Equally, this is not to say that *all* stereotypes are involved in such intensity or complexity. Nor that 'we' identify with either textual pleasures or stereotypes in some complete way. Identification after all is typically partial (selective in Dyer's phrase) and also depends on who 'we' are. Critics such as Judith Mayne (1993) and Carol Clover have explored the mobility of identification, with Clover exploring the implications of male viewers of the slasher film caught up in identification 'not just with screen females, but with screen females in the horror-film world, screen females in fear and pain' (1992: 5).

Work such as Laurie Schulze's analysis of the television movie situates the form within a context of production and reception, asking critics to look beyond a literal reading of popular cultural artefacts in terms of both the complexity of the texts themselves and of the range of possible responses. This is suggestive of a critical movement towards a more thorough-going critical engagement with, rather than dismissal of, not only popular mainstream cinema, but with what Carol Clover terms 'low film culture'. Her detailed investigation of the 'female victim-hero' in the modern horror film indicates not only that the operation of gendered discourses in the form is complex, but that many of the narrative devices showcased in big-budget movies are prefigured in the slasher films that exist, 'for all practical purposes beyond the purview of legitimate criticism' (1992: 43). If 'legitimate criticism' is to make sense of the developments in popular cinema, this may involve looking at the other media with which it intersects and on which it draws: from the television movie to stand-up comedy and music video.

1

CROSS-DRESSING, ASPIRATION AND TRANSFORMATION

Cross-class dresser: Tess McGill (Melanie Griffith) in *Working Girl*

'Just act like you belong' Tess McGill tells Jack Trainer (Harrison Ford) in Mike Nichols' *Working Girl* (1988) as they crash a 'society' wedding in pursuit of a business deal. Tess, played by Melanie Griffith, spends most of the film dressing up (in borrowed clothes) and acting as if she belongs. The 'imposture' both allows and necessitates her movement from white, working-class community to a middle management position in a New York company, though she clearly belongs absolutely in neither space. A critical and a commercial success, *Working Girl* is a sharp romantic comedy in which the heroine's ability to manipulate costume and other aspects of her physical and social performance (hair, voice, mannerisms) reminds us that cross-dressing isn't only an issue of gender, but also one of class. Or rather, the film underscores the extent to which these terms inform and give meaning to each other. For feminist criticism, the potential transgression of categories of *gendered* identity within and through cross-dressing holds an evident appeal, identified by Annette Kuhn in terms of a foregrounding of 'the socially constructed nature of sexual difference' such that 'what appears natural . . . reveals itself as artifice' (1985: 49). Subtly suggestive of transgression, of the erosion of boundaries rather than crass opposition or binary logic, the appeal of cross-dressing imagery can be further situated within 'queer theory', with its characteristic delight in the gender-fuck and its passionate, political challenge to binary conceptions of identity.[1] Movies such as *Working Girl* serve to reinforce Marjorie Garber's thesis that the separation of gendered dress codes (and their transgression) from discourses of class, race, ethnicity and sexuality produces only a partial understanding of cross-dressing and its cultural significance (Garber 1992). Garber's analysis of transvestism in the context of what such critics as Gail Ching-Liang Low (1989, 1996) have called 'cultural cross-dressing' (with T.E. Lawrence an exemplary figure) and her location of the theatrical cross-dresser in relation to traditions of, for example, minstrelsy, suggest the extent to which these different hierarchical discourses are inter-related. To reduce the analysis of cross-dressing to gender then, is to remove it from a complex historical relationship to constructions of race, class and sexuality and to particular lesbian, gay and trans-gender identities (drag, butch, femme). In turn, a narrow focus on the signifiers of gender neglects the extent to which narratives

21

of gendered cross-dressing often involve other kinds of transgression. Lola Young's discussion of *The Crying Game* (1992) and of reviewers' responses to it, for example, indicates how a discussion of race and nationality is sidestepped by the movie which 'self-consciously presents us with a disruption of sexual binarism whilst evading and failing to address racial binarisms' (Kirkham and Thumin 1995: 284). For Young, the attention paid to the 'shock' revelation that Dil (Jaye Davidson) is anatomically male was, for reviewers at least, at the cost of any discussion of the inter-racial relationship between Fergus (Stephen Rea) and Dil or the significance of the relationships between Dil and black British soldier Jody (Forest Whitaker), or Jody and Fergus in terms of either race or nationality.

For Christine Holmlund the butch clone and the femme lesbian, together with the passing black, are figures who are connected to 'resistance and power' through a refusal of the body as 'truth' (Cohan and Hark 1993: 219). Though acutely aware of the ambivalence of these identities/performances, she contrasts the familiar anxious masquerade addressed by feminist critics with the potential for pleasure that is located in both the cinematic and the social performance of identities, a process that might in turn open up the contradictions of hierarchical systems of gender and race. Elsewhere Jane Gaines has written of 'the radical possibilities of what might be called spectatorial cross-dressing', addressing the mobility of identification that is invited by the cinema (Gaines and Herzog 1990: 25). Popular texts offer both the powerful and the disempowered (though on quite different terms) a relatively risk-free identification with an other or series of others. The cinema produces fictionalised and fantasised versions of cultural identities. The cinematic spectator's participation in a proffered transgression is quite different from the account of public identification offered by Marjorie Garber in her discussion of transvestite and transsexual experience, one in which:

> The 'men's room' problem is really a challenge to the way . . . cultural binarism is read. . . . The public restroom appears repeatedly in transvestite accounts of passing in part because it so directly posits the binarism of gender (choose either one door or the other) in apparently inflexible terms, and also (what is really part of the same point) because it marks a place of taboo.
>
> (Garber 1992: 14)

The risks that cross-dressers take and the decisions made here are surely different from those taken by an audience in breathless moments of identification which are nonetheless (relatively) safe. Thus the specificity of the lives of drag queens (and kings), of transvestites and transsexuals are quite distinct from the fantasy space of the cinema. Without producing an artificial distinction between two separate spaces, one termed 'cinema', the other the 'social', it is important to consider the specificity of cinematic cross-dressing. If it is a commonplace that entertainment is escapist, that the pleasures of popular cinema lie in being transported elsewhere, Richard Dyer (1977) has attempted to codify the spaces into which audiences are taken and the needs that this might address. In attempting to specify the stuff of which the utopian aspects of popular cinema consists, Dyer stresses the experiential and the visceral aspects of 'our' response. Two recent movies involving drag are indicative here. Both *To Wong Foo Thanks for Everything, Julie Newmar* (1995) and *The Birdcage* (1996) work out their concerns around heterosexuality in terms of a fantasy opposition in which gay men and drag function as cyphers for some notion of 'liberation' set against stereotypical figures of repression (the small town, the Republican senator). To say that these movies are primarily about heterosexuality isn't to either dismiss them or to exhaust them, but to look at them in terms of the fantasies that they speak to. What they share with most of the movies discussed in this chapter is a desire for, pleasure in and anxiety around transformation which is signified through costume.

Cross-dressing: Class, sexual and national identities

For audiences who are not explicitly addressed by the mainstream cinema, questions of interpretation and the nuances of performance become significant. In this context Andrea Weiss discusses a process of 'reading in' on the part of the lesbian spectator of a classical cinema that kept lesbian desire implicit. A grainy image of Marlene Dietrich in trademark top hat, white tie and tails, provides the cover image for Weiss' 1992 study, *Vampires and Violets: Lesbians in the Cinema*. Dietrich's cross-dressed image evokes the sexual ambiguity so central to her star persona. Weiss elaborates on the way in which Dietrich's image could be constructed by spectators in relation to extra-textual rumour (rumours of Dietrich's affairs with women). She explores in some detail the moment in *Morocco* when a tuxedo-clad Amy Jolly/Dietrich admires and then kisses a woman in the club where she works, before transferring her attention to the male. Weiss argues the moment is not simply recuperated, in part since the signification of *costume* as well as action and star image works against the construction of Dietrich within the codes of a manageable, heterosexual femininity. 'Her costume', notes Weiss 'the tuxedo, is invested with power derived both from maleness and social class.' In contrast to Tom Brown (Gary Cooper): 'she is momentarily able to transcend both class and gender. Such an escape from societal limitations can be seductive for all viewers, male and female; for lesbian viewers it was an invitation to read into the image their own desire for transcendence' (1992: 35).

One of the most recognisable images of female-to-male cross-dressing in the world of entertainment is that of the female star body clothed in male evening dress: an image associated with cabaret stars such as Josephine Baker, and with stars of the 'classic' cinema such as Dietrich. This image is in turn reprised by Julie Andrews in the title role(s) of Blake Edwards cross-dressing musical, *Victor Victoria* (1982). The (northern) European associations of Dietrich's star image are echoed and modified in the Parisian setting of *Victor Victoria* aligning this 'aristocratic' variant of the female-to-male cross-dresser with European decadence, constructed throughout in opposition to American directness and simplicity (or sometimes, it is implied, vulgarity). Julie Andrews as Victor is an impersonator in terms of gender, sexuality, class and nationality (masquerading as s/he is as a male, gay, East European aristocrat). Both *Victor Victoria* and the cabaret image of the eroticised, tuxedo-clad, female star on which it draws, generate meaning not only in relation to gender and sexuality, but in relation to class, ethnic and national identities. In her comments on Josephine Baker, star of the period within which Edwards' movie is set, Garber notes how the occasional stage adoption of 'white tie and tails' was only one aspect of a thorough-going involvement with transvestism such that '[s]he seems to have found herself – or to have been found – almost constantly in contiguity with cross-dressing'. As a black American in Paris, and as 'an occasion for the theatricalization of scandal and transgressiveness' Baker orchestrated her image and her performances across different kinds of cross-dressing (1992: 279). Class and gender are foregrounded when Sarah Collins (Whoopi Goldberg) dons a ritzy black tux (complete with country and western-style bow tie) for the final competition scenes in her made-for-cable, romantic comedy poolroom movie *Kiss Shot* (1989). Her tuxedo signifies more than the sense of formality about the occasion, marking her transgression in gender terms. Early on we learn that Sarah's father has rejected her after the birth of her daughter. Yet if this grieves her, she remains a strong figure. In order to make money Sarah becomes a 'poolroom hustler', operating in opposition to a competitive male world throughout the movie. This transformation is actually a sort of rediscovery of the skills of her youth, a talent she 'remembers', following a strained visit to her distanced parents, whilst putting on a show for her daughter. The final match involves a battle of wills with her opponent, playboy/millionaire ex-boyfriend Kevin (Dorian Harewood). Sarah is playing to save her home for herself and her daughter, whereas he is playing just for the hell of it. The differences (class/wealth/gender) between them are both signalled and bridged through their (evening) dress as well as through the performance of the game itself.

If the Hollywood cinema has tended to sidestep any *explicit* address to class, it is nonetheless the case that the signifiers of class and of 'race' with which it is entwined are a constant presence, evident in a weight of unspoken assumptions and coded signs that are bound up with, but not reducible to gender and sexuality. Beverley Skeggs has argued that for working-class women, white and black, femininity can be understood as a costume or as a mode of performance that somehow does not fit. When put on it seems excessive, gaudy or parodic. For Skeggs this is no surprise since discourses of femininity have developed in and through the historical process of inscribing the difference of middle-class women in an industrialising society and a changing economy. Thus she argues that:

> Working-class women were coded as inherently healthy, hardy and robust (whilst also paradoxically as a source of infection and disease) against the physical frailty of middle-class women. They were also involved in forms of labour that prevented femininity from ever being a possibility. For

working-class women femininity was never a given (as was sexuality); they were not automatically positioned by it in the same way as middle and upper-class White women. Femininity was always something which did not designate them precisely. Working-class women – both Black and White – were coded as the sexual and deviant other against which femininity was defined.[2]

The extent to which femininities and masculinities are always already positions inscribed in terms of class and 'race' becomes apparent in a consideration of popular film images in relation to work, to labour and the bodies/costumes that this produces. Gender and class, that is, can be productively brought together around a notion of *work*, partially since labour is a defining term in both discourses. Manual labour defines a *gendered class position* just as much as genteel (indeed, gentile) femininity defines a *classed gender role*. Though the world of work is only rarely represented in popular cinema in terms of its mundanities (routine, repetition), an implicit or explicit reference to the status bestowed by work (or the lack of it) is nonetheless ever present, displaced into overdetermined signifiers of costume, speech or gesture. The populist rhetoric through which a classless notion of 'the people' has been constituted by American politicians and film-makers, has tended to imagine the proletariat as a male underclass. Male groups who are defined in terms of 'race' and ethnicity, such as Italian, Cuban or African-Americans, and situated literally on the street have come to signify 'class'. Sometimes suffused with nostalgia, their separateness is represented in terms of ethnically understood custom and ritual rather than work (labour) or, more precisely work as ritual in the most stereotypical form of gangster groupings with their elaborate and exclusive membership and rules of behaviour.[3] For women, as we've seen, entry into this space tends to involve a sexualised form of criminality: signified in the figure of the 'streetwalker'. If women tend to be marginalised within both gangster/gangsta narratives, the importance of dressing the part, of a physical, verbal and costumed performance within the context of the male group, remains central.

The successful horror hybrid *The Silence of the Lambs* foregrounds processes of transformation, offering a parallel between its two central cross-dressers, the serial killer Buffalo Bill who is producing a grotesque body suit from the flayed flesh of his female victims, and Clarice Starling (played by Jodie Foster), the cross-class cross-dresser who pursues him. Two types of cross-dressing: one extolled in a heroic character, the other pathologised in the monstrous figure of the killer. Starling's transformation, her ascent through the ranks of the FBI, is predicated on her discovery of Bill's predilection. Ultimately sidelined within the institution of law enforcement, left hanging on the phone by boss and mentor Jack Crawford, Starling's (intuitive) recognition of another cross-dresser leads her to the prize (advancement). As Elizabeth Young notes, the film's 'theorizing of gender as costume runs parallel to its recognition that class can be transformed by clothing: thus Clarice's self-fashioning materially represents her class ascension to professional career woman' (1991: 26). In their first interview, Clarice's sinister mentor, psychoanalyst and serial killer Hannibal Lecter, discerns immediately the history behind her dress, the contradiction between her 'good bag' and her 'cheap shoes'. Lecter taunts her with his cynical rendition of her personal history: an attempt to shed an embarrassing accent, to adopt the guise of the professional working woman:

> You're so ambitious aren't you? You know what you look like to me, with your good bag and your cheap shoes? You look like a rube, a well-scrubbed, hustling rube with a little taste. Good nutrition's given you some length of bone, but you're not more than one generation away from poor white trash – are you Agent Starling? And that accent you've tried so desperately to shed – pure West Virginia. What is your father dear – is he a coal miner? Does he stink of the land? And oh how quickly the boys found you – all those tedious, sticky fumblings in the back seats of cars, while you could only dream of getting out, getting any-where, getting all the way to the F-B-I?

In both *The Silence of the Lambs* and the earlier *Manhunter* (1986), Lecter's malevolent professional abilities are defined in terms of an intuition that allows him to identify and manipulate the weaknesses of his captors. For Starling this is her class/ethnic location, and the desire to escape it which makes it intolerable.

There is a particularity here which speaks of class and status in localised ways as well as the specificity of West Virginia and what it may mean for an international as well as a domestic audience (poor white trash). That origin provides a way of signalling more than poverty, suggesting the backward values of an uneducated people. More than an observation made in passing, the above exchange is marked as a moment of significance within the film: the music swells under Lecter's (Anthony Hopkins) 'actorly' delivery, his face intercut with Starling's so as to render the pain of recognition clear. Starling's ability to identify with ambition, and with the desire to be something other than what one is, ultimately enables her to find the killer. Yet she is different from the self-destructive, emphathising hero of Thomas Harris' novel *Red Dragon* and Michael Mann's *Manhunter* (also tor-mented by Lecter's insights) since Clarice Starling is a cross-class cross-dresser. Her cross-dressing is not played for comedy. It is subtle, nuanced: one part of her transformation, and of the broader 'rites-of-passage' narrative that the movie enacts. Her transformation through costume and through work is suggestive. For women in the cinema, cross-dressing is almost always about status – something which is doubly apparent when we understand femininity itself as a class position, one from which many women are excluded. In this context ambition, like desire or need, is unequivocally inscribed as 'unfeminine'.

Genres of cross-dressing

In her analysis of gendered cross-dressing narratives, which she terms 'films involving sexual disguise', Annette Kuhn suggests two broad generic locations: the musical comedy and the thriller. In these instances, she argues, not only does gendered cross-dressing become a source of comedy or of horror, but generic conventions offer particular ways in which to naturalise (or explain away) the activity of cross-dressing itself. Within the musical comedy, Kuhn suggests that cross-dressing is rendered plausible in terms of 'the work ethic and the necessity for economic survival', whilst within the thriller cross-dressing 'is naturalised through discourses on sexual deviance, psychopathology and criminality' (1985: 59). Though this does not provide an inclusive definition of cross-dressing as it is used here, excluding screwball and other non-musical comedies (*Working Girl, Mrs Doubtfire*), Westerns (*The Ballad of Little Jo*) and romantic dramas (*Up Close and Personal*), Kuhn's observation can be usefully adapted to identify two distinct narrative dynamics deployed in films which articulate cross-dressing across categories of gender, 'race' and class. The first is to do with transformation, whilst the second concerns a desire for knowledge. If the need to work operates as an 'excuse' for gendered cross-dressing in movies such as *Victor Victoria*, in which Andrews' character faces starvation or prostitution, it is also precisely cross-dressing which facilitates a movement from a context of privation to one in which needs are (provisionally) satisfied. Comedies and musicals offer generic pleasures of excess, spectacle and the possibility of change/escape, a context within which an imagery of cross-dressing articulates the precarious persistence of sexual and racial binaries.

Straight or gay, films of male to female cross-dressing (*Mrs Doubtfire, To Wong Foo Thanks for Everything, Julie Newmar, The Birdcage*), and of working-class women cross-class dressing (*Working Girl, Pretty Woman*) share a delight in sequences of transformation, enacting visually as well as narratively a process of 'becoming something other' that is conducted through/over the star body. Typically represented through montage sequences with an upbeat soundtrack, transformation is offered as cinematic spectacle that takes place, like the numbers in Hollywood musicals, in a space to one side of the narrative. The popular cinema has a tendency to minimise dialogue during moments of intensity – in scenes of action, horror or romance, for example. These are moments when words will simply not suffice, because what is offered seems unspeakable (in whichever sense) or because only clichés are available. The recurrence of sequences and images of transformation – typically showing performers as 'between', embodying both and neither of the characters that they play – are simultaneously awkward and fascinating. The pleasure and danger of such images indicate a structure of disavowal which bridges a delight in transformation and a sense in which the narrative seeks to reveal who the cross-dresser *really* is (or to suggest that such a truth exists). Of course disavowal also involves acknowledging the presence of the very thing or desire that its operation seeks to distance.

The presence of same-sex desire is perhaps the most obvious casualty here, raised in comic fashion to be quickly dismissed, just as the possibility of older women being sexually active is acknowledged and ridiculed in the misrecognised 'moms' of *Tootsie* and *Mrs Doubtfire*.

The desire for knowledge, a movement towards discovery or revelation involved in cross-dressing narratives is at least potentially more sinister, and to some extent sadistic. It is the tension between these two dynamics that generates comedy, pleasure and suspense within cross-dressing narratives. As with other comedies of cross-dressing, or more broadly of impersonation, there is an exhilaration to Tess McGill's series of successful transformation scenes in *Working Girl* – a sense of triumph that she has somehow got away with it. Yet in the Hollywood cinema 'passing', acting as if you belong across different social contexts, is also bound up with pain, associated as it is with a fear of discovery and exposure, but also with a loss of identity. Here is a classical narrative economy: loss, pain and violence on one side, pleasure and exhilaration on the other. In terms of narrative development, passing produces both mystery or suspense and a sense of transgression which may unsettle. It is no surprise therefore that cross-dressing features in both romantic comedy and the thriller or horror film. Julia Roberts appears briefly in drag in *Sleeping with the Enemy* (1991), a disguise she adopts to avoid detection by her violent husband. Here a fear of detection is related to the thriller rather than to comic anticipation. Yet this is only one of several 'dressing up' scenes in the film. During her marriage, Laura (Roberts) dresses to cover her bruises. Here dress is also a site of fear and trepidation: will she pick the right thing to wear (the husband's power is expressed in one instance through his choice of her dress for the evening)? Living under the name of Sara, her delight in her new identity and new love is signified by a montage sequence of Roberts in a whole series of different costumes. Her new beau Ben (Kevin Anderson) has taken her backstage into a magic world where dressing up is a source of pleasure.[4] No little irony then that it is also Ben, a drama teacher, who provides her with a moustache from his make-up kit. Though not a cross-dressing film, *Sleeping with the Enemy* is a thriller about the central character's transformation from victim to victor. Roberts in male drag offers one of the few truly perverse moments in this heroic tale of 'one woman's escape' from domestic violence, and from her victimised role, via the auspices of a kinder, gentler male lover. Indeed the moment represents a nice inversion of convention as Roberts visits her little-old-lady mother and avoids her psychotic, hetero husband through the adoption of male disguise. This in contrast to the more usual horror scenario of *Psycho*-style, cross-dressing mummy's boys.[5]

The cross-dresser is involved in complex narratives of belonging and exclusion relating to the categories that they transgress. In this way narratives of transformation emphasise a lack of place. In *Working Girl*, Tess McGill finds herself caught between the two worlds of monied middle-class finance and of working-class community. Heterosexual romance offers to bridge these worlds – providing a magical solution to the isolation of the individual achiever. And yet at the film's conclusion neither Tess, who approaches her new job tentatively, nor Trainer, her new love, seem secure. If heterosexual romance provides a sort of ending, the figure of the cross-dresser nonetheless remains troubling. Garber construes this sense of something left uncontained as a type of 'third' term, one which remains to trouble and disrupt binary systems:

> One of the most important aspects of cross-dressing is the way in which it offers a challenge to easy notions of binarity, putting into question the categories of 'female' and 'male', whether they are considered essential or constructed, biological or cultural. The current popularity of cross-dressing as a theme in art and criticism represents, I think, an undertheorised recognition of the necessary critique of binary thinking, whether partic-ularized as male and female, black and white, yes and no, Republican and Democrat, self and other, or in any other way.
>
> (Garber 1992: 10–11)

However, Garber is also clear that her third 'term' is not a term in any fixed sense, functioning instead to delineate 'a mode of articulation, a way of describing a space of possibility' (ibid.). Cinematic cross-dressers operate in transition, articu-lating the instability of the categories that they inhabit, marking out the possibility of an alternative space that remains ill-defined. Whether comically or brutally rendered, the 'revelation' that the cross-dresser is not what s/he seems generates responses from laughter to rejection or violence (or the threat of it). Some small detail of dress or performance inevitably gives the game away ('that's no dame'), a revelation which brings a host of other assumptions and meanings into play.[6] Yet as Garber suggests, moments of revelation do not somehow simply 'undo' the potentiality that the cross-dresser both signifies and produces.

Carl Franklin's *Devil in a Blue Dress* (1995) opens with T-Bone Walker singing his 'West Side Baby' who lives 'way across town'. Set in Los Angeles in 1948, the film operates across a city space that is divided and defined by hierarchies of 'race' and class. A period piece, the film is also a reinscription of 1940s *film noir* in terms of black America. To some extent it is also a reinscription of and ironic commen-tary on the stereotype of the 'tragic mulatto' who appears (and ultimately disappears at the end of the movie) in the form of Daphne Monet (Jennifer Beals). The narrative follows Easy Rawlins' (Denzel Washington) transition from laid-off aircraft worker at the start of the movie to self-employed private investi-gator at its close, via a complex tale of murder, scandal and political intrigue. At the heart of the narrative, in true *noir* style, is a mysterious woman, Daphne Monet, who Easy is employed by Albright (Tom Sizemore) to find. In this world constructed in terms of racial divisions, as Ed Guerrero observes, 'the fact that he's on the case at all is because he's black and can move and detect things in those cir-cles and that world forever closed to whites' (1996: 41). Easy accepts the dubious offer of employment since he needs to pay his mortgage. But Easy is also, he soon discovers, employed to 'take the fall', something he is not prepared to do. His pre-carious, but finally successful, management of the situation climaxes in a recourse to violence personified in the figure of Mouse (Don Cheadle), called up from their shared past.

Daphne is a destabilising figure who dramatises the instability of racial binaries and who serves to map Easy's transformation into private investigator in terms of movements within and across different social worlds. The 'passing' narrative indicates the extent to which the transgression of binary terms can be presented as both (tragic) endorsement of and undermining an essentialist understanding of identity. As Lola Young points out:

> Such ambiguous racial positioning may serve to re-confirm the legitimacy of racial categorisations whilst simultaneously problematising it. With regard to 'race' the act of passing, whilst potentially undermining absolutist notions of racial categorisation, is ultimately necessary because of these fixed, prescriptive racial taxonomies.
>
> (Kirkham and Thumin 1995: 276)

Repeated evocations of divided space and closed territories chart Easy's increasing confidence but still precarious position as both his transition to private eye and the revelation of Daphne's 'passing' articulate and question the divisions of the worlds in which they both operate. He begins the search for Daphne at a backroom jazz club; as he is shown upstairs a drunken white man, pleading to be admitted, is assured that there is no other room. Albright asks that Easy meet him out of town: while he waits a white girl casually starts speaking to him, a situation that brings trouble in the shape of her male friends (and which serves to demonstrate Albright's violence). Later Daphne has him drive her to a house in the hills where they find a corpse. Easy's uncertainties about driving Daphne through a white neighbourhood are realised when the police, already looking at him for another murder, threaten to frame him. It is when he goes directly to Todd Carter, Daphne's fiancé and a candidate for Mayor who has withdrawn from the race (his rival having threatened to 'expose' Daphne's mixed-race origins), that Easy takes charge of the situation, demanding an explanation and realising he is in a deep hole. And, ultimately, notes Guerrero, in 'a final act of double consciousness confirming his true powers as a black private eye, Easy Rawlins functions as go-between, negotiating the breakup of the miscegenous liaison' (1996: 41).

If the ostensible mystery to be solved is Daphne Monet 'passing', this is not the narrative problem. Indeed it is not her narrative. Guerrero criticises Beals' performance as 'flat', suggesting that she 'seems to play too close to the standard *vamp*, without looking deeply enough into the tense doubleness and marginality of the character' (1996: 40). Yet in the film, as in Walter Mosley's book, Daphne functions primarily as a screen onto which other concerns are projected. In the novel, Easy describes Daphne as a 'chameleon lizard' who changes 'for her man' (1996: 161). Her disruptive force is expressed not only in terms of 'race' (her passing) but in Mosley's portrayal of her as both strong and in need of protection, as simultaneously feminine and masculine. She seduces Easy in the hideaway he has taken her to (a seduction not included in the film, though the scenes between them are charged). Gently washing him, Daphne leaves Easy speechless ('I couldn't say a word'), implicitly unmanned:

> She stepped back from the tub and shrugged off her yellow dress in one long stretch then tossed it in the water over me and pulled down her pants. She sat on the toilet and urinated so loud that it reminded me more of a man.
>
> 'Hand me the paper, Easy,' she said.
>
> The roll was at the foot of the bath tub. She stood over the tub, with her hips pressed outward, looking down on me. 'If my pussy was like a man's thing it'd be as big as your head, Easy.'
>
> I stood out of the tub and let her hold me around the testicles. As we went into the bedroom she kept whispering obscene suggestions in my ear. The things she said made me ashamed. I never knew a man who talked as bold as Daphne Monet.
>
> I never liked it when women talked like that. I felt it was masculine. But, beneath her bold language, Daphne seemed to be asking me for something. And all I wanted was to reach as far down in my soul as I could to find it.
>
> (Mosley 1996: 159–60)

Franklin's film retains this sense of Daphne Monet as the site of contradictory qualities (a masculine femme fatale) rather than as a character. Just as the violence and disruption of categories triggered by Buffalo Bill's desire for a new body is juxtaposed with and echoes Clarice's desire for (class) advancement in *The Silence of the Lambs*, Daphne Monet's embodiment of the racially divided Los Angeles, through which Easy negotiates his way and unravels the mystery, echoes the hero's transformation.

Working girls?: Men cross-dressing

For feminist criticism the figure of both straight and gay men cross-dressing in Hollywood cinema is far from trouble-free, often read as travesty rather than transvestite. In both *Tootsie* (1984) and *Mrs Doubtfire* (1993) the cross-dressed persona is that of an older woman, the very possibility of her sexuality repeatedly used to generate comic implications.[7] Both prompt comparisons to 'mom', whilst Patrick Swayze's drag queen in *To Wong Foo Thanks for Everything, Julie Newmar* is both emphatically maternal and in command within a movie that reproduces, despite a few tart comments, the racial hierarchies of the buddy movie.[8] Citing Chris Straayer, Jane Gaines argues that 'such films as *Tootsie* and *Victor Victoria* . . . are finally reactionary in the way they reveal correct gender with a flourishing costume change confirming a "true" relationship between clothing and the gendered body beneath' (Gaines and Herzog 1990: 26). Though the trajectories of transformation and of revelation are in conflict, however, such a judgement may accord too much significance to narrative resolution and not enough to the work of imagery within these movies. In her comments on *Tootsie*, Garber argues for a recognition of the figure of transvestite that she suggests a feminist criticism focused on questions of gender (however astute) renders invisible:

> *Tootsie* is not a feminist film. Nor is it a film about a woman, or a man pretending to be a woman. It is a film about a transvestite. Its cross-dressed central figure, Michael Dorsey/Dorothy Michaels/Dustin Hoffman, is working within the established codes of female imperson-ation, but for feminists to see *Tootsie* as a film about men's view of women (and of feminism) is to erase or repress any awareness of that which the metadramatic nature of the film constantly stresses: the fact that 'Dorothy's' power inheres in her blurred gender, in the fact of her cross-dressing, and not – despite the stereotyped romantic ending – in either of her gendered identities. In *Tootsie* transvestism is an enabling fantasy, not merely a joke or a parody, whether the laugh is thought to be on men or on women.
>
> (Garber 1992: 6)[9]

Asking us to put aside the framework offered by a gendered binary, Garber seeks to acknowledge the existence of another space within the film and in relation to images of cross-dressing more generally. Across these different and distinct struc-tures, gendered cross-dressing seems both challenging to and predicated on a notion of 'essence', expressed in terms of a delight in transformation within a nar-rative that moves towards an underlying and ultimately unsustainable truth centred on the body. In an analogous fashion, Christine Holmlund draws out the sense that while the masquerader problematises binary systems and logic, there remains a suspicion or fear that 'there may be something underneath which is "real" and/or "normal"' (Cohan and Hark 1993: 224).

Both *Tootsie* and *Mrs Doubtfire* display a fascination, partly to achieve comic effect, with the processes of transformation, the accoutrements of the cross-dresser. Sequences of transformation in both films showcase the star performance: Hoffman's acting range, Williams' repertoire of comic voices. Performance is further emphasised through the evocation of a whole series of 'types' (Hillard/Williams tries on a host of different personas before settling on 'Mrs Doubtfire'). Both movies also include brief moments in which the cross-dressed character suddenly uses their 'real' voice or mannerisms; Dorothy resorting to Michael's deep voice to hail a cab, Mrs Doubtfire leering at a young woman in a bar. In both cases, the joke stems from behaviour counter to that expected of middle-aged or elderly women such as leering at younger women or behaving assertively. And yet, as Garber's comments suggest, if we look closer these are not the qualities we associate with the male characters in these movies: Michael Dorsey is signally unable to take command, whilst Daniel Hillard is presented as interested in little but his children. These moments offer a parodic masculine behaviour that underlines the distinctiveness of the cross-dressed persona rather than a revelation of the 'real' underneath. Think of the scene which takes place towards the end of *Mrs Doubtfire* in which 'Mrs Doubtfire' is finally, literally and very publicly unmasked. The moment follows a complex set of changes as Daniel Hillard/Mrs Doubtfire are both expected, by different parties, as dinner guests in the same restaurant. Comedy and confusion follow as the character's costumes (male/female), behaviours (raucous/demure) and scents (alcohol/perfume) over-lap and blur into each other. In the first of a series of quick changes, Mrs Doubtfire is caught entering the men's room by his wife Miranda and their youngest daughter. The rapidity of his subsequent change back into 'Daniel' is emphasised by the speeded up film – suddenly he catches glimpse of him/herself, in-between the two personas, and cries out loud at this grotesque apparition. Left behind in the restaurant, clad in a dress with a latex face-mask hanging around his neck, Daniel addresses the stunned clientele with a question: 'What are you look-ing at? Show's over' (an assertion that matches his comment on first appearing in the role of 'Mrs Doubtfire': 'Showtime!').

Both *Tootsie* and *Mrs Doubtfire* emphasise the *need* to cross-dress (for work), thus forming part of a group of narratives identified by Kuhn in which 'the story opens with the plight of an unemployed or otherwise desperate performer who resorts to sexual disguise in order to get work' (1985: 58). There is also an evident element of disavowal at play here (Daniel Hillard's quip to his kids 'It's just a job – I don't go to old lady bars or anything like that after work'). If a gendered inscription of class is a key element in narratives of cross-dressing, and class in American film is articulated partially through work, might there not be some sense in which what Garber terms 'the most conventional of motives' for cinematic cross-dressing, that is 'the need to work', is actually a little more than a mere nar-rative contrivance? Michael Dorsey and Daniel Hillard are both already performers, working in a notoriously unstable profession (one that involves dress-ing up). Both find difficulty not only securing work in the first place, but also in holding down a job. This is marked clearly as partly a consequence of unruly behaviour: they are men who don't submit willingly to the restrictions of the workplace. The credit sequence of *Tootsie* offers a montage of Dorsey (Dustin Hoffman) failing a series of auditions, educating younger actors and quitting a job after refusing to obey a director's instructions (walking off the stage). Hillard's instability and unreliability, also signalled in a credit sequence resignation, is underlined by his ability to slip in and out of different roles and voices. Both char-acters achieve a professional success as cross-dressers which eludes them as 'actors'. Dorothy Michaels becomes a star, though Dorsey renounces her, whilst Mrs Doubtfire hosts her own cable television show for children (ironically after a judge has dismissed his impassioned plea to have joint custody of the children as nothing more than the performance of 'a very gifted actor'). If narratives of female-to-male cross-dressing are about gaining status, then those which involve men putting on women's clothes are to do with accepting rules and limits. Daniel initiates a transformation ('make me a woman', he asks his brother Frank) through which he makes a spectacle of himself ('Showtime') but also turns that spectacle into professional success. Once again, what might be the significance of a scenario in which a man has to dress as a woman in order to hold down a job? We can locate this imagery in relation to an historical context of labour in the United States within which both white, male, middle-class incomes and job security are in relative decline. In this context, and without seeking to erase the figure of the transvestite, 'the most conventional of motives' for cross-dressing can be seen as pivotal. This is perhaps particularly resonant in the context of *Mrs Doubtfire*'s endorsement of a nurturing fatherhood over a repressive motherhood, providing the context in which Fred Pfeil situates both the women warriors of *Terminator 2* and *Thelma and Louise* and what he terms the 'sensitive guy' movies of the early 1990s, a context in which 'the female is simultaneously vindicated and doomed or thrust aside; while the male is simultaneously feminized and re-empowered' (1995: 54). Daniel learns control through his role as Mrs Doubtfire, just as he learns to cook and clean. In the restaurant scene, Daniel is torn between family and career. That it is the initial success of Mrs Doubtfire which prevents Daniel caring for his children after work only reinforces the different status of the two figures. Ultimately his impersonation becomes a form of labour (and not only a labour of love) as the space of Mrs Doubtfire's TV show recreates the domestic for national syndication. And, finally, it is she (Mrs Doubtfire) who is missed by both Miranda and the children, an inflection that recalls Garber's comments on the appeal not of Michael Dorsey but of Dorothy Michaels in *Tootsie*. These themes return in Chapter five in an exploration of the peculiar anxieties around women at work enacted in such movies of the 1990s as *Disclosure* and *The Last Seduction*, in which working women can both threaten and help men. At the same time the threat of unemployment (of becoming redundant in all senses of the word) hovers over these movies, incarnated or literalised in the figure of the contemporary *femme fatale*.

Working girls: Women cross-dressing

There is another 'working girl' in *Mrs Doubtfire* in the shape of Miranda Hillard played by Sally Field. Both Hillards are involved in a form of cross-dressing, and both undergo a process of transformation as the narrative develops. Miranda's costume, her stature and her 'harshness' with Daniel combine to associate her with a restrictive order defined in terms of the world of work. Our first view of Miranda, during the credit sequence, is at work. While Daniel is anarchic at work, she is authoritative, standing to address a group in a spacious office. Her costume, a tailored black trouser suit with white blouse styled to resemble a waistcoat, echoes the familiar cross-dressed image of male evening wear, an image which bears associations of social power. Miranda's profession as a design consultant underlines the significance of surfaces and the meaning that they are capable of generating. She reels off a rapid-fire list of qualities to be looked for in good design (including 'Arts and Crafts'). The camera then cuts to a close-up of one line picked out in Miranda's trademark clipped delivery: 'Don't be seduced by chintz'. This could be her motto for the whole movie. Femininity as fussiness, the vulgar parody invoked by 'chintz', has no place within Miranda's streamlined, organised world. In this opening sequence, which maps out in broad terms the opposition between the two characters, Miranda's rules and restrictions come into conflict with Daniel's anarchism. However anarchic, Daniel is aligned with not only pleasure (his orchestration of the children's party, for example) but moral value, a quality which is underlined when he quits his job for ethical reasons. He is quizzed when he arrives unexpectedly to collect the children (his assertion that he 'got off early' is contested by his daughter: 'you mean you got fired') indicating that this isn't the first time. In an understated fashion, it is implied that Miranda's income supports the family, and the pressures we see her under are those associated with what Fred Pfeil terms a traditional protector-provider masculinity: her constant worries, having little time for the family due to her long hours of work, and the recurrent image of her on the phone, a technology that takes her attention elsewhere. 'You chose the career', Daniel rebukes her, thus aligning himself with a kind of New Age contempt for over-investment in work. This opposition, and the terms that it enacts, is pursued in a sustained attempt to associate Fields' character with the regimented world of work or, more precisely, to distance Daniel from that space.[10] Though Williams' stand-up comic routines have included material on fatherhood, his film image frequently constructs him in terms of childishness (*Toys* (1992), *Hook* (1991), *Jack* (1997)). Indeed, as Pfeil argues, *Hook* involves a somewhat insidious narrative move to celebrate a fatherhood defined by childish pleasures from which female characters are excluded by definition (1995: 63–9). If Daniel learns about restrictions and limits, Miranda learns that work isn't everything, and is able to relax with Mrs Doubtfire as she never could with Daniel. The opening sequence then does more than simply establish a contrast between the two. It prefigures a whole series of issues around gendered dress, work and behaviour that are developed throughout the film, providing the source of its comedy and its narrative conflicts.

If anarchic men dress as women to learn about self-control whilst enjoying the evident pleasures of transformation, narratives and images of women cross-dressing relate to opportunity and achievement in different, though related ways. Both gendered and class cross-dressing is explicitly presented as allowing female protagonists an opportunity and a *freedom* (of both physical movement and behaviour) that they would not otherwise achieve. As the tailored image of Miranda Hillard in *Mrs Doubtfire* reminds us, the development of a wardrobe for working women continues to involve the negotiation of images and ideologies of gender and class. Women's entry into previously restricted areas of work in the 1980s (re)produced a 'new' stereotype (that of the independent woman) and a 'new' look – crystallised in the phrase 'power dressing'. The shoulder pad (and shoulder pad build-up) was to become a symbol and symptom of women's attempts to carve out a space for themselves in the world of work. Of course the figure of the New Woman is far from new: feminist historians have commented on her uncanny reappearance at different points in the twentieth century as a marker of first modernity and latterly of postmodernity (or even post-feminism). The image of the New Woman, which involved the adoption of selected 'masculine' features in dress and hairstyle articulates that which it also seeks to contain, the mobility of gendered identities and behaviours. It is in this context that Judith Mayne notes how the 'New Woman is at the very least a contradictory figure who both summons up and represses lesbian possibilities' (1994: 155). And as Barbara Creed points out, the representation of an active, 'masculinized' woman leads, via a steady chain of association, to the feared and fantasised lesbian body (Creed 1995). In her different historical guises then, the New Woman signals a limited independence and at least the potential for a transgression of gender that is aligned with a lesbianism which displaces the centrality of the male subject. A fundamentally ambivalent space, this returns us to Garber's 'third' possibility, one which resides not in the achievement of some happy compromise between two terms in a binary system, but works instead to question the very symbolic systems that gives it meaning. Contemporary articulations of the working woman against which, for example, Miranda is defined in *Mrs Doubtfire*, articulate both the sense of woman's 'masculinised' role in business and a critique of that role, enacted in the film through the reproachful, nurturing father.

Within this extended definition of cross-dressing, one in which 'passing' is not necessarily at stake, the development and mobilisation of types such as the tomboy action hero(ine) or the female gunslinger in recent Hollywood movies can be usefully located. Thus although, as Kuhn suggests, musical performance continues to function as a privileged site for the showcasing and the critical discussion of female-to-male cross-dressing, encompassing some of the best-known examples, I'd like also to highlight the Western and the action movie, discussed in Chapters two and three, as equally significant genres of gendered cross-dressing. Both the musical and the Western are Hollywood genres that foreground performance, though on rather different terms. In the Western an often stylised performance of masculinity is evident in scenes of heroic bravado, for example in the figure of men with reputations for violence that precede them and which they must act (and live) up to.[11] For white men the Western is a space defined in terms of a potential for physical freedom. The female gunslingers of Westerns made in the 1990s such as *The Quick and the Dead* or *Bad Girls*, involve an articulation of this performance of masculinity around the female body, which in turn serves to further denaturalise the Western hero. In mentioning the Western here I want to highlight the extent to which the form is in any case a site for cross-dressing. Within a genre that is so centrally concerned with the definition of white masculinities, the elaborate rituals of costume and performance through which the terms of gender, 'race' and class are enacted over the body draws our attention to activities of dressing up and acting out across a series of boundaries and borders. In terms of the involvement of class and gender with each other, it may come as no surprise that the image of the female gunslinger or cowgirl is articulated in direct relationship to two other roles: that of 'wife' and that of 'prostitute'. Neither the female gunslinger nor the figure of Miranda as working woman/career mom in *Mrs Doubtfire* are, in any traditional sense, immediately suggestive of cross-dressing. The term is associated most often with comedy in such movies as *Some Like it Hot*, *Tootsie* and *Victor Victoria*, for example. Maggie Greenwald's *The Ballad of Little Jo* (1993) is unusual in featuring a woman passing as male. Yet whether the female protagonist of the Western seeks to 'pass' as a man or not, her decisions are typically mapped quite explicitly in relation to the status and privileges this affords her.

Garber highlights the question of social status when she reviews a clinical literature which, in contrast to accounts of the male transvestite, refuses the very possibility of female transvestism. Thus '[w]omen who habitually cross-dressed were not psychotic; they merely wanted to be men, which in their society was a highly reasonable, indeed healthy, desire' (1992: 98). Similarly in the cinema, viewers are offered an explanation of female-to-male cross-dressing that can be understood as seeking to naturalise the transition, cast in terms of the desire for the privileges and freedom available to men. At the basic level of plot, the cinema offers us women who achieve freedom and/or success as male or masculine personas, their achievements typically presented as unique. However, the narratives considered in this book do not straightforwardly support the hypothesis that such a desire is 'perfectly natural', offering a critique of the attitudes and structures within which they are positioned. Both musical (*Victor Victoria*, *Yentl*) and Western (*The Ballad of Little Jo*) narratives work to offer a critique of dominant masculinities and to critique the structures which delimit both value and advancement in terms of the masculine. The narrative of cross-dressing offered in Barbra Streisand's *Yentl* is quite explicitly about opportunity. The film enacts a story in which the dutiful daughter, left without family obligations on her father's death, takes on the role of a male scholar. Though as Anshel, s/he falls in love with fellow scholar Avigdor (Mandy Patinkin) and marries Hadass (Amy Irving), Avigdor's former fiancée, Yentl ultimately eludes marriage. Or, more precisely, s/he eludes the passivity associated with marriage. In the early stages of the movie, she is set up as a poor cook – or at least an indifferent one, more interested in books than food. Her passion, shared with her father, is for knowledge. She is both carer and intellectual companion/pupil to him.

As Garber notes, Streisand's *Yentl* is a progress narrative of the New Woman, one in which Yentl's aspirations are contrasted with the passivity of Irving's Hadass:

> An active, learned, acceptably transgressive figure (as contrasted with the unliberated Hadass, who cooks, bakes, and smilingly serves the men their favorite dishes), Yentl is the 'new woman' of the eighties, a fit partner for a scholar – if she will only renounce her ambitions.
>
> (Garber 1992: 79)

Yet heterosexual romance does not function to provide a resolution for Yentl here, since it would involve surrendering the desire to study, the ambition which defines both her and Anshel. The marriage generates suspense and confusion around the possibility of discovery but also in terms of the relations of power between a woman and a transvestite. An image used for publicity features Anshel/Streisand dressed as a bridegroom, sitting in a 'masculine' pose, legs apart, feet planted firmly on the ground, Haddas/Irving standing devotedly behind him/her. The marriage between Anshel and Hadass operates as a site of tenderness and eroticism rather than exploitation or deceit. Quart reads the film in terms of 'woman's respect for woman', so that the portrayal of both Hadass and Yentl and the Hadass/Anshel marriage/romantic friendship are valued (1988: 84). Garber also writes that whilst the movie is 'at least on the surface normatively heterosexual', the portrayal of the scene between Anshel and Hadass 'smoulders with repressed sexuality'. She describes the wedding night as 'an extraordinarily tender and erotic scene of instruction' in which 'the forbidden sexual energy is deflected into a mutual reading of the Talmud, with Streisand (the woman play-ing a woman dressed as a man) teaching Irving how to understand the Law' (1992: 78). The energy associated with one forbidden (lesbian) desire is chan-nelled into another (study). One effect of this is to produce within the film an association between a repressed same-sex desire and the desire to study which is forbidden to Yentl but not to Anshel. Yentl's initial experiences as Anshel, as a man, are first of exploitation and isolation (his money taken fraudulently, sleeping alone in the woods) and then of an aggressive competition (arm wrestling) from which he is saved by Avigdor's intervention and study (which remains a refuge). The figure of Anshel has a transformative effect not only on Yentl but on both Avigdor and Hadass, who, it is suggested will have a marriage that is 'more modern and more equal' (Garber 1992: 79).

Whilst *Yentl* produces a heroine with a thirst for knowledge, *Victor Victoria* rehearses the 'need to work' scenario with Julie Andrews seeking to elude the twin threats (comically rendered) of prostitution and destitution. As we've seen, playing the role of a Polish Count involves Andrews in a series of disguises. Two primary deceptions are at work: that Victor is an aristocrat, and that he is male. Whilst we overhear a chorus-line gossip rejecting the first, the second disguise is held in place. Yet this is not such an outrageous impersonation, since it is clearly signalled to us that Andrews' character already has 'class'. She sings opera (high-brow) not schmaltz. Throughout the film she is defined in opposition to Lesley Ann Warren's showgirl. The movie's only other central female character, Warren is styled as a kind of grotesque cross between Mae West, Jean Harlow and Marilyn Monroe, presenting an artificial, vulgar 'femininity' marked as American. Her grating voice, chocolate consumption and heavy make-up serves to under-line the point so that it is *she* who primarily signals artificiality and constructedness (rather than either Victor or Victoria). It is class (as a gendered discourse) that underpins Warren's artifice. At the same time, Andrews' imper-sonation draws on representations of the male aristocracy as 'effete'. Perhaps it is this that allows Creed to read Andrews in terms of 'an increasing emphasis on the androgynous figure in popular culture . . . and the woman/man in the cinema'

(1987: 65). The androgyne and the woman/man are both bound up with gendered articulations of (upper) class identity. Here Edwards makes use of the Andrews image (restrained, refined and seemingly inextricably bound to *The Sound of Music*) to sustain the contrast with Warren.[12] Whilst Edwards' film opposes American artificiality to European sophistication (however artificial this in turn may be), *Yentl* ends with a move from (Eastern) Europe to an America which signifies a freedom for the immigrant, drawing on the imagery of America as a space of potential mobility in class, ethnic and gendered terms.[13] Not only is study (and the freedom required to pursue it) eroticised in *Yentl*, the production-number ending makes sense in terms of its star and her over-arching role as the film's co-writer, director, producer and star. The presentation of Streisand as controlling diva, a woman whom critics (with a certain predictability) have termed masculine, pervades not only this final scene but the movie itself. Stephen Maddison refers to 'one hysterically threatened MGM mogul' who reportedly said of Streisand: 'She's a man-eater. A regular ball-breaker. She wants to control the picture; she wants her own hairdresser, her own wardrobe, her own director – she wants it all' (1992: 62–3). 'And people wonder', adds Maddison, 'why she's such a gay male icon?' The extent of Streisand's success across music, stage and movies, her level of control over her work as star and director, all feed into the public circulation of her portrayal in *Yentl*, of a refusal to accept conventional limitations. Here as Garber notes, it is not 'surprising that the expression of [Streisand's] difference', a woman who 'displaces both WASP women and Jewish men in her dual roles as star and producer', 'should manifest itself in a transvestite vehicle' (1992: 80). The work involved in bringing Yentl to the screen frames the work of performance, so that *Yentl*'s project is not only one of portraying a cross-dressing achiever in which study (as men's work/God's work) is eroticised, but the production of Streisand as director, a role which both maintains and disrupts the couplet of female performer/male director (she is both womanly and manly) through which the equation of women's work and sexual performance is itself produced and sustained.[14]

Working girls: Cross-class dressing

'Being a "working girl"', writes Judith Mayne, 'means understanding economics in sexual as well as business terms' (1994: 101). This double knowledge is brought to bear by Tess McGill in *Working Girl*, an ambitious and efficient New York office worker up against the 'glass ceiling'. Despite her best efforts to progress, she is treated as a joke and/or sex object by male colleagues and senior staff. The film clearly deals with gender, but also foregrounds class concerns, once more highlighting the relationship between these discourses. Julia Hallam underlines this dual concern by indicating the movies reworking of elements from 'the proletarian woman's film and the career-girl comedy' of the 1930s and 1940s to 'construct "a woman's film" for the 1980s' (1993: 175). Tess has studied part-time at night school to gain a degree with honours, yet this cannot compare with qualifications from Harvard or Yale. The beginning of the film shows Tess to be proficient but going nowhere. She agrees to cut her apparently ceaseless round of self-improvement classes for a 'surprise' thirtieth party arranged by best friend Cyn (Joan Cusack). We see nothing more of the party than a brief image of her friends gathered in her apartment. We are not invited to associate Tess' private life with laughter; it is at work that she comes alive. As if to reinforce Tess' distance from her home-life, the next scene shows her standing in long-shot before a full-length mirror, dressing up in a gift of black underwear. This is not a scene of passion: 'Just once', Tess tells Nick, 'I could go for a sweater or some earrings – a present that I could actually wear outside of this apartment.' This is followed by a humiliating encounter with an executive Tess' boss has told her she might find an opportunity with, but who has little more than sex on his mind. Fetishised at home and at work, Tess' dissatisfaction is registered on two distinct yet linked levels. It is significant, in terms of the transformation that follows, that it is the gift of clothes which underlines her sense of disappointment and frustration. Most of the action takes place outside the home, which in itself is far from homely. Just as Tess is more alive at work, she seems more 'at home' in the apartment of her boss than her own place; though she is uneasy at times in this space, she evidently knows her way around.

Tess' new boss Katherine Parker (Sigourney Weaver) proffers the chance of advancement (a 'two-way street') and a mentor relationship. It is evident to the audience, (if not to Tess) that this is very much a relationship of power, little different from her other exploitative encounters with 'management', a configuration evident in their very different control of people and space, reinforced through the way in which Tess runs around after her boss, literally looking up to her in one scene which shows her helping Katherine try on ski boots. For Hallam, *Working Girl* disdains the female/male battles of the movies of the 1940s to which it alludes, operating instead in terms of 'a battle between women of different social classes fighting for status and economic rewards' (1993: 177). Katherine's status is marked by her origins (Boston), her arrogance, abilities (with languages, for instance) and her apartment with its wardrobe of expensive clothes, and touches of excess such as the chandelier and the Warhol-style multiple print portrait of herself. So when Tess takes a tentative idea to Katherine about the acquisition of a radio network it is no surprise to the audience that her boss appropriates it, presenting it as her own (a variant on the theme of exploitation). When Katherine has an accident skiing, Tess takes advantage of her absence to put the deal through herself. Borrowing the upper-class looks and voice of her boss, Tess crosses class categories as she calls them into question. 'Unmasked' in the final reel, Tess is revealed as a secretary rather than a manager and is forced to leave the boardroom in favour of Katherine.

The film thus enacts a narrative of Tess' transformation in which cross-dressing is an expression of agency. The film shares many of the characteristics of gendered narratives of cross-dressing: a pleasure in performance, a fear of discovery, the desire to escape limits and experience a freedom denied to the 'ordinary' woman.

Gender is explicitly involved to the extent that advancement is presented as a form of masculinisation, literalised in the powerful figure of Katherine Parker, but also implied in Trainer's phrase in defence of Tess: 'I'm telling you, she's your man'. Yet this alignment (of advancement as masculinisation) is nonetheless conducted in terms of gendered class position, rather than displacing class concerns wholly onto the adoption of male (dis)guise. The different social status of Griffith's and Ford's characters also informs the articulation of gender and sexuality in the film's romance plot. When Trainer rebukes her for her pretence, Tess responds with what is seemingly her only moment of cynicism, or indeed of incisiveness about her situation: 'If I'd told you I was just some secretary, you would never have taken the meeting. Maybe you would have fed me a few drinks and then tried to get me into the sack. End of story.' Of course, we don't see Trainer behaving in this way, a fact which distances him from the more exploitative aspects of the work environment, along with his evident distance for 'the kill'. Trainer's relative passivity also underlines the extent to which, caught between two competing women, he is, in Hallam's words, 'the prize for success . . . not the reason for seeking it in the first place' (1993: 177).

Hollywood cinema uses signifiers of dress and speech to locate white, working-class women: Joan Cusack's nasal twang, big hair and big earrings played for comedy in *Working Girl*, or, tragic rather than comic, the way in which Glenne Headley's dress underlines her powerless status in *Mortal Thoughts*. When Tess invites her new boss to comment on her appearance, Parker suggests (looking distractedly at a computer screen) that 'you look terrific – you might want to re-think the jewellery'. A brief scene follows in which Tess contemplates herself in the mirror whilst two other women chatter in the background. She then removes her bracelets and checks her eye make-up, the first stage in her remodelling. The beginning of her transformation is significantly located in the women's room, the space of so many cross-dressing comic confusions. Initially Tess' transformation is based on mimicry. However, Katherine's theft of her idea makes explicit that their relationship is one of power. Tess resorts to theft herself, appropriating Katherine's identity. Access to Katherine's apartment is crucial, providing Tess with the outfits she needs to pass with class. Tess' first (revelatory) visit to Katherine's apartment her fascination with the accoutrements of power is evident, conveyed with a sense of discovery, of seeing things previously unseen or with new eyes.

Working Girl sets up two frequently juxtaposed areas of dissatisfaction for Tess: the perception of her as a sexualised object at work and at home. The parallels between the romance plot and the narrative of achievement in work, already encapsulated in the phrase 'working girl', underline the extent to which class and social status are inextricably bound up in some way with sexual performance. After discovering that Parker has appropriated her idea, Tess returns home to find Nick in bed with another woman. After this double betrayal Tess is seen looking out across the river, a recurrent image that signals both her isolation/difference and the geographical inscription of class difference.[15] Her imaginative leap is to cross this boundary – signified by the speed of a camera movement which offers a

41

fantasy extension of Tess' point of view, taking us over the river at night before cutting to Tess sitting in Katherine's office in daylight, her long hair pinned up tightly. She uses her 'own' voice to play secretary and an imitation of Katherine's to play the executive. Here then, cross-dressing is triggered not so much by the need to work, but by the desire to succeed in work. Tess transforms herself with the aid of Katherine's wardrobe into an executive: from the big hair and jewellery that signifies her working-class status, to a guise of short hair and business suit. There is a short-lived, interim look, adopted before Tess determines to get 'serious hair'. Here, as some reviewers commented, Griffith looks like nothing so much as her mother Teppi Hedron's famous screen incarnation 'Marnie', another class interloper and shape-shifter, a thief disguised as a secretary. The daughter of a pathologised prostitute, she is, for Barbara Creed (1995), a phallic woman ultimately saved for heterosexuality.[16] Though the evocation of 'Marnie' situates Tess' dilemma within the terms of class, gender and sexuality, her position as *protagonist* within this scenario prevents the production of her transgression as neurosis.

Tess' imposture produces both pleasure (for example, in the scene where she confuses Katherine's snooty colleague) and suspense around the anticipation of discovery: when and how will it occur? Will some small detail give her imposture away? The film also maps the increasing distance between Tess and her existing social world, so that her cross-class cross-dressing, and the aspirations that it signifies, takes her away from the community of which she is part. Thus an opposition between the terms of belonging and exclusion expresses the contradictory sense in which Tess, like other cross-dressers, is both deceitful and yet honest. The social world that she is leaving behind, but with which she is still associated, is represented, somewhat sentimentally, as a space of warmth and friendship. Having refused Nick's proposal of marriage, Tess gazes across the river to Manhattan, from a community in which she no longer belongs to one in which she is equally out of place. Indeed the values of this new world are askew (as Cyn exclaims on seeing the dress borrowed from Katherine's wardrobe, 'Six thousand dollars? It's not even leather!'). Seeing her again at Cynthia's engagement party, Nick notices the transformation in Tess: 'You look different – classy; what, did you have to go to traffic court or something?' If Nick notices her new look as *classy*, on *their* first meeting, Jack Trainer (Katherine's intended fiancé and the man Tess wants to help her with the deal) also notices her difference from the world in which she finds herself, but expresses it in terms of sexuality. Once more costume provides the clue. In a tortuous compliment he tells her that 'You're the first woman I've seen at one of these damned things who dresses like a woman, not like a woman thinks a man would dress if he was a woman.' After a few drinks, Tess retorts that she has 'a head for business and a bod for sin'. The confluence of sexuality and work figures Tess as working girl. Yet her move 'up' in class terms works to problematise the definition of working-class women in terms only of sexuality.

Tess' transformation in dress signals her aspirations, just as Clarice Starling's 'good bag' and 'cheap shoes' encapsulate her state of being in-between, her provisional status as trainee FBI agent. And like Clarice Starling, who is able to put herself in others' shoes, Tess has a special facility. It is her familiarity with the popular press and gossip columns that gives her the idea for the entertainment merger and which enables her, clutching a folder of clippings, to prove the idea as her own to captain of industry Oren Trask at the end of the movie. Following Garber we could see Tess' new identity as a disruptive possibility – neither one thing nor the other. Following her humiliation at being unmasked at the board-room meeting, Tess renounces her ambitions, and resolves to 'just wise up and not take the whole thing so seriously'. After the intervention of Jack Trainer ('she's your man') Tess is given the chance to make her case. Having come to clear her desk, she is dressed casually in blue jeans, black sweatshirt, her hair a mess. In this guise she is believed by the boss and is rewarded with a management position (at entry level). Her transformation then is not into the predatory version of middle-class management which Parker represents. To some extent this is secured by Tess' 'girl' status: which in turn owes much to Griffith's star persona (her breathy delivery, for example).

Working Girl ends on an ambiguous note. We see Jack and Tess together, both preparing for work, both in suits: he gives her an executive lunchbox, and speaks to her as if she is a child. The infantilising gesture of the lunchbox, together with his name, 'Trainer', suggests a paternalistic relationship. Yet Trainer is himself vulnerable in the cut-throat world of business. His character is identified early on as somehow uncomfortable at the 'kill', distancing himself from the more ruthless aspects of business. Trainer practises a deception of his own on their first meeting, refusing to give his name so they can 'meet like human beings'. If it is an anxious Tess who asks him on their first meeting 'Do I look like I don't belong here?', it is Trainer who is out of his depth when they pose as guests at a wedding to secure a meeting with businessman Trask ('Just act like you belong'). In yet another bathroom scene he tells her 'you're like one of those cops no one wants to ride with'. Yet both of them enjoy the pretence which, fuelled by cocktails, turns to exhilaration. Earlier, Jack has revealed his fears to Tess, telling her that he has been 'in a slump', and talks of the 'good men' who have been made redundant from just 'one lost deal'. His fear (the food hanging out of his mouth underlining his lack of 'polish'), like Tess' impersonation, produces them both as uncertain of themselves. In this context Trainer prefigures the paranoid world of *Disclosure* with its ghostly redundant male executive who takes the ferry like a zombie, seemingly out of habit. Tess is a young woman with aspirations in the world which men fear being displaced from whilst women accept temporary contracts and entry level pay as a first step on the ladder. If the film celebrates achievement, it also associates dynamism and energy with women.[17]

Pretty Woman (Garry Marshall, 1991) and *Up Close and Personal* (Jon Avnet, 1996) are both romantic films in which the progress of heterosexual romance involves the heroine in social mobility against the backdrop of work. The attainment of femininity is as clearly marked in class terms in these films as is Tess' struggle to climb the management ladder. For *Pretty Woman*, transformation is about consumption, though there are moments when the very possibility of the heroine's assimilation is questioned. The film casts the Cinderella-heroine as prostitute, a profession to which the title of Marshall's film alludes. Pat Kirkham and Janet Thumin view *Pretty Woman* as a scenario in which 'the proletarian woman "moves up" out of her class through her charming personality, moral integrity, and prowess in bed' (1995: 19). Once more, the conflation of sex and work in the figure of the prostitute (and the female star) provides a way of talking about class difference. At one level then, *Pretty Woman* offers a fairly transparent fairy tale in which the working-class woman achieves advancement through heterosexual romance. Yet the film also underlines the work involved in romance (and for the 'working girl'). Though on rather different terms from Tess, Vivian/Julia Roberts is also a class cross-dresser. Different in that Vivian is not so much involved in achieving freedom through crossing classes, but providing freedom for employer Edward/Richard Gere. She teaches him to relax and to conduct business ethically; he starts to build things (ships) rather than rip companies apart. Her cross-class movement via heterosexuality is, that is, involved in shoring up rather than questioning masculinity.

In contrast to *Working Girl*, Vivian's/Roberts' body is not valued for its difference, but as a site to be subjugated. She is dressed up by others rather than dressing up herself. And as Radner points out, the body that we see at the beginning of the movie is not her body, but a body double (Collins et al. 1993). The film operates as an exercise in disciplining the working-class female body and its excesses – producing it as middle class through the codes of femininity. Class is signalled through bodily excess in *Pretty Woman*: Vivian blows her nose loudly (a comic sign of vulgarity often found in the cinema), cheers in a raucous fashion, fidgets (for which she is repeatedly rebuked) and spits her gum on the street. On her first visit to Rodeo Drive, a cold shop worker (female, of course) tells her 'you're obviously in the wrong place'. Although she ultimately takes her revenge on the shop women who disdain her, taunting them over lost commission, Vivian is disciplined, taught to correct her posture and to conform, to become a class act. Like Tess McGill, Vivian has some sense of irony about the situation: she responds to Edward's offer of a condo with the observation, 'that's just geography'. Thus *Pretty Woman* offers itself as a narrative of transformation through cross-dressing, at the same time that the narrative suggests Vivian was already essentially middle class, belonging in the penthouse rather than on the street. Unlike Tess in *Working Girl*, there is little sense that Vivian has anything to lose in her transition (she is leaving a sub-cultural world marked by drugs and death, one in which she never really belonged) rendered as a process of discovering (uncovering) what was always there.

The performance of femininity, class mobility and professional success are again linked in *Up Close and Personal*'s romantic narrative of transformation. Sally Atwater (Michelle Pfeifer) is transformed by mentor, and later, lover, Warren Justice (Robert Redford) into Tally Atwater, a successful network news anchor. Justice's character is a composite of romance fiction clichés, the name signalling how he should be read (as an idealised, rather two-dimensional figure). His hero-ism relates to his former career as an investigative journalist, a role that he has abandoned but will take on once more through the course of the film. Thus the characters act on each other, producing a sort of mutual transformation. Ultimately, however, they end up apart: Justice dies in 'the field', a re-masculinised figure pursuing and breaking a major news story in Panama. Although romance is transformative within the film, with frequent demonstrations that Tally 'falls apart' without Warren, this is also a narrative of 'one woman's professional success'.

Up Close and Personal begins its narrative towards the end of its story, with the confident image of Tally Atwater. The camera pulls out from a close-up of her eye in a red artificial light, revealing her image displayed on a monitor. As the camera pulls further back we see her sitting on a tall stool, on the left of the screen, set back, dressed in black and relaxed in the studio setting. The right half of the screen is taken up by two monitors which show her face in medium close-up. Right from the beginning of the film, we are asked to consider her image as a work in progress. This opening sequence constructs a biography which the rest of the film will add to, flesh out, clothe, through her transformative relationship with Justice. Tally is invited to talk about how she got started, to say 'something cute'. 'You went to college?' she is prompted: a rhetorical question. But this is a different sort of tale: responding contrary to expectations, Tally talks of how 'I temped, I waited tables. The minute I was old enough I dealt craps'. She begins to warm to the subject of her hard work/small town origins. Accompanying this voice-over we see a brief shot of a gaudy, lit-up street – little movement is evident which con-firms the smallness of the town that Tally is remembering (this is not even Vegas). She tells how she went to college at night, but already we are back in the studio: the story of her self-education is not of interest (just as in *Working Girl* we do not see this aspect of Tess' life). Tally's multiple images tell how she made a demo-tape which we see something of – she is shown as gauche with a frizzy blonde perm and wearing a bright pink suit that will recur at various points in the movie, quite different to the contained, tailored image she presents in her later life. We see how much she has changed and the film will tell the story of how she has moved from a gaudy pink suit to a pastel pink one, from small-town girl to success story through the mentoring of a successful man and through wearing the right outfits. We see her first day at work in a Miami TV studio – asking the woman who greets her, 'Do you think I'm overdressed?', confessing her nervousness about what to wear, dropping her bag, awkward and embarrassed. 'Overdressed' here, as in both *Pretty Woman* and *Working Girl*, relates to a distinction between a simply stated middle-class femininity and a gaudy, decorated working-class show. When Justice keeps calling her 'sweetheart' she rebels, though it is evident (from the movie poster and the conventions of romance) that this is just so much tension *en route* to falling in love.

The clear contrast between the novice Sally and the later, confident persona of Tally leads us to expect a story of transformation. Sally recognises Warren Justice as a former White House reporter (trailing here the connotations of Redford's role in *All the President's Men*) so that some rapport seems to be established (though he tells her 'you'll still have to make coffee'). At this point she turns and is finally positioned centre frame within her own flashback. We hear Justice asking 'You always wear that much make up?' The camera closes in very slightly as she looks out at us/him, giving no response. The moment allows us to contemplate her image, to compare again this Sally to the Tally she will become and to judge her. Sally's next two costumes are more relaxed – as fits her 'behind the scenes' role at the studio – jeans and T-shirt. Yet having talked her way into the weather-girl slot her pink suit re-emerges, covered by a giant sou'wester: already suggesting her disastrous on-air debut. Her failure is compounded by Justice's seemingly spontaneous decision to rename her on the autocue – Sally becomes Tally, the name she will retain. Justice will mentor her through her career in terms of wardrobe and, to a lesser or equal extent, journalistic skills. The two are explicitly bound up together since, according to Justice 'You don't want the look to get in the way' (to look 'overdressed' or, excessive would render her too visible). Thus a makeover of sorts takes place in which the garish pink suit is replaced by a pastel pink outfit and her hair is cut. These decisions are taken without her consultation – literally over her head as Justice asks an assistant 'You can do something about the hair?'. Sally's success as Tally leads to the offer of a job in Philadelphia where she flounders in competition with upper-class anchor Marsha (Stockard Channing) whose snootiness includes snide social remarks ('Is that *actually* a banana daiquiri?' and professional put-downs (rebuking her in turn for being too intuitive and for lingering too much on statistics). It is not that *Up Close and Personal* suggests the impossibility of women working together, but somehow this is conducted through the agency of men (as when Tally is advised by Justice's ex-wife Joanna). As she becomes more successful, there is some attempt at a turnaround, with Tally calling in favours to get Warren hired. But he is not grateful, being no good at dealing with people in authority over him (resenting their attitude in the light of his glorious past). The cinema typically portrays television news as a cynical, superficial world, though one in which solitary figures of integrity may be found, struggling to represent the unwelcome truth. The sense that this superficiality is also unmanly is evident in, for example, *Broadcast News* (in the faked tears of the William Hurt character) and provides a context for Justice's reluctance to take part in Tally's success.[18]

On only one occasion do we return to Tally's past as Sally in anything other than reminiscence. She is suddenly called away to help her sister, whose boyfriend has left her without paying the rent. We know that she has raised her sister, though no reason is given. The rain-soaked small town is the occasion of another battle between the couple as Justice follows her to provide the money needed. Tally accuses him of humiliating her, speaking with resentment of men who spoil women's dreams of success and hold them back. Justice stops her as she is about to embark on a familiar narrative of struggle. He is only 'interested' in hearing a well-turned out version of the tale, of the desire to escape – not talk of the banality she wished to escape from. This emotional outburst becomes another lesson in journalism, in the correct way to tell a tale of transformation. The film ends with Tally, an assured and independent woman, assuming the role of network anchor. She may depart from the script but, unlike the maverick Justice, not in a particularly threatening way. His vastly enlarged image on the screen behind her suggests how much her success is also his. Achieving professional success is once more the achievement of containment, of a movement from an undisciplined working female body marked as working-class to a (classy) star body. The attainment of an adult independence through heterosexuality plus professional success, producing Atwater/Pfeiffer in *Up Close and Personal* as both a romantic construct and a media construct.

For women, narratives of cross-dressing are almost always about gaining status – in both class and gender terms. Though these terms inform each other, discussion of the latter has tended to displace the former. In their account of *Pretty Woman*, Kirkham and Thumin do note that '[i]n cinematic representations career success is frequently imbricated with class and also with social mobility'. Thus Vivian's 'new class position' is 'that of her husband-to-be', just as Sally becomes Tally through her marriage to Redford's character in *Up Close and Personal* (1995: 19–20). Romantic and professional success are at stake in both films and though they are conflated, they are not reducible one to the other. Across comedy, romance and horror narratives, the dual dynamics of pleasure in transformation and fear of discovery generate an ambiguity around cross-dressing that is suggestive of the masquerade. For Holmlund, masquerade both challenges and infers the existence of some essence, some truth hidden 'underneath' the literal surface (written on the body) (Cohan and Hark 1993). At the level of gender, class and race, the routing of aspirational narratives through cross-dressing accepts the very binarisms questioned through the act of crossing over. The conflation of romance, sex and work, and the production of women's work as sexual performance (through the different configurations of prostitute/career girl/professional woman, in, that is, the image of the 'working girl'), simultaneously conceals and reveals the complex interdependence of gender and class within popular discourse.

2

COWGIRL TALES

'You can't resist her': Sharon Stone as Ellen ('The Lady') in Sam Raimi's Western pastiche *The Quick and the Dead*

The idea of a 'female Western' may be both as useful, and as risible, as that of 'male melodrama', both formulations being predicated on a supposed exclusivity of terms which are actually closely entwined. Gendered identities, the meaning, experience and parameters of masculinities and femininities, are at issue in both the Western and the melodrama, regardless of whether the fiction revolves around men or women. The perception that genres might in some senses be gendered has nonetheless persisted with narratives of crime, science-fiction, adventure and the Western acquiring and retaining a reputation as male spaces. Yet, as Pam Cook points out, women have had a long and a significant role in the genre. Writing in 1988, she indicated that women's historical role in the west, at least as far as the Western was concerned, had foregone the 'dubious luxury of a liberal reassessment', adding that it is:

> tempting to put this down, as many critics have, to the male Oedipal bias of the Western, a narrative based on a masculine quest for sexual and national identity which marginalizes women. Fruitful though this approach may be, it has not really come to terms with the dual, contradictory role of women. On the one hand she is peripheral. . . . On the other hand she is central.
>
> (Buscombe 1988: 241)

The significance of women in the 'traditional' Western, with its insistent inscription of sexual difference in the context of homosocial bonds between men, lies, as Cook suggests, in this peculiar position of marginal centrality. Discourses of masculinity in the Western are defined in relation to female figures such as the showgirl, and a structuring opposition between wives and whores, just as much as on the national, racial and ethnic hierarchies (implicit or explicit) within which white men and women of the Western both battle and depend on native, Black, Chinese, Mexican, Irish, Scandinavian (and other) Americans.

It may come as no surprise that the saloon-owning, business-savvy Vienna in *Johnny Guitar* (1954) is styled as a self-made woman whose status, it is implied, has been achieved through sexual performance. Her success in business marks her

51

as 'working girl' in both sexual and economic senses. Like Joan Crawford's star image, Vienna's costumes and costume changes (first butch, then femme, then butch again) suggest her mobility in terms of gendered signifiers.[1] The stylised geography of the saloon (Vienna's itself) both offers up and questions the division between gendered spaces of business, sexual performance and sex as business. In the Western, women 'upstairs' in a saloon are typically prostitutes, a convention reiterated in such recent movies as *Bad Girls*. Yet Crawford's Vienna insists 'down there I sell whiskey and cards: all you can buy up these stairs is a bullet in the head'. If the representation of white womanhood in the Western is structured in terms of an opposition between wives and whores, it is not the case that individual female characters or protagonists are simply fixed in one position. Just as critics need to acknowledge the significance of women's role in the genre, Cook insists, any 'demand for more realistic images of women' should also take account of:

> the fact that what lingers in the memory, refusing to be dismissed, is a series of extraordinary heroines, from Mae West's Klondike Annie and Doris Day's Calamity Jane, to Joan Crawford's Vienna and Barbara Stanwyck's Jessica Drummond. The search for realism is perhaps self-defeating in a genre which is more concerned with myth than historical accuracy. It might be more illuminating to shuffle the deck (bearing in mind that female card-sharps in the Western are few and far between) and see what permutations emerge.
>
> (Buscombe 1988: 241)

Ten years on, these comments have a resonance for an examination of the latest batch of revisionist Westerns to revisit the myths of the open range. We might note that the only female card-sharp to appear in recent Westerns is the decidedly femme Annabelle Branford in Richard Donner's *Maverick* (1994), a film that produces the unexpected spectacle of Jodie Foster, known from her days as a child actor for her tomboy roles, as a fraudulent Southern belle romancing Maverick Junior (Mel Gibson) and Senior (James Garner).

Cook's litany of strong women (stars and roles), whether 'masculinised', aggressively sexual or some composite of the two, provides a frame through which to consider those recent Westerns with female protagonists including *The Ballad of Little Jo*, *Bad Girls*, *The Quick and the Dead* (1995) and *Buffalo Girls*. The combination of sexuality and bravado in movies of both past (*Johnny Guitar*) and present (Sharon Stone in *The Quick and the Dead*) can also be understood in terms of the extent to which the Western has been a prime genre for the eroticised display of masculinities as spectacle, a spectacle typically enacted over the male body.[2] The genre's long history includes dandified singing cowboys who rub shoulders with glamorous stars such as Marlene Dietrich, Marilyn Monroe and Angie Dickinson. The Wild West show, paperback fictions, comics and songs all contributed to the production of the 'cowboy' as a spectacle of masculinity even in the nineteenth century within which many of the films are set. Indeed the production of the west as spectacle, and the relation of this production to truth and history has been a regular concern of the cinematic Western itself.[3] The Western as a cinematic genre has been understood as a set of fictions articulating discourses of American history. Yet it is also rather camp and is centrally concerned with the activities (however earnest) of dressing up and putting on a show. The androgynous eroticism of such images as Doris Day in/as *Calamity Jane* (1953) or Crawford in *Johnny Guitar* (in her battle with Mercedes McCambridge) also provides a context within which to consider the lesbian connotations of the cowgirl/female gunslinger.[4]

If the Western is noteworthy for its foregrounding of masculinity as a form of performance which, at least potentially, links the showgirl and the cowboy, it is also and pre-eminently a genre in which freedom is the central term. The Western is a genre in which white men and women achieve a freedom in class terms that is simply unimaginable in other genres. Though some Westerns have worked to open up the role of African-Americans, this has tended to focus on men. *Posse* (1993), for example, features Pam Grier, an action star of the 1970s. Yet she does little more than fire off a few rounds, relegated to cutaway shots.[5] The Western then, offers a (limited) textual space for tomboys/cowgirls to flourish, producing the set of archetypal roles that Cook refers to. Within the rhetoric and imagery of freedom, which is in turn bound up with colonial expansion, vagrancy has a romance attached to it (the open range). The vagrant/wandering Western hero(ine) signifies the freedom that stems from colonial expansion whilst not necessarily being an explicit part of it (as a property owner for example). The romanticism of the vagrant/wanderer provides a framework within which the double meaning of the word 'tramp' is also quite suggestive. Or rather the term means something distinct when applied to women, with tramp taking on sexual connotations (ironic then that Vienna's trouble stems from her desire to settle down). A strong element of the loss involved in the framing 'present-day' sequences of Ford's *The Man Who Shot Liberty Valence* (1962) is the contrast between a slow, restrained, repressed Hallie (Vera Miles) and her younger self which has been lost with the development of the west. This loss is not only to do with the passage of time (as ageing) but a loss of mobility, energy and agency. As Hallie has become literate she has lost her voice. The white woman in the Western has, at least some of the time, a strength and an independence to match the struggles that she faces.

Outlaws and gunslingers

Styled by B Ruby Rich as 'the closest thing to a female Western so far', Ridley Scott's *Thelma and Louise* (1991) successfully deployed the iconography of the Western within a narrative that explored the genre's themes of self-reliance and self-discovery (1993: 20). The film's reworking of the road movie format around two women (Susan Sarandon and Geena Davis), which provoked substantial critical and popular debate, called up the history and imagery of the Western (through costume, gunplay and the desert) whilst also touching on a series of other generic reference points. *Thelma and Louise* mobilises a powerful imagery involving the movement of its 'outlaw' protagonists into an 'empty' landscape that operates as an environment for self-discovery, with the women heading towards a mythicised Mexico that they never ultimately reach. The scene in which their car drives through the night, illuminated from within, recalls the campfires of the stylised movie Western landscape (sharing a sense of human isolation within nature). The climax set in Monument Valley is also rich in Western connotations. At a thematic level, the representation of Thelma and Louise as outlaws by default, their actions the result of circumstances as much as intent, makes sense not only within feminist discourses about sexual violence but in terms of the conventions of the Western. Scott's film both capitalises on and contributes to an iconography of independence associated with signifiers such as guns, country and western music and denim, signifiers which also define the figure of the cowgirl. Just so, films and television movies of the 1990s, including *Bad Girls, Buffalo Girls, The Ballad of Little Jo* and *The Quick and the Dead*, have in quite different ways situated women as protagonists within the Western. Moreover, again as with *Thelma and Louise*, they have intersected with a broader reappropriation and redefinition of the cowgirl style by lesbian audiences and within music (new country) and advertising.

Just as *Thelma and Louise* was greeted with some ambivalence on its release, of the movies cited in this chapter, only *The Ballad of Little Jo*, with its distinctly arthouse touches, has received much favourable response (or indeed any response at all) from feminist critics. Leslie Felperin's *Sight and Sound* review asserts that: '*Bad Girls* is about as politically correct as a L'Oréal hair mousse commercial, which it resembles far more than *The Searchers* or *Johnny Guitar*.' Of course she is right, since the feminist discourses on which the movie draws are those also deployed in advertising: that is, your right to choose the way you want to be.[6] Critics such as Hilary Radner have commented, in this context, on consumer culture's particular articulation of feminism as identity politics, consumption as self-production (Collins *et al.* 1993). If *Bad Girls* was not the type of Western which feminist critics might have looked for neither was it, according to Felperin, the movie that was initially envisaged, having been conceived originally as a more experimental affair directed by Tamra Davis.[7] The film's exploitation of sexual violence, toying with glossy magazine versions of both femme lesbianism and feminist posturing, for example, were almost guaranteed to produce the kind of uneasy response which greeted it. Whilst *Bad Girls* betrays self-consciousness about its project, most evident in its references to *Johnny Guitar* (the bank robbery, for instance), the fact that women are central to the Western landscape is not played for comedy. They are not, that is, *out of place*. *Bad Girls* has its precedents and reference points not only in a sexy cowgirl chic or the stylised figures of strong women found in Westerns of the 1950s and in country music, but in the comic book characters of the 1940s and 1950s such as those discussed by Jack Shadoian

(1979), including Buffalo Belle and Rhoda Trail. From this basis, the film introduces the stereotype of the independent woman, more often located in an urban environment, and the themes associated with her into the Western setting: the struggle to be financially independent from men, a feminist-inspired critique of violence and of women as property.

This juxtaposition of the 'independent woman' and the Western setting is also prefigured in an earlier, slow-paced film, Alan Pakula's *Comes a Horseman* (1978). Set during the end of the Second World War, the film stars Jane Fonda as Ella, a tough woman who is struggling to keep her ranch going through another season. She is helped by an old man, Dodger (Richard Farnsworth) and, later, by Frank (James Caan) an outsider recovering from a gunshot wound. The movie rehearses a melodramatic terrain in which Ella is pitted against Ewing (Jason Robards) who wants her land at the same time, it is revealed, that he is in danger of losing his own. The familiar opposition of farmer versus cattle is supplanted by cattle versus oil as the ranchers attempt to hold out against the drilling of their land. At the same time, the film addresses the implications of its female protagonist (very much a 'novelty') through its use of both Fonda's star image and the iconography of the Western. Citing diverse examples, including *The Doll's House, Nine to Five* and *Coming Home*, Tessa Perkins characterises Fonda's films of the 1970s as scenarios in which her character, through the course of the film, 'changes and moves closer to the Jane Fonda star-image of an enlightened, independent, radical woman' (Gledhill 1990: 247). Here, though, from the outset she is defined as tough, independent, but also isolated. The film charts Ella's struggle with Ewing alongside her movement from a silent, gruff figure to a warmer persona through her developing relationship with Frank. The portrayal of the work of the ranch is central to the film providing, with the expanse of the landscape, a key element of its spectacle. Yet Ella is also frequently positioned in the house, her face looking out (in close-up) from behind net curtains. It is not until Frank has begun to work with her that we see Ella on horseback, linked firmly with the iconography of the Western. The sequence in which they agree to work together has Ella in her car (noisy, awkward in the landscape) driving alongside Frank on his horse. Both are small figures within the landscape. Their first kiss follows their efforts to contain a stampede, an image that both sublimates their energy into their work and provides a counterpoint to the low-key scenes of the couple which follow. Pakula's film is not only concerned to situate its female protagonist within the Western, but to bring out contemporary aspects of the genre: the returning soldiers of the war refer back in terms of the genre to the Civil War and, in contemporary terms to Vietnam. Ella's precarious but iconic position, her enmity with Ewing and his destruction of her house (the movie ends with her and Frank building a new place) locate the film's themes, through gendered and generic discourses, in terms of an opposition between inside and out, past and present, tradition and modernity.

The opening shot of *Bad Girls* echoes the contradictory positioning of Ella/Fonda both within the landscape and within the house, seen through net curtains. The camera is positioned outside a saloon window, revealing both Anita

(Mary Stuart Masterson) inside with a client (whose death will trigger the women's flight) and, superimposed, the Western landscape reflected in the glass. The movie begins in Echo City with the four women working as prostitutes, Eileen (Andie McDowell taunts the Christian marchers gathered on the street below. If, within the classic Western, the woman poses a problem for the hero, here the narrative 'problem' is posed (fairly loosely) in terms of sexual violence and exploitation. Kaplan's movie followed the success of Clint Eastwood's *Unforgiven* (1992), an exercise in demystification the narrative of which is triggered by a knife attack on a prostitute, Delilah. When Gene Hackman's 'Little Bill', Sheriff of Big Whiskey, demands that the cowboys responsible should bring the brothel-owner horses in exchange for damaging his property, the women team together to pay for a gun-fighter to avenge them. Here then the motivating factor is the women's refusal to agree with the definition of themselves as property. Similarly, when a customer hits Anita in the opening sequence of *Bad Girls*, Cody shoots him, an action which leads (almost instantaneously) to the mobilisation of a Christian-led lynch mob, her rescue by the other three women, and their subsequent efforts to escape pursuers including Pinkerton detectives and Kid Jarrett. Thus the four women's stylised struggle for independence begins in a brothel. Here, as in *Klute*, prostitution simultaneously stands in for some notion of sexual 'liberation' and exploitation. The opposition between 'bad girls' and citizens of the town works in terms of a contrast between moral freedom and restriction expressed as absolutes. The asso-ciation between the lynch mob and the Christians (dressed in funereal black) confirms their delight in death over life. The film thus foregrounds and pursues themes of status, property and justice in order to establish the inevitability (and the legitimacy) of their outlaw status. (Anita's deed to 'her' land is worthless without her husband: prostitution and marriage are both envisaged as forms of exchange). The move from barely sanctioned role of 'bad girl' (prostitute) to outlaw evolves through the women's reliance on each other and themselves, rather than either of the 'communities' associated with men encountered in the film (Jarret's outlaw gang, Tucker's ranch). The individual stories that gradually emerge relate to famil-iar narratives in which women take on 'male' responsibilities following the loss or failure of a significant man. Cody Zamora's (Madeleine Stowe) past was with a gang of outlaws who picked her up as a teenager. Anita had travelled west with her husband to stake a claim. His death leaves her without legal claim to their land. Eileen left her father's small Texas farm when it was taken by the bank. Lilly (Drew Barrymore) was left with the debts of her father's Wild West show in which he had been a famous trick rider. In providing motivation for their outlaw status, the film combines the women's anger at the (sexual) violence to which they are subject with long-standing Western themes of the individual pitted against the institutions and finance and government: banks, the law and small-town morality.

The climax of *Bad Girls* features the four protagonists in a *Wild Bunch*-style gunfight in which Cody wishes to exchange a captive for her lover, Josh (a 'pretty boy' who helps her elude capture and later takes care of her). The gang kill him anyway and, after a long fight, Cody challenges chief villain, Kid Jarrett, to a gunfight that is simultaneously parodic and conducted in earnest (throwing him a bullet she drawls, 'pick it up, put it in; die like a man'). If *Bad Girls* seems at times parodic, it nonetheless draws upon and rearticulates the iconography, themes and narrative concerns of the Western. Its distinctiveness stems from the other sources on which it draws: the iconography of country and western, advertising images, soft pornography and fantasy comics. At the same time, however, its use of a group of women as central characters involves renegotiating the terms of the genre at some level. *Bad Girls* was marketed as a (sexy) post-feminist Western, employing a language of liberation and independence, of women's right to control their own bodies in an uneasy combination with cleavage shots and the fetishistic use of whips and weaponry. It is in this context we can understand the film's rather exploitative aspects – the sexualised display of the female leads in their various prostitute costumes, the hint of an undeveloped lesbian relationship between Lilly and Eileen, the images of sexual violence. Though the film's 'novelty value' was undoubtedly central to its marketing, *Bad Girls* also depends to an extent on a generic basis for its intelligibility. However, its exuberant production of a girl-gang Western results in an avoidance of the complexities of the iconography that it invokes, sidestepping any interrogation of the Western itself.

Sam Raimi's *The Quick and the Dead* stars Sharon Stone as Ellen, an 'enigmatic stranger', referred to through most of the film as 'The Lady', a designation which suggests a femininity quite at odds with her gunslinging image (leather pants, cheroots and even shades in one scene). From the opening scene in the desert through her arrival in and triumphant departure from the small town of Redemption, the film operates a sustained pastiche of the spaghetti Western which casts Stone, strong and silent, as a figure beset by doubt and the desire for revenge. *The Quick and the Dead* capitalises on the iconic status Stone, who also co-produced, has accrued as signifier of a strong, independent and dangerous sexuality through her early role in *Total Recall* and, most notoriously, in *Basic Instinct*. Like the prostitutes-turned-outlaws of *Bad Girls*, Ellen as The Lady offers a sexualised version of female strength defined in relation to the positions of 'Lady' and whore. On arrival she rides into Redemption, walks into a bar and asks for a room. Still an unknown quantity, she is met with the response 'whores next door' from a barman who doesn't even turn round to look at her. Ellen's response is to kick his chair out from under him, catching a bottle of beer with bravado. Here, as in the scene in which she reveals her shooting skills (rescuing outlaw-turned-preacher, Cort), the film reprises a familiar scenario in which the hero's powers and abilities are at first kept hidden. While the unknown male is designated weak (subject to laughter), the unknown female is designated a prostitute, as just another working girl. The comic exchange in which Ellen replies to the invitation 'I need a woman' with the put down 'You need a bath' further situates her in relation to the terse one-liners associated with cinematic tough-guys. This in contrast to the spectacular Ace (Lance Henrikson) whose bravado and dandy costume is revealed to be an imposture.

If the movie refutes a wife/whore opposition, Ellen's 'masculine' status does not render her asexual (something that Stone's image might not allow). The night before the final contest, Ellen storms into the brothel where Cort (Russell Crowe) is being held and takes him for herself since they may both be dead the next day. As in *Bad Girls*, it is suggested that her character can use her sexuality. 'You Can't Resist Her', the posters proclaimed, conflating her sexual attraction with her capacity for violence. The motivation for Ellen's actions is uncertain at the film's outset. She seems distant from the other gunfighters who are in town for an annual competition organised by its boss, Herod (Gene Hackman). This is in part because of her sex (and, of course, she is the only female gunfighter in the film: construed as exceptional). Apparently repelled by violence, she leaves town after the first round, turning her back on plans for vengeance. Her fury at the sexual exploitation of the bar-owner's daughter (she 'wriggled like a fish' gloats her attacker) leads her to kill him, effectively going through to the next round of the contest. Clearly there is some affection or empathy between Ellen and the young girl, expressed in a series of looks. Yet when she seeks to idolise Ellen ('I think you're great'), she is dismissed and is told to 'grow up'. Just as *Bad Girls* picks up and runs with the commodified images of female rebellion familiar from advertising, magazines and music video, *The Quick and the Dead* looks to other popular cultural reference points: the black humour of director Sam Raimi exercised in the horror classic *The Evil Dead*. Here the Western combined with more than a little of the conventions of the horror/slasher film enables Stone to function as a kind of composite of the Eastwood/Bronson gunslinger and the 'final girl' identified by Carol Clover (1992) in the slasher movie. For once, the woman with a past is not seeking to avenge her own sexual violation, though the theme is nonetheless invoked in the figure of the young girl Ellen avenges. Instead she is her father's daughter, acting in his stead. Towards the end of the film however, it is revealed that as a young child Ellen inadvertently shot her father when offered a chance to save him by shooting through the rope by which he was to hang. The revelation produces an ironic comment on the masculine woman's supposed identification with the father. There is also a generic reference here in the allusion to Bronson's 'harmonica man' in *Once Upon a Time in the West* (1968).

Cross-dressers and tomboys in the Western

The Western has long been a privileged site for gendered cross-dressing. Whether or not she seeks to pass as a man, the 'masculine' Western heroine, as tomboy, gunslinger or cowgirl, is a recurrent figure in the genre, past and present, with Calamity Jane perhaps the best-known example. 'Male' attire serves to further underline her strength and independence, drawing on the physical freedom which working clothes suggest in advertising images, a freedom constructed in relation to 'feminine' costumes of restraint. Ella's costume of cowboy hat, jeans and plaid shirt in *Comes a Horseman*, Vienna's more stylised 'gunfighter' look in *Johnny Guitar*, Ellen's Eastwood-style garb in *The Quick and the Dead*, all function as appropriations of cowboy clothes that signify the uncertain status of the heroine.

Transgressive in her refusal of her place, the tomboy is typically explained and contained in terms of her relationship to her father. Her 'masculine' qualities stem from a distorted upbringing in which she has had to rely on herself, whether this is expressed in terms of the loss of the mother or an identification with the father deemed excessive for a woman. The four 'bad girls' all tell different stories which define them, as we've seen, in relation to failed or absent men. Frank tells Ella in *Comes a Horseman*: 'Lady, you got balls the size of grapefruit.' Later, in a cowboy bar, old-hand Dodger explains how Ella's father had raised her: 'tried to make her a son that he needed but he never did have – she was weaned on war; she never knew nothing else'. Ellen in *The Quick and the Dead* produces herself as gunfighter to avenge her father. Neither does she have any ambitions to embody the law, tossing her father's Sheriff badge to Cort before riding out of town.

Though tomboy types are often 'explained' in terms of their relationship to men/fathers, they are also iconographically lesbian figures. In this way Barbara Creed terms *Calamity Jane* (1953) a 'lesbian Western', commenting on the Oedipal narrative of transformation in which Doris Day 'relinquishes her men's clothing, foul language, guns and horse for a dress, feminine demeanour, sweet talk and a man'. This movement also involves giving up Alice, the woman 'with whom she has set up house and whom she clearly loves' (1995: 95). Pam Cook also identifies a 'characteristic trajectory of the Western heroine from tomboy to wife' (Buscombe 1988: 243). The distinctiveness of at least some recent Western narratives involving female protagonists lies in their refusal of that Oedipal trajectory. Or, more precisely, a refusal of its implications: such as the renunciation of activity for passivity, masculinity for femininity, female friends for a man. Like Crawford's Vienna, both Ellen and the 'bad girls' of Kaplan's film shift between butch and femme guises. The construction of Ellen, for example, involves no contradiction between her 'masculinity' and her active sexuality. Fonda's Ella may wear a frock to dance with Frank, in a scene that emphasises their happiness as a couple, but his first gift to her is a set of chaps. If these protagonists are tomboys or cross-dressers, they are not, it seems, necessarily destined to give up pleasure for marriage.

In the CBS mini-series *Buffalo Girls* Anjelica Huston stars as the cross-dressed heroine Calamity Jane, from whose point of view the sprawling narrative of the 'Old Wild West' is told. She is one of a range of stock characters (including Wild Bill Hickock, Buffalo Bill Cody, General Custer, Annie Oakley, Sitting Bull and so on) in a production which seems at times to be a Wild West show itself. Calamity's voice-over addresses this history to her daughter Jane who, during the course of the film, she gives up to a wealthy English couple travelling in the west. At the very beginning of the narrative she speaks of her adoption of male clothing thus:

> In them days, Jane, there was only two ways for a woman to survive out west; 'wife-ing' and whoring. As I wasn't cut out for either one, I had to find my own way of surviving. So I lived like a man and sometimes even passed myself off as one. Got a little sticky at times but give me a kind of freedom that few women ever knew.

Later, Jane 'tells' her daughter that 'I never really thought of myself as a woman'. Her cross-dressing is, once more, explicitly to do with status and work. The opening sequence has Calamity/Huston passing as male to get work in Custer's army. Shuffling her feet, she is a tall, gawky figure who looks at the ground. But when challenged, Calamity wields a whip to flick the cap off the recruiting officer and thus demonstrates her prowess. On discovery (her breasts give her away whilst washing in the river), Calamity is set to 'humiliating women's work' washing clothes. If there seems to be something of necessity in Calamity's cross-dressing, this is no rites of passage tale in which she will ultimately adopt female clothes and institutionalised heterosexuality. Indeed in the final sequence, left caring for the baby of her buddy Dora (Melanie Griffith), Calamity is still in her male garb, in mythic tones telling of how she needs to just take off sometimes and ride in the hills. Even Ellen Barkin's lovesick Calamity in Walter Hill's *Wild Bill*, is at a distance from the roles of wife or whore (though she spends the film mooning over Bill Hickock).[8]

In Maggie Greenwald's *The Ballad of Little Jo*, Josephine Monaghan (Suzy Amis) finds a space out west as a small man ('little' Jo). She has been expelled from a position of femininity, designated 'society girl', which is clearly marked within the film as a class position through the expression of her sexuality (she has given birth to an illegitimate child). Having lost her class position she goes west, engages in the colonial adventure and becomes a man, owner of land and a 'husband' of sorts. Living in a hidden relationship with Tinman Wong (David Chung), who s/he has saved from the townsmen, Jo takes on the role of patriarch. Jo's choice, like that of Calamity Jane is mapped in relation to the two options of marriage and prostitution. Thus the promotion for Greenwald's film ran: 'In the Old Wild West, a woman had only two choices. She could be a wife or she could be a whore. Josephine Monaghan chose to be a man'. But of course the line means a 'poor white woman'. Rather than live as a working-class woman (as classless) s/he scars herself and sets out on a life as a small man, needing patronage but independent after a fashion. Jo's decision is not really constructed within the film as a matter of choice. The opening sequence shows her in woman's clothes, walking down a busy road, haughty but encumbered by her luggage and her parasol. 'I'm not a vagrant' she declares, but does not know where she is going. She is given a ride by a salesman, Mr Hollander, who betrays her, selling her to some soldiers from whom she escapes, her clothes torn. Mr Hollander seems to offer one possible career. She sells a chair on his behalf and is delighted when he pays her: 'the first money I've ever earned' she tells him. The scene underlines the dangers of remaining Josephine, though the woman who runs the store where she buys men's clothes (there are no dresses to be had) tells her 'it's against the law to dress improper to your sex'. Jo's transformation, in which she undresses, cuts her hair and scars her face, is intercut with flashbacks that tell her story. The sequence is eroticised, the first shots framed as if through a window, spying on her. The intercutting suggests a relationship of cause and effect between past and present, the conception of an illegitimate child, her father's condemnation of her as a 'whore': all of which produce her decision to become male. Later in the film the undertaker's undressing of her dead body is intercut with Jo's friends reminiscing in the saloon bar, a reminiscence disrupted by the news that 'Little Jo' was a woman.

As do other cross-dressing narratives, *The Ballad of Little Jo* takes pleasure in mapping Jo's successful disguise, while at the same time is haunted by the threat of discovery. This threat leads to isolation, for example with Jo taking the job of shepherding, the loneliness of which would drive other men crazy. Revelation does indeed bring danger, as Percy Corcoran's (Ian McKellen) angry attack demonstrates. Corcoran's earlier attack on Elvira, a deaf-mute prostitute who is led into the town on horseback, indicates the precarious position of women among this community of men. The final revelation of Jo as Josephine, in death, brings humiliation as his erstwhile friends marvel at the female corpse, dressing it up and setting it on a horse to be photographed. Jo's cross-dressing generates a cinematic commentary on masculinity and on the Western, with the restrictions within which other female characters operate framed through her perspective. We watch her/him learning how to eat like a man, acquiring shooting skills to protect the sheep s/he is guarding. Her gun also protects her from Percy and from the incursion of the land-hungry cattle company. Though a 'little' man, Jo gains respect within Ruby City by situating himself outside of it: 'You are a free white man now', Tinman tells Jo. She has saved his life of course, though Frank spares him on the condition she hires him to cook and clean. Jo thus gains, and at least initially exercises, power over Tinman, shutting him out in the rain to protect her own identity, to hide her secret.

If Greenwald's film thus involves the movement towards heterosexuality characteristic of the 'tomboy' scenario, this movement is problematically located in terms of the hierarchical relationship between Jo and Tinman, relations of master/servant (the parts they play when Frank visits) which also intersect with discourses of gender and with the portrayal of their inter-racial romance in a genre that is, as Pam Cook notes, 'haunted by the fear of miscegenation' (Buscombe 1988: 242). Their romance does not involve Jo returning to the role of woman. As they lie in bed together, she shows him a small, framed photograph of herself as 'society girl', formal and posed. Tinman prefers her as she is, saying 'this white girl would never do this with me'. Later, Jo angrily demands he leave the house, dressing herself as a woman and trying to make a pie: 'What man would want you?' he asks. Frank's perception of Tinman as a housekeeper disguises his role as Jo's lover, just as he cannot see Jo for what s/he is (though he repeatedly terms him 'peculiar', 'unfriendly'). The film draws on, and to some extent cuts across the Hollywood cinema's recurrent inscription of Chinese men in terms of 'femininity'.[9] Jo's 'male' guise, her short hair, is set against Tinman's long hair; her scarred face against his body, scarred from assaults and from years of work on the railroad. Their developing relationship is constituted and functions in terms of their shared exclusion from the society of white men: both face the threat of violence and fear the town. Of the three occasions on which her secret is discovered, the moment when Tinman recognises Jo as a woman ('You are not Mr Jo') is defined not by violence but mutual interest, one in which they both ask each other for their 'real' names (his mispronounced, hers shortened).

The classic Western rarely portrays women together. The fact that *Buffalo Girls* is a television production, albeit a big budget, all-star movie, allows the narrative to focus more directly on its female protagonists than is usual in the Western.[10] Indeed, the friendship between Calamity (Anjelica Huston) and Dora (Melanie Griffith) structures the film. Dora is an ultra-femme madam, to whose (whore)house/saloon Jane continually returns and who has known her, we are told, for twenty years. Unlike the cinema's many male-bonding movies, the sexual implications of this butch/femme friendship are not disavowed through comedy. Arriving at Dora's place in Deadwood for the first time in the movie, Jane enters her bedroom where she is asleep with romantic interest Gabriel Byrne, and leaps on the bed, embracing them both, at which point Byrne's character retreats to another room. While Dora immediately uncovers the secret of Jane's love for Hickock (whilst cleaning her up with a bath), it is their relationship that is constant. When Jane wants to seduce Wild Bill Hickock, Dora lends her woman's clothes. This is one of only two occasions when she will be dressed as a woman – contemplating herself in the mirror she expresses her wonder: 'I don't look anything like myself'. She must learn to walk like a woman (just as Jo in *The Ballad of Little Jo* must learn to act like a man), but her greatest humiliation also comes in these clothes as Hickock announces her identity to the bar and she becomes an object of ridicule.

If the first time Jane self-consciously dresses in female clothing is as a prospective lover, the second is in her role as mother, during an ill-fated trip to London to reclaim her daughter. She is quite out of place in the context of the 'old world', a lack of place played for comedy when she shoots up a pub. The contrast is further underlined as she looks on (unacknowledged) at her daughter riding a pony in the park, sat 'gracefully' and quite different to her mother. And in their final meeting Jane gives her daughter a horse, so much associated with the Western, which they ride together. Yet the film does not suggest that somehow Calamity's masculine dress and behaviour is an impediment to motherhood. When Dora dies in childbirth (the seemingly inevitable corollary to female friendship) Jane takes on the job of raising her baby. If the two women operate as a kind of butch/femme couple, it's also worth noting that Dora too keeps moving from town to town, as restless in her own way as Calamity. She consistently refuses marriage to the man she loves, a refusal that Calamity explains to him/us as a fear of being trapped on a ranch, of being away from the town. Yet Dora's independence and her friendship with Jane also suggest another story, one which reinvents the familiar Western relationship of cowboy and townswoman in terms of an eroticised female friendship. The image of the cowgirl, tomboy cross-dresser that she is, evokes the figure of the lesbian. Perhaps wary of these connotations, Hollywood movies have frequently cast her either as an isolated figure or set within an Oedipal narrative that ultimately produces her as a wife. Sharon Stone's Ellen is a solitary, revenge-driven figure in *The Quick and the Dead*, while Ellen Barkin's lovesick Calamity Jane in Walter Hill's *Wild Bill* exists only in relation to Hickock dashing upstairs in the saloon to fetch him her guns, she hands over her power to him. As a movie about a group of four women, *Bad Girls* can, it seems, spare one of them for domesticity/heterosexuality whilst retaining the image of the remaining three women riding off into the sunset together to the sounds of an upbeat soundtrack. Eileen's decision to stay on the ranch with William Tucker at the end of *Bad Girls*, though it is also a rejection of tomboy Lilly (with whom she shares kisses), stems from a 'femme' persona that is constructed as extreme, artificial and out of place. Her allusions to her status as 'a fine Southern lady' are undercut by Lilly, for example, repeatedly emphasising the artificiality of her performance.

The appropriation of 'masculine' clothing that defines the cowgirl produces her as a transgressive figure who is frequently androgynous, sometimes decidedly butch. *Even Cowgirls Get the Blues* (1994), Gus Van Sant's adaptation of Tom Robbins' book, offers a loving rendition of the lesbian/cowgirl scenario on the Rubber Rose Ranch complete with a k.d. lang soundtrack including such songs as 'Cowgirl Pride'. The Western/road movie provides a generic setting for a parodic tale of transformation, politics and lesbian love in which Sissy Hankshaw (Uma Thurman), a hitch-hiking misfit falls for cowgirl Bonanza Jellybean (Rain Phoenix). B Ruby Rich links the film's uneven critical reception to divisions of 'gender and generation', with straight male critics left cold by the humour and the film's lesbian/cowgirl articulation of the road movie/Western, reading the film as dated rather than as a commentary on 1970s-style collectivism (1993: 21). Van Sant's explicit appropriation of Western iconography and the figure of the cowgirl for a lesbian love story picks up on the genre's (increasingly) evident homoeroticism. *Johnny Guitar* constructs and exploits what Victor Perkins (1996) terms the 'eroticism of hatred' between Vienna and Emma, a move that, in Paula Graham's words, both underlines and draws on 'the lesbian-erotic implications of the "cat-fight", which in turn draws on homoerotic subtextual elements in Westerns' (Wilton 1995: 175).

In turn country music, whence cowgirl chic was long banished, both operates and undercuts extremes of (white) gendered identities, partly through its array of strong (often tragic) womanhood.[11] Louise Allen notes that k.d. lang's 'fame as a country singer has helped to popularize a country and western style lesbian style', whilst cowboy/girl iconography also features 'specifically within gay and lesbian cultural production' including *Desert Hearts* and Van Sant's earlier *My Own Private Idaho* (1991) (Wilton 1995: 81). Elsewhere Rosa Ainley and Sarah Cooper show how New Country has attracted a lesbian audience by keeping the elements of country and western that hold a 'camp' appeal (its '"spunky" women performers, and great clothes', for example) whilst offering an updated 'cowgirl brand of feminism that was first seen in numbers like Dolly Parton's "Dumb Blonde"' (Budge and Hamer 1994: 47). The comic fantasy sequence in which Dolly Parton's character in *Nine to Five* pursues, lassoes and ropes her sexist boss (Dabney Coleman) comes to mind. Parton's elaborate performance of femininity (she has observed more than once that 'if I hadn't been a woman, I would have been a drag queen') has its counterpoint in k.d. lang's androgynous, latterly out-lesbian persona (her latest release is titled 'Drag').[12] Madonna famously referred to k.d. lang's androgyny as 'Elvis is alive and is she ever beautiful', a phrase that signals both her gender ambiguity and the strong element of performance in her image.[13] Performance in the sense that, as Marjorie Garber notes, '[i]t is almost as if the word "impersonator", in contemporary popular culture, can be modified *either* by "female" *or* by "Elvis"' (1992: 372). Of course Elvis was an ambivalent figure who articulated a peculiar feminised, objectifying version of white working-class masculinity as aggressive sexual display. Presley's image was built on a sexual and racial ambiguity that produced him as both feminised and macho, appropri-ating black American music for the white mainstream. One of his two Westerns, *Flaming Star* (Don Siegel, 1960), picked up on the sense of racial ambiguity asso-ciated with the Elvis persona, casting him as a son of white/Native-American ancestry who is torn between two identities.[14]

If the cowgirl is already a type of cross-dresser, the Western is a genre in which an elaborate, ritualistic performance of masculinity and activities of dressing up are central. In this context it may be no surprise that Jackie Stacey terms *Desert Hearts* a 'fantasy of transformative and successful lesbian romance' (Wilton 1995: 94). She suggests that the cumulative effect of the Western setting, and the jux-taposition of the country soundtrack with this narrative of lesbian romance is ironic, drawing attention to the conventions of Hollywood romance. Already stylised when played by a man, women's enactment of the cowboy/girl image only heightens the element of self-conscious performance, of a dressing up often associated with childhood. The framing of the romantic couple, Cay and Vivian, serves to contradict 'the meaning of the "Wild West" as the place where anything goes', reminding the viewer 'that, for lesbians, romance always take place within the "frame" of heterosexual culture' (ibid.: 109). It is surely significant that *Desert Hearts*, *Even Cowgirls Get the Blues* and *Thelma and Louise* (three movies that draw on the lesbian connotations of the cowgirl, country music and the Western) involve journeys, using the metaphor of travel as escape from social con-vention (transformation) set alongside the development of a strong central relationship between two women. In a quite different way to the sort of revisionist Western typified most recently by *Unforgiven*, the evocation of the cowgirl here works to question assumptions made in the Western about violence or about gender. *The Ballad of Little Jo* adopts both strategies, framing its gritty (revision-ist) portrayal of the west through the eyes of a woman from the east who is living as a western man. Whether stylised, comic, musical or revisionist the Western still has stories to tell.

3

ACTION WOMEN

Muscles, mothers and others

Mother/Other: Geena Davis as 'Charly' in *The Long Kiss Goodnight*

'It's not because you're a woman', so psycho-bomber Howard Payne (Dennis Hopper) reassures Annie (Sandra Bullock) who he has decked out in a vest of dynamite and shackled to a moving subway train during the climax of *Speed* (1994). Annie moves through the film in various guises, appearing first as civilian participant in the action-drama, then as driver of the bus set to explode if its speed drops below fifty miles per hour. With only a very brief romantic interlude, she moves from driving a bomb-laden bus to becoming a walking bomb herself. Back in the role of civilian caught up in the action, she must wait for the hero Jack (Keanu Reeves), to come to the rescue. It's not because she's a woman? Perhaps not, since Jack's cop partner Harry (Jeff Daniels) is also held hostage, and later killed, by the vengeful bomber.[1] Though Annie's plight may not be *because* she's a woman, the fact that she *is* one certainly has significance, produces meaning. While women have long been both actors and agents in the action genre, the figure of Annie – as victim/bargaining chip/feisty heroine (dubbed 'Wildcat') and tomboyish cheerleader – is symptomatic, an indicative composite of agency and passivity. As indeed is Jack himself who is portrayed as largely reactive, even as he, like the camera, charges around the set in a manic fashion. Clearly marked as the 'dumb' one against Harry's brains, Jack is the one who tells the passengers on the bus in air-hostess-fashion to stow their bags under the seats while Annie drives.[2]

This chapter explores aspects of the sporadic integration of women into the action cinema in the late 1980s and the 1990s, considering some of the different roles and narrative strategies developed and deployed in the process. Though there have been some spectacular (and much debated) exceptions, including *Alien* and its sequels, *Terminator 2* or the more recent *The Long Kiss Goodnight*, the majority of big-budget action movies continue to focus primarily on male protagonists and to position women in supportive, often romantic, roles. Janine Turner as Sylvester Stallone's colleague and romantic interest in *Cliffhanger* (1993), Halle Berry as the air hostess assistant to Kurt Russell's hero in *Executive Decision*, Tea Leoni caught in the middle with Will Smith and Martin Lawrence in *Bad Boys*, Cindy Crawford as lawyer in peril alongside William Baldwin in *Fair Game* (all 1995): such sidekick/romantic roles, though diverse, indicate the place of the female character. At the same time, women have featured as protagonists within low and medium budget action and crime movies. Thus although high-profile movies with female protagonists such as *The Long Kiss Goodnight* or *Twister* are considered in this chapter, they should also be understood in the context of action genres more widely. Though there are specificities to the construction of the female action hero, those action films in which women *have* taken central roles were not developed in a *separate* generic space. Indeed, the increased inclusion of women in action roles has both contributed to and been part of the ways in which the genre has evolved in recent years, a process also evident in the so-called 'revisionist' Western.

In developing roles for women as fighters, action and crime movies have made use of stereotypes and images including the 'butch' type, the tomboy and the 'feisty heroine', alongside the conventionally glamorous and/or sexual action women who continue to populate the genre. Although in different ways, both the tomboy and the feisty heroine offer an articulation of gender and sexuality that foregrounds a combination of conventionally masculine and feminine elements. The tomboy is, as we've seen, a type who is frequently situated within an Oedipal narrative of cross-dressing, one in which she will ultimately discard her male clothing. Cross-dressing, and sometimes 'passing', is explicitly at work in the Western which shares with other action genres a foregrounding of performance, of 'acting tough', of confrontation and bravado which is in turn tied to gendered imagery. Cross-dressing is also foregrounded in another reworking of a genre associated with the classic Hollywood cinema: the pastiche of the swashbuckler enacted in *Cut-Throat Island*, with Geena Davis as tomboy pirate hero(ine) Morgan Adams. Yet it is not the masculinised hero(ine) in 'male' clothes that is most explicitly to do with cross-dressing. It is when Davis is dressed as a 'lady', and later as a 'whore', that she is most apparently cross-dressing, performing an artificial identity with the aid of elaborate 'feminine' costume. Her guise as a 'lady' inevitably falls apart with the chase that ensues characterised by an enthusiastic lack of decorum: charging through a shop Morgan leaps onto the coach temporarily driven by Matthew Modine, her dress torn off and in disarray, she quips 'I must visit that shop again when I have more time'. The physical abandon of a delight in movement and in casting off the gender/class impersonation of a 'lady' tallies with the opening scene which introduces Morgan as someone who is confident and sexually active. The opposition between the two sides of the Davis character in *The Long Kiss Goodnight* also constructs a tension between femininity and masculinity which is expressed through costume and behaviour. Samantha's long hair, embroidered sweaters and floral prints contrast with her alter ego Charly's 'masculine' outfits: leather jacket, leggings and vest. Like the costumes worn by Ripley in the *Alien* films, by Sarah Connor in *Terminator 2*, or by Jo in *Twister*, Charly dresses in a distinct style of women's high-street fashion which can be defined as 'butch femme' (with more emphasis on the butch than the femme). Thus the costume of the cross-dressing action hero(ine) draws on a stock of extra-cinematic images and sources. This sense of cross-dressing within and across genders reinforces the ambiguous gender identity of the female action hero, or rather points to the instability of a gendered system, and the production of an alternative space through that instability. In turn, the ubiquitous check-shirts, vests and jeans of the action movie are class-based signifiers of masculinity, used to signal the populist transformation of characters in movies such as *Independence Day*.

Distanced from a classed and raced 'femininity' which is defined by passivity and hysteria, the female action hero offers a fantasy image of (proletarian) physical strength showcased within narratives that repeatedly seek to explain her (and to explain her away). Female action heroes are constructed in narrative terms as macho/masculine, as mothers or as Others: sometimes even as all three at different points within the narrative. The maternal recurs as a motivating factor, with female heroes acting to protect their children, whether biological or adoptive (*Terminator 2, Aliens, Strange Days*) or in memory of them (*Fatal Beauty*). *The Long Kiss Goodnight* is a little more ambivalent in its use of child/mother themes and imagery. For Sam her child is paramount, but for her alter ego Charly, the child is easily left behind (at least initially). The return of 'Charly' as Samantha's memory recovers is expressed first in terms of new physical abilities. Gleefully enjoying her skill in chopping vegetables ('I used to be a chef') her talent with knives proves to be rather more deadly. The reappearance of Charly is also evident in Samantha's impatience with her daughter's tears, shouting at her as if in the army. Ultimately, of course, Charly is overcome by the maternal: we discover that she was already pregnant in her former life. Alternatively, the female hero may be represented as identified with the father, in search of authority and, sometimes reconciliation with authority. Her heroism is somehow legitimated in relation to a lost or loved father in films as diverse as the two *China O'Brien* movies with Cynthia Rothrock, *The Silence of the Lambs* and *Twister*. These latter tales mobilise the stereotype of the 'tomboy' who is framed by an Oedipal narrative in which she must 'grow up' and accept limitations and responsibilities within the terms of heterosexuality. However, the action cinema is a genre which celebrates the refusal of (physical) limitations so that different aspects of the narrative may pull in different, contradictory, directions. A third articulation of the female hero is as a fetishistic figure of fantasy derived from comic books and soft pornography involving an exaggerated statement of sexuality: performed quite precisely in the action/porn hybrid *Barb Wire* (1996) with Pamela Anderson.[3] The female action hero poses a challenge to gendered binaries through her very existence: her qualities of strength and determination and, most particularly, her labour and the body that enacts it, mark her out as 'unfeminine'. In relation to the definitions of femininity discussed in the previous chapters, it is clear that this applies both to the fetishised and the masculinised images of action, though functioning differently in each instance.

There is then a tension between the images of strength accruing to the female action hero and the narratives within which they are contained, narratives which frequently attempt to offer some explanation for her actions, to define her as exceptional. *Images* (not characters) such as the masculinised or the fetishised female body in action, evolve from and engage with an iconography of female independence derived or developed within sources including advertising and soft pornography (where strong women are the stuff of fantasy). Yet these sources do not fix the meaning completely. As with pin-ups of muscular male bodies, the very qualities that are foregrounded in still images pose problems for narrative. As Richard Dyer (1982) has pointed out, the built male body already contains a contradictory sense of masculine strength in relation to the objectification and display involved. There is also a tension between an image built, designed for contemplation in static poses and the situation of such images within the context of action. By extension it is possible to understand the difficulties involved in putting the eroticised female image from pin-up into 'action': both she and the male bodybuilder are subject to display and to the need to 'pose'. There is an evident difficulty in reconciling the 'Don't call me babe' tagline featured throughout *Barb Wire* with the images of Barb Wire/Anderson herself in the movie. Barb Wire, as her name suggests, exhibits an eroticised toughness, both inviting and returning a sexual gaze. The movie begins, as might be expected, with a staging of erotic performance: Barb Wire is sprayed with water as she swings from a trapeze wearing a fetishistic dress that is cut to reveal her breasts. This erotic act, we discover, is designed to take her undercover into a club. To prove her sassiness, she greets a comment from the audience with a hurled shoe, thus transforming her garb into a weapon.[4] An aggressive, pouting version of female sexuality, familiar from fashion spreads or still images in magazines, both mainstream and pornographic, seems less plausible within the context of narrative. Poses of independence feature in adverts for a range of products aimed at women from cosmetics to holidays. The difficulty of narrativising a repertoire of powerful images is discussed further in Chapter eight around the interchange between music video and cinema and the location of female musical stars, such as Cher or Madonna, with highly sexual images within the context of narrative. More generally the marketing of 'babe' and 'girl power' to young women in the 1990s produces a commodified context within which to understand these images.[5]

Musculinity and motherhood

The 1980s and early 1990s saw the emergence of a few female action heroes defined by a quality of 'musculinity', an enactment of a muscular masculinity involving a display of power and strength over the body of the female performer. Linda Hamilton's role in *Terminator 2*, dubbed a 'buff warrior-mom' by Fred Pfeil (1995: 53), or that of Ripley across the four *Alien* films invoke a 'musculinity' linked to the maternal. Ridley Scott's *Alien* and James Cameron's follow-up *Aliens* became two of the few action/horror films to receive sustained critical comment. There are evident links between Cameron's sequel and his later *Terminator 2* in terms of the place assigned to motherhood as a motivating factor for the female hero. The extent to which the *Alien* films also address the 'horror' of reproduction, discussed at length by Barbara Creed, is both reaffirmed and to some extent problematised in the final scene of the third film in which Ripley's suicide/birth is celebrated in slow-motion. In Creed's words: 'Despite her integrity and courage, Ripley/woman is betrayed by her body, unable finally to preserve her own flesh from contamination by the abject alien other – the monstrous fecund mother' (1993: 52). A more clinical reproduction, though undoubtedly equally monstrous in its implications, is promised for the upcoming fourth film.

Alien³ is perhaps the bleakest film in the series (thus far), with Weaver playing Ripley as a weary veteran of alien battles: 'You've been a part of my life so long, I can't remember anything else', she mutters darkly. This after yet another encounter with the bureaucratic disbelief that greets heroes in action movies who try (and fail) to convince those in authority that 'it' is 'out there'. As Creed argues, *Alien³* aligns Ripley/Weaver more explicitly than the other films with the alien, as a figure of Otherness (1993: 51). 'The Bitch is Back' ran the line on the poster for the film, under a close-up of a butch Ripley, head shaven military fashion, face-to-face with an alien. Set within an all-male maximum-security prison, populated largely by British actors, the American Ripley/Weaver is more than ever out of place.[6] She is far from submissive however: told by one of the prisoners that he is 'a murderer and rapist of women' she replies calmly, 'I guess I must make you nervous'. Indeed her arrival on Fiorina 'Fury' 161 produces consternation among the inmates, a panic and uncertainty associated with the very presence of a woman (a presence deemed 'intolerable'). Not only does Ripley bring her own (monstrous) body, but she brings the alien with her, her investigations ultimately leading her to her own body, invaded by 'foreign tissue'. She is 'part of the family' now, prowling the labyrinthine corridors under the prison looking for death. Both mother and Other, Ripley represents a sort of authority on Fury 161, she is the one to whom the prisoners look for 'some leadership', at the same time she is a sufficiently different figure who can be resented and blamed for the chaos and death that surrounds them. Continuing the anti-corporate theme of the previous *Alien* films, the prisoners eventually realise that the company (authority) will bring no respite, will save none of them. In this context the prisoners can unite under her leadership: since their death is inevitable the only question that remains is how it will occur and how they will face it.

Appearing in different versions across the three films, Ripley functions as a sort of reference point for the contemporary female action hero. In Fincher's version Ripley's is a decidedly butch body, an androgynous body pregnant with an alien infant. The contradictory articulation of a female body which is masculine, a body that is simultaneously maternal and destructive is symptomatic. The butch/androgynous/tomboy action heroine brings with her associations of same-sex desire, suggesting a lesbian body. As Barbara Creed writes:

> One does not need a specific kind of body to become – or to be seen as – a lesbian. All female bodies represent the threat or potential – depending

on how you see it – of lesbianism. Within homophobic cultural practices, the lesbian body is constructed as monstrous in relation to male fantasies

(1995: 87)

If all female bodies are potentially lesbian bodies, Creed nonetheless notes that some types are more explicitly or specifically lesbian bodies: the 'lesbian body as active and masculinised' (ibid.: 88). It is such active/masculinised bodies that we find in the action cinema. The lesbian connotations of the action hero(ine) are both expressed and comically undercut in *Cut-Throat Island* when Morgan Adams (Geena Davis) looks a prostitute up and down before asking her 'how much?'. The film quickly goes on to reveal/explain that it is the woman's clothes she is interested in, not her body. Often situated within the Oedipal narrative of the tomboy, this body 'undermines patriarchal gender boundaries that separate the sexes' (Creed 1995: 96). If the shaven-headed image of Ripley produces her even more as a (butch) lesbian body than before, it is in this film that she has a (hetero)sexual encounter with disgraced doctor Clemens (Charles Dance) who is dispatched fairly shortly after. This equivocal play with gay and lesbian desire and identity has become a defining feature of the genre, though it is handled in diverse ways.[7]

Action cinema in the 1990s

The movement of the action cinema into big-budget (and indeed mega-budget) production, and thence into the mainstream represented a significant shift in the popular American cinema in the late 1970s and 1980s. Expensive effects-driven action and adventure films increasingly dominated domestic and international box-office in this period. The continued production of action movies in the 1990s has confounded those critics who felt the genre was dying away at the beginning of the decade, and was perhaps giving way to 'softer' versions of masculinity showcased in melodramas and comedies around families and fatherhood.[8] Of course the articulation of masculinity on offer in the 1980s action movie was not in any case straightforward, producing complex gendered identities in relation to class and racial divisions and hierarchies. In effect evolving discourses on masculinity in relation to men, work and fatherhood have informed, rather than displaced, the action genre. For Fred Pfeil the 'sensitive guy' movies of the early 1990s, such as *Regarding Henry* and *The Fisher King*, have a lot in common with the caring-killing machine played by Schwarzenegger in Cameron's *Terminator 2*.[9] The family and domesticity, for example, are central to James Cameron's *True Lies*, an expensive, special-effects showcase that was too violent to target itself directly to a general (or 'family') audience.[10] Though there are many continuities with the 1980s, the action cinema has reformulated itself in the 1990s. The continued appearance of female protagonists in the genre is part of, as well as a contributing factor in that reformulation.

If in the 1980s two trends or types of narrative could be distinguished, that which emphasised the suffering of the hero on the one hand and that which was either comic or parodic in tone on the other, then it is clearly the latter that is dominant in the 1990s. The contemporary action cinema has tended to erase or to play down the figure of the suffering hero, though he has not disappeared.[11] The hero is treated as something of a joke, with films opting most often for a comic buddy partnership defined by an eroticised banter. If the typical action scenario of the mid-1980s featured an embittered, silent and sole male protagonist, the typical action movie of the mid-1990s is comic (whether light or cynical) even parodic in tone. Though McTiernan's *The Last Action Hero* (1993) was an expensive flop, the kind of tongue-in-cheek mockery of Schwarzenegger's persona which characterised the film has been repeated across a range of other movies. This, crudely put, has followed the displacement of the embittered, countercultural Vietnam veteran as a central figure by the more confident Gulf War veteran. Though temporarily triumphant, there is already an increasing stock of representations which register (if indirectly) concerns about that conflict, such as Gulf War Syndrome and friendly fire. This broad shift can be related to the triumphalist tone of *Independence Day*, for example. Yet even *Independence Day*, a thoroughgoing pastiche of its generic reference points, invokes the Gulf War as some lost point of certainty, a time when things were simpler and, as the President says in the film, 'we knew what we had to do'.

The broad move to a lighter tone in American action movies has also allowed a space for female characters to take on more central action roles. The camp excesses of *Streetfighter*, its video-game origins and its clear debt to Hong Kong action films allows both Kylie Minogue in pigtails and camouflage leggings and Ming-Na Wen as journalist Chun-Li who has trained in all the martial arts so as to avenge her father, to seem no more or less credible than Jean-Claude Van Damme with a tattoo of the Stars and Stripes on his bicep. And female fighters do not appear only in such vehicles, as the ambivalent, slow-paced investigation of heroism and betrayal in *Courage Under Fire* (1996) demonstrates. The suffering, betrayed female hero, played by Meg Ryan in Zwick's film, almost inevitably means something different from her male counterpart as we also see in the very different scenarios of *Terminator 2*, *Alien³* and *The Quick and the Dead*. Indeed, the latter two are perhaps best understood as pastiche in any case. Vowing to go in search of the alien herself, Ripley mutters through gritted teeth that 'it's down there in the basement'. Aaron, the officer with such a low IQ that the inmates jokingly call him '85', tells her, in a bemused tone, 'this whole place is a basement'. 'It's a metaphor' Ripley whispers in return, a remark that serves as commentary on the by now epic battle between her and 'the' alien(s). The irony is underlined (with hindsight) since even death has not stopped the series. The development of the female hero in the Western as gunslinger/tomboy/cross-dresser/mother could be said to set the pattern for the development of other action-based genres in the 1990s: from *Streetfighter* to *Bad Girls* to *Cut-Throat Island* or *The Long Kiss Goodnight*, action roles for women were perhaps not those that films of the 1980s suggested, but nonetheless both signalled and form part of generic shifts.

Buddies and partners: From homo- to hetero-bonding

The summer of 1994 saw the successful international release of two blockbuster action films incorporating female protagonists in quite distinct ways, *True Lies* (James Cameron) and *Speed* (Jan de Bont), to which I've already referred. Commenting on *Speed*, Dyer notes that while Annie (Sandra Bullock) 'does get the thrills of extreme physical danger and the exultation of mastery of a machine', the film nonetheless 'conforms to the pattern of contemporary action films by constituting her as helper' (1994: 10). Though her successful guiding of the bus over a fifty-foot gap in the road is greeted by a fellow passenger with the shout 'you are the *man*!, you are the *man*!', Annie is not, as Dyer reminds us, 'the main man'. Rather she is one of a range of supporting characters, typically played by white women or black men (less often, though sometimes, black women) who follow the white male hero 'but never quite as equals, never with quite the same access to the speed of worldly sensation' (ibid.). Such sidekick roles are related to but distinct from the buddy partnerships so common in the genre. The distinction, though difficult to draw precisely, lies with the extent to which the film emphasises hierarchies of knowledge and skill: the relationship between two cop partners, however hierarchical is more equal than that of the professional and the amateur in need of protection. Contrast, for example, the relation between the two male cops in *Bad Boys*, one freewheeling and risk-taking, one domestic and cautious, with that between Vanessa Williams and Arnold Schwarzenegger in *Eraser* (1996). In the film, Williams plays a witness in danger, Schwarzenegger is the Marshal assigned to protect her. Whilst her role is not an 'hysterical woman' (what might be termed a 'screamer') since she shows herself capable with a gun among other things, she is nonetheless defined in relation to Schwarzenegger who, we are frequently reminded, is 'the best' in the business.

Against this background, it is interesting to note that whilst sole female protagonists remain relatively rare, central male/female partnerships are increasingly common in American action films. Recent examples include *Speed*, Kathryn Bigelow's *Strange Days*, discussed further in this chapter, and John Woo's *Broken Arrow* (1996). Woo's film begins with familiar ground: a competitive male friendship – defined further by their different places in a military hierarchy – between Vic Deakins (John Travolta) and Riley Hale (Christian Slater). Quite quickly, Deakins is revealed as the villain – a man who steals nuclear weapons and plots to blackmail the government. Their friendly competition becomes lethal, or rather the barely suppressed hostility evident in the opening scene boxing match comes to the surface. Once Deakins has left Hale for dead, ranger Terry Carmichael (Samantha Mathis) comes to his aid. As the film progresses they work together, and separately, to defeat Deakins. Such narratives offer a variant on the mismatched male partnership theme which serves to make explicit the romantic/sexual aspects of that relationship within a heterosexual context. Yet in highlighting this aspect of 'partnership', the male/female action narratives come across the 'problem' of (hetero)sex. The sparks which fly when male buddies

74

banter with one another become more transparently sexual when transposed onto the male/female pair. And if the convention of the male buddy pairing is that the two will *not* kiss – though they may joke about it incessantly, or perhaps exchange tender glances, as in the *Lethal Weapon* films – it is almost inevitable that the male/female buddy pair *will* end up in an embrace. The foregrounding of romantic/sexual possibilities may be a 'problem' since it potentially halts the action and generates vulnerability: a scenario highlighted in *Fair Game* when William Baldwin and Cindy Crawford pause in their flight from high-tech Russian pursuers for a sexual encounter on a moving freight train. Such moments have the additional effect of 'exposing' the homosexual as well as the homosocial aspects of male buddy relations, even as the contrast is maintained. Further, as we'll see across a range of genres including the crime film, discussed in Chapter four, this movement serves at a narrative level to reaffirm the idea that women are a disruptive force who somehow bring sexuality into the (male) world of work.[12]

True Lies has deception and transformation as its central terms. Cameron's film offers spectacle, expensive special effects and too much screen violence for a family audience, yet it gives a substantial amount of screen time to domestic themes. The film's central conceit revolves around Schwarzenegger's duplicity as a husband who masquerades as a dull, computer sales representative who actually leads the glamorous life of an international spy (The film's poster read: 'When he said I do, he never said what he did'). This is a fairly recognisable fantasy, one in which the ordinary is a mask for the extraordinary, of escape from everyday routine. Yet, in contrast to Schwarzenegger's comparable role in *Total Recall* (1990), the audience is left in no doubt as to the veracity of Schwarzeneggers's spy identity via the film's spectacular opening which reprises *Goldfinger*, with the star as Harry Tasker as Harry Renquist (his alternate identity) emerging from a lake by a Swiss mansion and peeling off his wetsuit to reveal uncrumpled evening dress. Tasker/Renquist proceeds to enact his role in the operation with some precision, finding time to tango with glamorous villain Juno Skinner (Tia Carrere) and making a spectacular, explosive shoot-out exit. At this point, within the context of the fantasy of a sales rep who dreams he is an international spy, one might expect his character to wake up, disappointed to find out that, after all, it was just a dream. Indeed there is a sort of waking up as Renquist/Tasker returns to his 'ordinary' life/wife and daughter in their suburban home. In fantasy-land Renquist overcomes two aggressive Dobermans, smashing their heads together and commanding them to 'stay'. In suburbia he takes a tiny lapdog for a walk in the rain, a cover to allow partner Gib (Tom Arnold) to plant a tracking device in his wife's handbag. In fantasy-land Renquist dances in a vast ballroom and has high technology at his command; in suburbia the darkly-lit rooms seem too small for his physique.

Schwarzenegger is not the only star body in *True Lies*; Jamie Lee Curtis co-stars as his wife Helen Tasker. Whilst Harry Renquist tangos in his European action-fantasy, Harry Tasker neglects his wife. Helen becomes involved with a used-car salesman who is masquerading as a spy in order to attract bored middle-class women. Thus the territory with which the film deals is fantasy – clearly marked by its references to Bond-style glamour and, more disturbingly, in the casual racism and cardboard villains. The film offers a double fantasy of double lives – Schwarzenegger as a computer salesman with a dysfunctional family who is actually a spy, Curtis as a legal secretary who seeks escape from dull routine through the pulp fiction spy narrative offered by Simon (Bill Paxton). *True Lies* works to produce a reconciliation between the polarised gender roles that it has established as the basis for its central characters – Helen as frustrated wife and Harry as both duplicitous and deceived – between the routine of the domestic and the excitement of action. Once he discovers the 'affair', Harry is obsessive in his attempt to find out about Helen's private life, arranging surveillance of her activities, tapping her phone, tracking her with a helicopter, but not, of course, speaking to her. This pursuit culminates in her 'arrest' and interrogation, a scene which articulates and underscores his failure to communicate and her frustration and isolation. Harry can see her, but Helen has only a mirror to contemplate, as her husband quizzes her in a voice distorted by technology. Tearful then angry, she talks of her desires, which Simon has exploited: her need to 'feel alive' to 'do something outrageous', 'to be needed and to be trusted and to be special'. Harry as her interrogator, offers her 'a little adventure' which, unsurprisingly, involves a sexual assignation (with Helen playing the role of prostitute) with himself in disguise, an adventure that leads to a hotel room but which is disrupted by the arrival of a gang of terrorists. Later, the interrogation is briefly reprised in reverse when Harry is injected with a truth serum and Helen takes the opportunity to ask some questions. Yet it is not until almost the end of the film that they reunite as a couple. Ultimately Harry and Helen join together to defend America against the caricatured Arab terrorist group led by Aziz (Art Malik). Here Harry reveals his skills whilst Helen helps out accidentally, screaming and grimacing as her automatic weapon falls down a flight of stairs killing adversaries unaided. She is still largely an ineffectual observer, recaptured at the end of the sequence. It is work that separates the family and threatens it, but it is also ultimately work that (re)unites them, or at least a fantasy version of work.[13]

In the attempt to bring the 'wife' into the Bond-style action, *True Lies* uses strategies through which she is subject to sustained surveillance/punishment and ultimately functions by positioning her as a sort of Bond girl. We follow Helen, daughter Dana, but also Harry himself through a process of transformations designed to stitch up the heterosexual family. Initially Curtis' 'star body' is concealed in what might be conventionally understood as dowdy (though not tomboyish) dress, with glasses, her awkward movements, hunched shoulders and a late 1970s hairstyle. It is only at the very end of the film that she is able to demonstrate physical agility while dancing the tango. Thus in the final sequence Harry and Helen are united as 'spies' located within a world of glamour and romance. Dana's transformation is in line with the typical development of the tomboy's narrative. She moves from scruffy petty-thief in trousers and Dr Martin shoes to feminised and cleaned-up 'daddy's girl' who wears a frock and a string of pearls in the 'one year later' happy family scenario at the end.[14] If *True Lies* disdains the explicit parody of macho roles found in Schwarzenegger's double role in *The Last Action Hero*, this is hardly surprising given the spectacular financial failure of a film generally taken to be too smart for its own good. In the film, 'real' women and 'cartoon' female characters were played off against each other, explicitly discussed in relation to a notion of 'male' perceptions. The film shares with *True Lies* a combination of parodying the action hero whilst still taking pleasure in his exploits. Cameron's film also picks up on those 1990s narratives that chart a nurturing masculinity defined largely through fatherhood. This is alluded to (of course as a joke) in Gib's suggestion that Harry get in touch with his 'feminine side'. Yet in the moment of discovery of Helen's 'affair', Gib confronts Harry with an exasperated: 'what did you expect? She's a flesh and blood woman and you're never there'. Perhaps the central point of interest in the drawn out and tortuous attempt to address themes of domesticity versus action is that all the hero's achievements (real or fantasy) count for nothing when they exclude his wife/family. In this context the use of a female *star*, Jamie Lee Curtis, alongside Schwarzenegger is surely significant. Curtis brings a history of strong but persecuted roles from her lengthy involvement in the thriller and horror genres (*Halloween, Blue Steel*).

José Arroyo has suggested that '*True Lies* might not be good Cameron, but it is good Schwarzenegger. Racist, sexist and shallow, it is escapism into a white boys' fantasy land' (1994: 28).[15] The film also attempts to take the white female star into the shared 'fantasy land', after a fairly thorough humiliation. Yet Helen's destruction/reconstitution is not the only 'cost' in this narrative economy, as Arroyo's comments suggest. Just as the couple kiss against a background of a nuclear cloud mushrooming across the Florida skyline, the terrorist plot functions as a cardboard background against which, and through which, the couple can be reunited. And just as Harry is constructed in relation to a caricature racial enemy (Art Malik) and his incompetent terrorist gang, Crimson Jihad (who are unable even to work a video camera effectively), Helen's transformation into a glamorous action heroine is through an opposition to and ultimately conflict with Juno Skinner. In the film's final sequence Helen and Harry are firmly in fantasy-land together. The two of them humiliate Simon, who is seen in the guise of a waiter playing the same 'spy' act. Thus Helen takes on Gib's role as buddy partner, relishing the superiority of their position. This reuniting of the heterosexual couple troubles the other central relationship in the film which is that between Harry and Gib. The relationship is a sort of marriage: they spend most of their time together, know each other's secrets, foibles and faults and engage in banter. They complement each other physically and in terms of characteristics: short/tall, soft body/hard body, vocal/silent. The final line of the film is Gib's. His pleading voice-over accompanies the Taskers' tango in fantasy-spy land (he insists they should get back to work). Gib resents being left outside, being ignored. He complains that he's 'been in the van for fifteen years'. This comic monologue emphasises the extent to which the romantic action pairing is both different from and similar to the buddy relationship (for example, in verbal exchanges). Thus in the final sequence, Harry and Helen also tango, reprising the opening sequence in which Harry as Renquist dances with Juno Skinner. Even the two women's dresses are similar, suggesting that Helen is occupying the space of glamour and sexuality that Juno signifies in the film. Helen initially seeks adventure and excitement with fraudster Simon in Chinatown, Hollywood's privileged location of an exoticised otherness.[16] At the conclusion, she has moved from ineptitude to physical grace and control, taking the place of the 'other' woman. In *True Lies* it is not so much that the marriage overcomes the buddy relationship, but that Harry and Helen must *become buddies*. Helen and Harry are produced as a couple in terms of the homosocial codes of the buddy partnership (laughing at a weaker man) and the heterosexual codes of marriage (their dance).

By contrast, the male/female double-act in *Speed*, with Keanu Reeves' cop and Sandra Bullock as the citizen co-opted into action, spends little time on emotion – focusing instead on action. The film is too frenetic to engage explicitly in much of the battle of the sexes-style comedy found in *True Lies*. So, although there is clearly a romantic/flirtatious aspect to the partnership that evolves (again defined as professional male and amateur female) the film is not particularly concerned to explore this. Both central characters are composites of agency and passivity, active and reactive in turns. Jack Travens/Reeves is brave but stupid: cautioned by Dennis Hopper's villain not to 'try to grow a brain'. This complements Reeves' developing star image: 'Young, dumb and full of cum', as he's described by an FBI boss in *Point Break*. In *The Making of Speed* Reeves plays up to this image (his *Bill and Ted* persona) enthusing about the dressing up that the film involved: 'I get to wear this really bitching SWAT outfit – this really cool uniform.' Whilst the hero is concerned with showing off his clothes as much as his mind, Annie is driving the bus, and some of the action in *Speed*. When Jack has a tantrum, she holds his hand and calms him down. 'I've never seen driving like that' enthuses Jack, and sure enough it is revealed that she takes the bus because she lost her licence for speeding. Annie's outfit functions as a sort of 'femme tomboy' guise, with the combination of butch/femme elements found in high-street fashion (chunky boots and lacy socks, vests combined with floral prints). This is quite different from the frumpy-to-glamorous transition enacted around Curtis in *True Lies*. Annie is already dressed for action. Her collegiate sweatshirt suggests a cheerleader type: the sort of perfect teeth and sweet smile role which Bullock played as Lenina Huxley alongside Sylvester Stallone in *Demolition Man*. She displays qualities of capability, first in demanding to know what is going on, later in her calmness in contrast to the panic-stricken passenger who leaps to her death. However, Annie is also scatty: she is late for the bus, running to catch up whilst smoking and balancing a cup of coffee. Ultimately Annie shifts from the driving seat to heroine awaiting rescue. This allows her to move directly into the less interesting role of the 'romantic interest'. The film was a major breakthrough for Bullock, establishing her as a box office star (she went on to make a series of romance movies, and starred in the high-tech thriller *The Net*). That it was Bullock's presence which was a key element in green-lighting *Speed 2* (1997), even after Reeves turned down the chance to reprise his role, is indicative of the centrality of her role in the scenario.[17]

The implications of the introjection of central female characters and concerns of 'family life' are exemplified quite differently in two further blockbusters of the 1990s: *Independence Day*, in which the President of the United States (Bill Pullman) saves the world through his heroic labour and his special skills as a fighter pilot/populist leader, and *Twister*, in which researcher Jo (Helen Hunt) acts as the locus of a heroism defined through a romantic search for scientific knowledge. Though family, and the need to reconcile spaces of public labour and private life, provide an important reference point in both films, the deployment of the 'independent working woman' and of the action hero(ine) (with action as heroic labour) is distinct, revolving around signifiers of class. *Independence Day* enacts a tongue-in-cheek pastiche in which a set of science fiction clichés are rehearsed against spectacular special effects that threaten to overshadow the characters at every turn. At a narrative level, working women are a problem to be solved. We are presented with four male and three female central characters, all of whom are involved in discrete narratives which come together in different ways. The female characters can be precisely located in relation to the types already outlined, undergoing transformations that involve their role in relation to the action, largely conducted by men, and, crucially, signified through costume. Jasmine (Vivica Fox), the girlfriend of Steven Hiller (Will Smith), is a stripper (and a mother) whose work is presented as standing in the way of his career (he wants to be an astronaut but, it is suggested, either he isn't doing enough respectable living or he isn't the right type). We briefly see Jasmine dancing at the club, the Stars and Stripes in the background. Ironically, no-one is looking; the customers are all fixed on the television with the news of alien spaceships displacing an interest in sexual display. This indifference perhaps prefigures her transformation as apocalypse-survivor-cum-nurse to marry Hiller on the eve of the final battle. From stripper/mother to carer/wife, Jasmine's transformation is mapped in relation to the already overdetermined cinematic portrayal of black women as either sexual or nurturing. The First Lady, played by Mary McDonnell, a power-dresser in the style of Hillary Clinton, is caught in the blast, rescued by Jasmine and finally dies in a defining fictional space of governmental conspiracy made notorious by *The X Files*, 'Area 51'. Her dying words to her President husband are: 'I'm so sorry that I didn't come home when you asked me to'. Redemption is also available, though not through death, for Constance (Margaret Colin), the other power-dresser in the narrative. Connie, the President's aide and a type of Public Relations manager, is the ex-wife of hippy he-man hero, David (Jeff Goldblum). Both the President and his PR aide must exchange their suits for a different kind of attire: a gradual transformation in costume that signals a process of redemption, of movement away from bureaucracy and big government to a populist identification with the people. The President swaps his suit for a jumpsuit for his change back to the role of pilot – a role in which he is evidently most comfortable.[18]

Connie's transformation is perhaps most indicative of the symbolic functioning of two distinct types of 'cross-dressing'. Recall here that both the power-dressed working woman type and the 'masculinised' attire of the action hero(ine) involve costumes that incorporate elements of supposedly male clothing as part of a negotiation of the presentation of women's (aberrant) bodies in relation to women's role. Thus the fact that Connie moves from pinstriped shirt suit and heels in her working woman mode, to green vest, check shirt, casual trousers and trainers not only produces an echo of David's costume but equates her with a different type of labour: one that is also masculine, but located within a distinct class base (manual). The moment when she first appears in this new costume is when David has figured out how to stop the alien attack ('now he gets ambitious!'), a moment when she must also admit, when asked what's going on, that she has 'no idea'. If the image of women in business suits or evening dress has connotations of success in a male environment and aristocratic decadence respectively, it is not the case that when women step into 'male' attire it is always class cross-dressing at stake. Dressing as a proletarian man has featured extensively in high-street fashion and is reserved in the cinema for the action heroine as a tomboy cross-dresser. Within the action narrative the tomboy and the power-dresser present two distinct appropriations of 'male' attire, with the latter a figure of fear.

Twister also uses costume to suggest and reinforce an opposition between different kinds of female cross-dressing. It is Jo, dressed in a white vest, brown slacks and a leather jacket, an outfit marked clearly as working clothes, who brings the hero Bill (Bill Paxton) back into the world of robust (if nebulous) science as a space of integrity. This is set against the glamourised media world to which he has succumbed in his new role as TV weatherman. In both *Twister* and *Independence Day* heroism is linked quite precisely to *action*, operating within a populist framework that opposes real work (action, manual labour) to superficial work (characters who have careers in the media, PR or politics) – an opposition frequently mapped in turn onto masculine and feminine. Wooden characters are opposed to the spontaneity of the heroes, static to mobile camerawork, sedate to orchestral music.[19] In *Twister* both the tomboyish, discreetly cross-dressed Jo and Melissa, Bill's new fiancée, are doctors, though neither is a medical doctor. Yet Melissa's profession, as a 'reproductive therapist', is played for laughs: as the truck follows and is swept around by a tornado, her mobile phone is forever ringing, allowing her to dispense advice that has come to signal the ludicrous aspects of therapy-speak ('she did not marry you for your penis'). Her mobile phone is counterpoint to Jo's use of CB-style radio. Melissa's distance from the world of Jo's team is underscored when she confesses that when Bill had told her he used to chase tornadoes 'deep down I always thought it was a metaphor'. Which of course it is. The final seal on the reunion of Jo and Bill in *Twister* is their experience of the tornado together. Jo relishes the action and excitement whilst Melissa is fearful, telling Jo she is the craziest of all. Just as throughout the tools of the trade are contrasted. However, Melissa is not a bad character, unlike the villainous Jonas, seduced by corporate research grants (he's in it for the money not the science). If we needed reassurance on this, she changes clothes: from linen suit into jeans, white vest and a (man's) blue and white striped shirt.

Tomboys and other cross-dressers

When female characters are cast as tomboys, as muscular or as cross-dressed in male proletarian guise, they can be incorporated fairly easily into action narratives as both *Twister* and *Speed* demonstrate. The tomboy is by now a staple of the action and adventure narrative. There are evident similarities with the figure of the 'Final Girl' identified by Carol Clover in the slasher film:

> The Final Girl is boyish, in a word. Just as the killer is not fully masculine, she is not fully feminine – not, in any case, feminine in the ways of her friends. Her smartness, gravity, competence in mechanical and other practical matters, and sexual reluctance set her apart from the other girls and ally her, ironically, with the very boys she fears or rejects, not to speak of the killer himself.
>
> (Clover 1992: 40)

Clover distinguishes between horror and action fairly sharply, suggesting that they operate in different modes, with the horror film emphasising the victim.[20] The tomboy hero(ines) of the action cinema share with Clover's Final Girl a peculiar gender status, and an ambivalent relationship to sexuality. The sense of a transitional state is sometimes played for eroticism – as if the 'masculine' clothing forms a disguise behind which the 'real' figure of the woman is glimpsed. Paula Graham observes in this context that the tomboy's 'masculine clothing emphasizes her girlish sexual attractiveness' (Wilton 1995: 169). In *Bad Girls* Drew Barrymore's tomboyish character Lilly resents being perceived as a sexual object at the same time as the camera insistently presents her in that fashion. For Creed the active, masculinised body of the tomboy as a potentially transgressive image is framed (contained) by an Oedipal narrative of transformation. This, she suggests, is a male fantasy through which the desire to act without restraint (and by association, lesbianism) can be understood as a phase within a narrative which charts the acquisition of an appropriate heterosexual attachment and identity. *Twister* spins a fairly explicit Oedipal yarn around its hero(ine) in which Jo must learn to accept the death of her father during a storm (which we see in the opening scene, set some twenty years before when Jo is a young girl) and focus on what she has 'right in front of her' (i.e. Bill). Yet this acceptance does not necessarily involve putting away childish things, but a drawing of women into the infantile pleasures of the action film. Scientific work is evoked through the joys of driving around the countryside very fast and playing hard rock music. '*The laboratory is nature*' intoned the trailer for *Twister*: offering a gutsy, frontier version of scientific research in which Jo as frontierswoman is at the centre.

The tomboy is variously identified with her father, may seek to take his place, to fulfil or run counter to his expectations: in each case an intense relationship of some kind is foregrounded to provide an explanatory framework for the hero(ine) as masculinised, as active. In *Cut-Throat Island* Davis literally carries her father with her: one third of the treasure map is tattooed on his scalp which she removes on his death. While the film ends with the formation of a heterosexual couple (Adams and Shaw), the future pleasures of a life of piracy (and of a sequel, of course) are retained. Captain Morgan Adams offers her crew the choice of either retiring to the Caribbean suburbs (a mock statement of the typical fate of the tomboy) or continuing a life of notoriety in search of treasure; the former hardly seems an option. Of course there are no other action women in this world – only the society women duped by Shaw at the beginning of the movie and the prostitute whose clothing Davis purchases at one point. 'You're more active than other women I've known,' Shaw tells her in the middle of a set-piece fight, another reminder perhaps of her 'exceptional' status. Graham writes of Jean Peters' role in *Anne of the Indies* (1951) that '[h]er cross-dressing symbolizes freewheeling, masculine attitudes to sexuality, money and aggression' (Wilton 1995: 169–70). This is constructed throughout in contrast to the 'feminine' Debra Paget in the role of good and loyal wife with both women competing for the affections of Louis Jourdan's LaRochelle. Renny Harlin's film dispenses with this opposition entirely so that Adams can be constructed as both 'masculine' (tomboy) and as actively heterosexual. In *The Long Kiss Goodnight* (the second collaboration of then husband and wife team Harlin and Davis) the conflict between Davis' two personas, 'Samantha' and 'Charly' represents this distinction quite precisely through codes of costume and behaviour. If Charly's desires are unfettered, Samantha is defined by her motherhood, community role, and thence by the needs of others.

The refusal of an opposition between a masculine woman and a feminine woman, which is also a refusal of the tomboy's successful Oedipalisation, in part depends on the employment of a related stereotype of popular cinema, the 'feisty heroine'. She is characterised within movie discourse as a woman with a strength and spirit that is defined as atypical (sometimes through a contrast to other weaker women). If the tomboy is an ambivalent, transitional figure, the feisty heroine is both clearly adult and clearly inscribed as heterosexual. Consider, for example, Rene Russo as an Internal Affairs officer in *Lethal Weapon 3* (1992) and as an agent protecting the President in *In the Line of Fire* (1993), or the roles taken by Mary Elizabeth Mastrantonio in *The Abyss* (1989) and *Robin Hood: Prince of Thieves* (1991) (in which she is cast as a supposedly 'feminist' Maid Marion who ogles Robin and betrays an ability to fight). An earlier and indicative example of the feisty heroine is Carrie Fisher's role as Princess Leia in the phenomenally successful *Star Wars* (1977), *The Empire Strikes Back* (1980) and *The Return of the Jedi* (1983). A self-conscious pastiche of the adventure serials of the 1930s (among other generic reference points), the character recalls Dale Arden in the *Flash Gordon* series, origins that also serve to remind us of the longevity of these types.[21] Princess Leia constantly requires rescue, whilst at the same time fulfilling an active, take charge, role. Is this by virtue of her rather vague 'royal' status? She clearly has a leadership role in the second film in the series, *The Empire Strikes Back*, in which she reprimands love interest Han Solo (Harrison Ford) for his seeming self-interest. As in *Cut-Throat Island* there are scarcely any other women in the three films, good or bad. Thus the heroic female stands alone, as an exception to the rules and (at least in narrative terms) determinedly heterosexual.

By contrast to the tomboy, the feisty heroine moves between modes in a non-linear fashion, functioning simultaneously or alternately as romantic interest, sexual object and active protagonist within the narrative. The association of feisty heroines with male/masculine qualities is marked by her very inscription as feisty: she 'has balls' as well as guts, she is 'spunky' and so forth. These qualities can be acquired seemingly through association with men/masculinity. Charly in *The Long Kiss Goodnight* was adopted/recruited by CIA boss Perkins on the death of her father. 'Suck my dick, every one of you bastards' spits Charly at her grittiest, driving a truck with chemical weapons on it into a brick wall. Morgan Adams was raised by her pirate father. In *Lethal Weapon 3*, Cole (Russo) tells Riggs (Mel Gibson), before a display of martial arts skills and a comparison of scars gained in the line of duty leads to the inevitable clinch, that she was brought up with four brothers, a history which suggests an 'explanation' for her familiarity with the codes of laddish masculinity. The comic 'misunderstanding' that follows as Riggs tells partner Murtaugh about the encounter confirms that the masculinised Cole can be incorporated into the buddy relationship:

> Riggs: 'I slept with Sergeant Cole.'
> Murtaugh: 'Sergeant Cole from traffic?'
> Riggs: 'No not Sergeant Cole from traffic – Lorna, Lorna. Sergeant Cole from traffic's her Uncle.'

One of an incessant series of references to relationships between men, the joke also reminds us of Lorna's masculine qualities (which, after all, allow her to take part in the final showdown and to survive the movie, albeit wounded). The exchange also serves to emphasise the involvement of Cole's family in the institution of the police force. Cole personifies authority in the film, at least initially, surprising Riggs, Murtaugh and their boss with the revelation that Internal Affairs had secretly installed video cameras in interrogation rooms. Though they are of equal rank, as an officer of the 'police police', Cole is at first in a more authoritative position.[22] Later, Riggs holds Murtaugh back to watch her fight five men, commenting 'that's my girl' (so that she seems like a pet, well trained like the Rottweiler he pals around with and of which she is afraid). *In the Line of Fire*, by contrast, does not so much offer an integrated working relationship between male and female, as the ending of *True Lies* might suggest, but a handing over of responsibility. As Gill Branston notes, Clint Eastwood's infirmity 'allows gestures on the part of Raines/Russo which are part professional/part maternal concern for this 63-year-old man'. Further, '[a]t the end of the film we are left to imagine Clint as retired house husband, in a reversal of the status quo at its start' (Kirkham and Thumin 1995: 48) For Pfeil (1995) this ending suggests a withdrawal from a public space in which Harrigan's instinctual skills are not required (in contrast to Raines who is both a career woman and a team worker). Once more the consequences of women's entry into the workplace/space is mapped in terms of evolving discourses of masculinity.

Like both 'working girls' or 'bad girls', the image of the 'tomboy' captures a sense of immaturity – of both a freedom from the responsibilities of adult life and a sense of incomplete development. A mapping of transgression that can be contained, the tomboy signals a composite of experience and innocence – of capabilities and energies together with sexual *naïveté*. Or rather she is a sexually ambiguous figure. Her ambiguous state allows the tomboy to accompany the hero on his travels, even to drive the bus. She is a kind of cross-dresser, discreetly, rather than excessively muscular in her proletarian male guise. And as Barbara Creed suggests, the image may exceed the narrative that seeks to contain it:

> The narrative of the tomboy functions as a liminal journey of discovery in which feminine sexuality is put into crisis and finally recuperated into the dominant patriarchal order – although not without first offering the female spectator a series of contradictory messages which may well work against their overtly ideological purpose of guiding the young girl into taking up her proper destiny.
>
> (Creed 1995:88)

Indeed, as in the Westerns discussed in Chapter two, these hero(ines) are crucially distinct from the Oedipal tomboy-type in that they don't ultimately grow up. Heterosexual romance doesn't equal the abandonment of liberty in these adventure tales. Instead Lorna Cole as feisty heroine, like the heroes of these comedy action films has access to a juvenile anarchy – taking pleasure in scars, guns and fighting.

Buddies, bonding and racial difference

What Ed Guerrero terms the 'bi-racial buddy movie' has proved to be one of the most successful action variants of the 1980s and has continued into the 1990s with films such as *Money Train* (1995) reuniting Wesley Snipes and Woody Harrelson who scored a success in *White Men Can't Jump* (1992). Underlining Dyer's comments on the gender and racial hierarchies of hero and helper in the action movie, *Bad Boys* remains one of the few action films to team two black men. The period features no examples of an action movie with female pairing, unless one includes *Thelma and Louise* as a variant on the road movie.[23] The reluctance to put money into such vehicles is telling on a number of counts: perhaps it is the lesbian potentialities of the active body identified by Creed that so often preclude narratives involving two women together. Political conservatism and economic rationale come together in Guerrero's view to produce the bi-racial male buddy formula. It offers, he argues, a form in which to exploit the economic appeal of black male stars whilst containing the political impact of their presence on the screen. Thus 'Hollywood has put what is left of the Black presence on the screen in the protective custody, so to speak, of a White lead or co-star' (Diawara 1993: 239). How then has the shift of buddy banter in the mainstream action movie towards an increasing number of male/female partnerships, impacted on the formula? While bi-racial buddy movies foreground racial difference in part to deflect attention from the homoerotics of the formula, it might be thought that any male/female variant of the genre would be troubled by anxieties to do with the recurrent taboo on miscegenation. Hollywood action films have regularly matched white male stars with black, Asian and Latina performers in supportive sidekick roles. Yet these have rarely acknowledged either 'race' or racial difference in any explicit fashion. Here I'd like to explore two recent movies that foreground the politics of 'race' and racial difference in a heterosexual rather than a homosocial context: *The Long Kiss Goodnight* and *Strange Days*.

The Long Kiss Goodnight pairs Geena Davis and Samuel L. Jackson in a narrative that revolves around the uncovering of Samantha Caine's (Davis) buried/forgotten identity as a government agent/assassin, with the help of Jackson's private eye, Mitch Henessey. The film makes use of the conventions and the serio-comic texture of the buddy movie – verbal banter, mutual rescues, a movement from antagonism to affection and support – but pulls away from developing a romantic or a sexual scenario between the two. Kathryn Bigelow's millennial *Strange Days* is not a buddy movie in the same sense: making no resort to comic exchanges, the film operates in a hybrid terrain of horror, thriller, action and science fiction. Yet it does involve a central action/investigative partnership and shares similar themes around identity and memory (though articulated in more complex fashion with nuanced performances). Here it is the hero, Lenny Nero (Ralph Fiennes) whose stability is at issue, as he hopelessly pursues lost love, Faith (Juliette Lewis). Lenny's perception of reality is blurred from hours spent 'reliving' the past of their time together through the recorded memories that are the basis of his trade. Lornette 'Mace' Mason (Angela Bassett) is a long-time friend and personal security expert, initially cast as Lenny's reluctant helper; together they become involved in a complex investigation which centres on the party of the century, New Year's Eve 1999 in Los Angeles. It becomes evident that Mace loves Lenny, though it takes him most of the movie to realise it. Their relationship develops in the context of a narrative which takes as an explicit part of its substance conflicts around racism, policing and urban America.

The Long Kiss Goodnight involves several recurrent features of recent action narratives: bi-racial buddy bonding; an aggressive action hero figured as mother; doubled identities and alter egos. The latter allows the production of an old style, Cold War warrior to re-emerge and then be laid to rest in the film's final, dreamlike images of a knife-wielding Samantha/Charly composite in a white dress (following a joke reference to *Thelma and Louise*). The aggressive Charly who (re)emerges from the past is defined by her physical strength and sexual aggression, but is also violent and unstable. 'Samantha', we learn, was always a fiction, a parodic performance of down-home domesticity invented as a cover that Charly, waking up without a memory, has fallen back on. She gradually remembers and avenges her own 'death', finally reinventing herself as a composite of the two personas, complete with New Man-style partner who has promised to love her whatever she finds out about her past (whoever she is). Samantha has employed Jackson's Mitch Henessey, a down at heel private investigator, to try to trace her true identity; when a clue as to Samantha's past life surfaces, the two depart together to investigate, quickly finding themselves the target of Charly's former colleagues now engaged in a complex plot to extract government funds for their work by faking a terrorist incident. Thus the doubled identity of Samantha/Charly is matched in the villains who are both 'terrorists' attacking America and employees of the American government. In turn, we first see Mitch impersonating a police officer to extort money from a hapless man he and his assistant have entrapped. *The Long Kiss Goodnight* further exploits the familiar buddy hierarchy of oppositions: male/female, father/mother, black/white, professional/amateur. The latter opposition shifts across the pair as Davis' schoolteacher is revealed as an assassin (amateur to professional) who rescues Mitch (the detective). If this implies a complete reversal, it is Mitch in turn who finally comes to Charly's aid. Similarly while the scam that introduces Mitch suggests he is unethical, it is Charly's ruthlessness that is exposed.

The prohibition over sexual expression associated with the male buddy movie is here displaced, in similar fashion, on to racial difference. Yet the fact of their attraction for one another and the possibility of a sexual relationship developing between them, is explicitly raised (and rejected) by the film. In her aggressive, confident Charly persona, Davis' character bleaches her hair, wears heavy make-up, and indulges in hard liquor and smoking before making a pass at Mitch in their hotel room. Charly's sexual assertiveness underlines her distance from Samantha (who is defined as mother), another sign of her 'masculine' identity. Manohla Dargis writes that while the 'sex' scene makes 'nothing . . . of the colour of their skins':

> Of course colour does matter, especially when white skin and black work such a chromatic and vivid contrast: Davis isn't just white, she's blindingly white, with milky skin, movie-star teeth and peroxide hair; Jackson isn't just black, he's deeply, richly black. Both are also dressed to accentuate this – she in jet black, he in emerald green – and both are *undressed* enough to show off their lustre .
>
> (Dargis 1996: 8)

At a visual level then, the movie foregrounds and eroticises the visual marks of racial difference. Yet Mitch accuses Charly of wanting him to prove her difference from 'Samantha': 'to kill a schoolteacher, to bury her once and for all'. Charly's attempt to seduce Mitch, and the inter-racial romance that it posits, is produced as part of her disruptive alter ego, that of the anti-mother who returns to the small New England town not to visit her daughter but to ransack her room in search of a key. Mitch confronts her with a photograph of her past life that she has thrown away, telling her 'I kinda liked that schoolteacher: when she comes back you give me a call, all right?' and reproaching her for not having phoned her daughter. If this is in part an attempt to relocate Charly as Samantha (as mother) the rebuke also makes sense in terms of an early scene which frames Mitch as a father, estranged from his former wife and excluded from the family. The two do kiss once more, in an almost tender moment when the schoolteacher, or the love for daughter Caitlin that defines her, has returned and Charly is about to go in to rescue her. Yet at the close of the film, Samantha/Charly is back with her daughter and 'New Man' partner in a romanticised (soft focus) 'nature' setting.

If Samantha is determined by motherhood, Charly is (over)determined by an excess of phallic imagery: from the moment she reaches for the gun hidden in her former mentor's crotch to her open challenge to 'suck my dick'. Yet the film can't seem to resist somehow enacting this transformation partially at the expense of Jackson's Mitch, whose abilities are repeatedly undercut.[24] It is in such awkward negotiations that Guerrero understands the popularity of the bi-racial male buddy movie in the 1980s in terms of its 'ability to transcode, even into terms of fantasy, social unease over rising racial tensions' and indeed to provide 'escapist fantasy narratives and resolutions, which in some instances articulate allegorical or metaphorical dimensions that mediate America's very real and intractable racial problems' (Diawara 1993: 240). *Strange Days* produces both a scenario of social unease that becomes a fantasy of reconciliation and a 'masculine' woman in Angela Bassett's 'Mace'. Dressed for most of the film in 'masculine' attire, first in tuxedo-style dress for her role as a limousine driver, then in leathers and heavy boots; clothed in muscles and toughness, the Bassett character's nickname suggests her strength. She wears a dress for the final scene, in which she and Lenny crash the New Year's Eve party at the Bonaventure Hotel; if this is the moment in which Lenny finally 'sees' (notices) Mace, complimenting her on her appearance, she still has a gun strapped to her inner thigh (undercutting the idea of a narrative journey towards 'female' attire and/as heterosexuality that the ending might imply). Mace is defined by more than physical strength however, but by her stability in a chaotic world (a stability in part articulated through her role as mother). She is the only character to reject the pleasures of 'playback' ('you sell porno to wireheads' she tells Lenny), only once consenting to wear the device by which Lenny makes his cash and which she sees destroying him. While Lenny wallows in recorded memories of Faith, Mace tells him it's 'time to get real', to think of the present and the future. Here she 'sees' the racist murder of musician and activist Jeriko One (Glenn Plummer) by two white policemen, an execution-style killing that is at the heart of the plot and which evokes the infamous video images of Rodney King being beaten by LA police officers.

Both *Strange Days* and *The Long Kiss Goodnight* include serio-comic reference to *Driving Miss Daisy*, through which the script both draws attention to and seeks to make a joke out of the black/white hierarchy which structures the Hollywood cinema.[25] Mitch makes a quip about his driving role when Charly is in take-charge mode. Lenny calls Mace when his car has been towed, the first in a series of favours he asks of her; 'Driving Mr Lenny' she observes with some bitterness. He tells her Japanese business client that he is Mace's supervisor, putting himself in a position of superiority to which she responds by throwing him out of the car. There is much bitterness in the film as Lenny is fixed on the morally bankrupt Faith, Mace is in love with the desperate, pathetic Lenny. Her barely suppressed rage gives way on other occasions, yet it is when Lenny intends to trade the clip of Jeriko One's murder for Faith that she threatens to reject him completely: 'If you pawn that tape, you're nothing to me'. Lenny disappears into the crowd, only to reappear from nowhere, having, it seems, changed his mind. The chaos of the crowd/party scenes, like the use of rapid editing and fluid camerawork, echo the movement of the characters in and out of 'reality', memory and clips. The concluding scenes of *Strange Days* produce a sequence of events leading to a fantasy/surreal ending in keeping with this sense of unreality: it is revealed that the murder of Jeriko One was random rather than the result of organised police violence; Lenny's best friend is revealed as Faith's lover and the film's deranged killer; Lenny finally sees Faith for what she is; Mace captures and handcuffs the killer cops, but is beaten down by other cops, triggering a riot; Mace is rescued by the intervention of the (white) Chief of Police; Lenny attempts to protect Mace from a deranged cop, disappears into the crowd and re-emerges once more for a final kiss in the slow-motion finale that sees the new century in. The scenes in the hotel room which unravel the plot involve the juxtaposition of clips (recorded images) and 'real time' events in the same setting. The scenes outside are rendered dreamlike by the contrast between the image-track (with its violence, crowds, neon lights and confetti floating from the sky) and the soundtrack, with its slow-paced music. In a genre defined by cynicism about authority, the honest cop makes a surprise appearance. In a film which revolves around the violence of 'race' in America and the damage caused (as well as the pleasure generated) by fantasy images/constructed memories, the romantic image of the couple is ambivalent. The film has certainly explored their friendship and Mace's love with some care. Yet if Mace represents 'reality' ('this is real time') against Faith as illusion (as image), the use of fantasy/cliché images of romance to suggest *their* new relationship seems ironic. Their partnership-cum-romance, then, both covers over and reveals the faultlines in the narrative.

4

INVESTIGATING WOMEN
Work, criminality and sexuality

Pursued and pursuers: Helen Hudson (Sigourney Weaver) with Ruben Goetz (Dermot Mulroney) and M.J. Manahan (Holly Hunter) in *Copycat*

In popular literature the figure of the female investigator has long been a staple, with Sara Paretsky's V.I. Warshawski and Patricia Cornwell's Kay Scarpetta only two well-known recent examples from a line that extends back to the 'golden age' with Christie's Miss Marple.[1] Alongside a boom in feminist crime writing led partly by small publishing houses in the 1980s, feminist critics have reappraised crime fictions, greeting with some enthusiasm the move to the fore of female investigators across a range of independent and popular media. The development of the television crime series, from the 1970s' success of Angie Dickinson in *Policewoman* or the glamorous investigators of *Charlie's Angels* through to the more evidently 'socially aware' and award-winning *Cagney and Lacey*, can be read in terms of a popular response to feminist concerns and to the changing social position of women.[2] The cinema success *The Silence of the Lambs* (1991) took its central character, Clarice Starling, from Harris' best-selling book and, arguably, derived its repertoire of imagery – via an Oscar-winning performance from Jodie Foster – at least partially from the groundbreaking work of the television crime series.

The combination of female buddies, light-hearted comedy and evidently fore-grounded 'issues' (including sexual harassment, racism, abortion) in the long-running police series *Cagney and Lacey*, suggests a movement of women in crime fictions from a typical position as *object* of investigation to that of investi-gator, acquiring the symbolic authority invested in that position. Such a move would seem to correspond with the development of the independent woman 'types' in the American cinema of the 1970s. Indeed, though the mainstream cinema has only rarely approached the confidence of either television or literature in regard to the characterisation of the female investigator, the 1980s and 1990s have seen a variety of films in which female protagonists are cast as crusading lawyers, private investigators, police officers or FBI agents. At the same time the rearticulation of the independent woman as an archetypal *femme fatale* within the context of work (discussed in Chapter five) also produces a rather different inscrip-tion of the 'strong woman', one in which her strength is defined as threatening and her identity functions as an enigmatic object of investigation. Thus *Basic Instinct* pursues a tortuous and contradictory plot in which an exploration of female sexuality suggests a juxtaposition between desire and death, whilst diverse films such as *Presumed Innocent, Disclosure* and *Final Analysis* all feature white male heroes who are entrapped by, or between, deadly women.

This chapter explores the ambivalent articulation of female sexuality in contemporary crime narratives. The developing involvement of women in cinematic crime genres, as the foregoing suggests, has not been by any means straightforward, often conflating the transgression of conventional norms or behaviour with criminality. In the cinema, popular genres dealing with crime overlap to some extent with variants of the action film explored in Chapter three and with the 'new *film noir*' which forms the focus of Chapter five. The thriller or the legal drama, for instance, may adopt the light-hearted tone of the comic action film (the *Lethal Weapon* series or *Legal Eagles* (1986) which paired Debra Winger and Robert Redford, for example) or the more enigmatic shades of *film noir* (*Basic Instinct, Presumed Innocent*). The crime films discussed in this chapter are informed by a variety of generic roots which include police procedurals, legal drama, soft pornography, *film noir* and horror. Films such as *Impulse* (1990), *Bodily Harm* (1994) and *Judicial Consent* (1994) involve some of the conventions of soft pornography or erotic fictions (such as dissatisfied heroines in unhappy relationships, the trademark confession of fantasy within therapy sessions), and are fundamentally different in tone from, say, *The Accused*. This is not to say that these diverse films may not inhabit similar thematic territory, but that their different generic locations allow the production of different types of crime narrative. If this suggests that crime is little more than a type of content, there is nonetheless a distinctiveness to the crime fictions and the scenarios enacted within them which form the basis for this chapter.

Female protagonists and characters can be understood as located across three sites or realms within crime genres: the active, knowledgeable (or at least inquiring) space of the investigator, that of the criminal/object of investigation, and that of the victim of crime. Whilst it is the first that might be held to be have arrived only recently, it is nonetheless the case that female characters and protagonists frequently exist across or move between these three textual realms or positions. The rape/revenge narrative for example involves, as Carol Clover has suggested, an articulation of the protagonist as victim and as survivor/aggressor/vigilante. Indeed Clover suggests that the revenge scenarios she discusses are very much '*about* that transformation', charting the development of the victim-hero (1992: 123). Megan Turner (Jamie Lee Curtis) in *Blue Steel* (1990) initially aspires to a position of agency, moving from rookie cop through her role as victimised object of Eugene's (Ron Silver) attentions to that of active agent once more. Films such as *The Silence of the Lambs* and *Black Widow* (1987) make substantial use of a crime genre convention through which the identity of the investigator is dissolved or called into question through the acts of identification with the killer that their roles require (imagining the killers' thoughts, fears and desires in order to effectively entrap them). If female characters can be seen to inhabit the positions of victim, investigator and investigated in a fluid sense within many crime narratives, it may come as no surprise to note that these sites or realms are bound up with the articulation of sexuality. Women, it seems, are involved in transgression even and to the extent that they are represented as law-makers or enforcers. Partly this is to do with a working out of issues around women's sexuality which, like women's ambitions and their friendships, is a realm seemingly in need of almost constant policing in the Hollywood cinema.

Just as female characters may inhabit more than one of these three positions, or may move between them in the course of the narrative, the examples discussed in this chapter can be mapped in terms of a broad opposition between the crime film (or crime series) as a site of 'realism', whether in terms of an exploration of the 'social' or the conventions of the police procedural, and, alternatively, the crime film as a site of the 'fantastic', including the psychological thriller or a *noir*ish articulation of the law. An association between women, criminality and sexuality is evident in two stereotypes explored across different genres in this book, the *femme fatale* and the prostitute. These two stereotypes might be said to corre-spond to a distinction between those narratives in which enigmatic women pose a problem for the hero/heroine and 'realist' crime fictions. Yet this distinction repeatedly breaks down, as does that between investigator and investigated in nar-ratives as diverse in tone as *The Accused, Impulse, Blue Steel* and *Copycat*. It may be more productive then to consider realism/fantasy in terms of a continuum rather than an opposition. The criminal investigations which structure the narra-tives of *Impulse, Blue Steel* and *Bodily Harm* all involve an exploration of the sexuality of the female investigators alongside, and complexly entwined with, the central case itself. *Impulse* has undercover cop Theresa Russell increasingly attracted to the life of her alter ego. *Blue Steel*'s Megan Turner is the fetishised object of killer Eugene's obsession. And in *Bodily Harm*, Linda Fiorentino's ice-cool Las Vegas cop is drawn into a sexual relationship with the chief suspect in the murder she is investigating.

The repeated recourse to a narrative device in which a female police officer finds herself undercover as a prostitute functions both to comment on and reaffirm the extent to which women's work involves sexual display and/or sexual perfor-mance. The figure of the prostitute (and of the female cop as prostitute) recurs repeatedly in the crime film, primarily but not only as criminal subject and subject of violence.[3] As corpse or character she is a female criminal who may signify a more generalised notion of promiscuity and/or deception (fake passion). She is also a classed and raced subject, both allowed and required to be 'on the street'. The criminality of the prostitute's 'down to earth' (street level) sale of sex can be set against the *femme fatale*'s more mysterious/glamorous exploitation of her allure. Both are involved in deceit it is suggested and yet, at the same time, the prostitute is repeatedly invoked to signify a position of relative 'honesty' (the 'tart with a heart'). The direct, aggressive sexuality of the prostitute – images of groups of women on the street, shouting and strutting are commonplace – is set against the prostitute as victim, most extremely (and repeatedly) cast as victim of violence or as a corpse. The role of the prostitute varies then from a corpse that society does not grieve over to a good-hearted caricature who is, for example, more than will-ing to share information with male detectives – a generosity which suggests no relation of power. *Pretty Woman* makes use of these extremes, opening with the corpse of 'Skinny Marie' found in a dumpster and warm-hearted Kit who has helped and befriended heroine Vivian. It is also Vivian's simplicity and honesty which marks her out as 'different' (and therefore perhaps as redeemable?). Iris, the child prostitute played by Jodie Foster in *Taxi Driver* (1976), becomes the object of Bickle's obsession with moral corruption. His desire to redeem her triggers the climatic bloodbath whilst also clearly functioning as a projection (like Cybill Shepherd's character, a blank screen).[4] The recurrent depiction of women officers working undercover as prostitutes represents a trope that signals her problematic location within the force (it is invariably a subject of comment) at the same time as it functions as a fairly straightforward voyeuristic strategy for showcasing the body of the star/performer. Both Whoopi Goldberg in *Fatal Beauty* (1987) and Theresa Russell in *Impulse* walk the streets in the opening sequences before being revealed to be cops (by the detectives listening in the case of the Goldberg movie, by the arrest of Russell's client in the latter film). Helen Mirren's character in the award-winning British television drama *Prime Suspect* succeeds in part because she deems prostitutes worth speaking to and values their dead bodies (as worth inves-tigating). The prostitute is more than simply a backdrop to the crime narrative, recurring as a central figure who articulates in class terms the confluence of work-ing women and sexuality, returning us to the complex connotations of the 'working girl'.

Women as officers: Police procedural/police series

Television can be said to have led the cinema in positioning women in the role of investigator and in demonstrating the commercial viability of the female cop character. Crime series featuring women characters which emerged in the early 1980s were also part of a wider reformulation of the genre, partly in response to concerns about television violence. Action-based shows from the same period, such as Michael Mann's stylish *Miami Vice* (which had its quota of undercover cops as prostitutes) were met with ongoing conservative hostility, accusations of 'designer violence' and so on, whilst fairly light-hearted crime series such as *Legwork* (in which Margaret Colin played a private investigator) passed with little comment. If analyses of the crime series in the late 1970s had focused on the rep-resentation of relations between citizens, the law and the State, the entry of women into the genre transformed it into a different critical object with the pri-mary concern shifting to gender, concerns which feminist critics had already foregrounded. More than any other series, *Cagney and Lacey* reflected explicitly on such feminist concerns. The developing format of the show serves to indicate both the potential and the seeming parameters of the female cop format during the 1980s. Building on successful images from the 1970s, the show's central characters were defined as 'real' women, self-consciously distinguished from media stereotypes. This is made quite explicit in an episode from the 1986/7 series, 'Role Call', in which the pair are assigned to look after an actress named Vicky Barrington. Barrington, who plays 'Detective DeeDee' in a network crime series and wants to learn 'how to make her show better', brings chaos to the squadroom. Her glamorous looks and the 'inauthentic' nature of the character she plays are set against the real business of women police officers. Barrington is however revealed to be a 'person of integrity', a mother who struggles over issues in her show such as the gimmick that has her keep her gun in her bra ('I fight the producers on that one *every* season'). Here *Cagney and Lacey* simultaneously engages in a comic critical commentary on media stereotypes and defines itself against the alternatives presented by popular media (including, by implication, the cinema which holds itself superior to television).

In the *Cagney and Lacey* pilot movie (1981), Christine Cagney (Loretta Swit) is introduced as (hetero)sexually active in her first scene. We see her the morning after with an unnamed conquest who enthuses about how good she was: 'New York's finest' is her reply, a re-inflection of the phrase for the police (a professional designation) in terms of sexual performance. Meanwhile Mary Beth Lacey (Tyne Daly) spends the film frustrated that husband Harvey isn't interested in sex, a lack of interest related explicitly to his unemployment and a sense of failed masculinity in having to rely on her wages. The two women start out in uniform but get promotion after busting a drugs ring: there is a dissolve from Cagney holding a gun on the suspects and saying quietly, and with some relish, 'next week plain clothes' to the station house and to the women dressed as prostitutes in the Captain's office (Cagney's world-weary voice on the soundtrack pleads 'You call this plain clothes?'). They find themselves on 'john detail' despite their protests that prostitution is a 'victimless crime' (as opposed, they argue, to 'real crime'). Thus the pair are first introduced to a hostile male squad room *already* dressed in prostitute's guise. Cagney pursues a case that isn't her own, attempting to (im)prove herself, and making alliance with Petri, a (differently isolated) black male officer. The case, it is finally revealed, involves a former Nazi now living as a Jew, a device that draws attention to themes of disguise and impersonation. Meanwhile, Lacey becomes involved in establishing a prostitutes' union, sympathetic to the way in which the women are pushed around (and getting beaten up herself). It is a black prostitute, however, a single parent named 'Female' (which suggests something of the symbolic weight she bears in the narrative as both mother and 'other') who first resists the collectivisation attempted by Lacey and provides the link in the murder case, neatly ensuring that both plots come together.

The series drew on and reshaped the popular device of the 'buddy' cop pairing. Julie D'Acci (1994) outlines how the development of a female buddy duo was conceived by Barbara Avedon and Barbara Corday as a response to Molly Haskell's critique of 1970s' cinema, with its increasingly marginal portrayal of women, displaced by a male buddy format. The characterisation conforms to now familiar versions of the active heroine: Cagney identifies with her father (those blue uniforms and brass buttons), while Lacey is identified as a maternal figure. Tyne Daly, who played Mary Beth Lacey throughout the long run of *Cagney and Lacey*, had already played a cop character alongside Clint Eastwood in the third 'Dirty Harry' film, *The Enforcer* (1976). Appointed as an equal opportunities 'stunt', she shares the fate of the majority of Harry's partners when her character is killed off at the end of the film. Despite this inauspicious precedent, it was the male/female heterosexual buddy format that was to become more common, though such formats have given way to group dramas (perhaps as a response to the potential power the earlier format gave to performers). The evident taboo over representing female friendship, addressed further in Chapter six, has persisted. *Cagney and Lacey* remains the only long-running crime show to focus on the relationship between two women. Whilst CBS produced a pilot for a series based in Chicago, *Angel Street*, this has so far run for one series only. Robin Givens played a middle-class, educated, wealthy cop given her choice of assignment, with her Polish partner portrayed as down-at-heel, working class. If the cops in *Angel Street* don't start out undercover as prostitutes, they are given cases regarded as 'unsolveable'. A familiar set of oppositions are played out within the evolving buddy partnership: African-American/white Polish, upper-class/proletarian, smart/scruffy, femme/butch. The tension between the two women is primarily focused around class and racial difference and racial politics within the context of policing the urban streets of Chicago.[5] (Givens' character accuses her partner of not caring about black deaths.) *Cagney and Lacey* began with the cop partnership already established – whilst they are clearly different and this creates conflict, they are also allied against the authority that is hostile towards them.

Other examples of female pairings are overwhelmingly comic in tone. The light-hearted buddy movie *FEDS* (1989), for example, follows trainees Ellie (Rebecca DeMornay) and Jan Zuckerman (Mary Gross) through the FBI training programme. The movie establishes the by now familiar two mismatched characters: military/college education, blonde/brunette, physically confident/academically gifted, butch/femme, and so on. As the closing credits roll the two find they have both been assigned to LA – an occasion for hugs and screams, but not, it seems, for a follow-up series. Executive producer Ivan Reitman's comic credentials are more than evident: the movie combines the tone of the *Police Academy* series with that of those multiple comic 'Revenge of the Nerds' scenarios in which the underdogs win out against preppie snobs. Thus in the final exercise, sidelined by Brent Shepard (from a third generation FBI family), the two women team up with resident geek Howard Butts to win the day. Ellie accepts the special award on behalf of her and Janice with the words 'I hope the people of the United States of America will be able to sleep better knowing that women like us have guns – thank you'. As the acceptance speech might suggest, though *FEDS* is structured around the premise of female trainees as novelty, the producers are unable to make anything of this scenario.

To some extent it has been the emphasis on dialogue in television crime series and TV movies that allowed the success of *Cagney and Lacey* in terms of its portrayal of a friendship between women. Over its long run the two characters had trademark 'women's room' conversations on a host of issues and problems. If the idea of serious female buddy crime-fighting partnership has not been taken up in the 1990s, a rather more long-lasting legacy of the 1980s has been the 'ensemble' shows or 'cop-soaps' which followed the launch (in 1981) and subsequent long run of Steven Bochco's *Hill Street Blues*. Whilst *Hill Street Blues* and later *NYPD Blue* mixed public and private lives, male and female characters, they also addressed subjects such as the difficult position of women and various ethnic groups within predominantly white male institutions. Such ensemble programmes brought female characters into the TV crime/detective narrative without running the perceived ratings risk of putting them centre screen alone. For Lidia Curti *Hill Street Blues* represented a 'predominantly male series' within which the 'emergence of female characters . . . has, however, slightly, altered the quite powerful all-male feel of the show' (1988: 156). John Fiske also compared *Hill Street Blues* with *Cagney and Lacey*, suggesting they both offer 'interesting mixtures of masculine and feminine' (1987: 216). Whilst the idea of masculine and feminine forms or genres is a problematic one, these critics are pointing to the distinctive hybrid mix that television was developing, one that existing (cinematic and television) genres did not quite describe.[6] A more recent Bochco production, *Murder One*, indicates some of the potential and pitfalls of serial form. Spanning twenty-three episodes (or 'chapters'), *Murder One* represented a fairly self-conscious attempt to explore the limits of a serial crime narrative as distinct from the crime series. The show follows the development of a single case from discovery through investigation, prosecution and delivery of a verdict. The audience's point of identification was to be the legal offices of a wealthy firm (with shades of another Bochco success, *LA Law*). Each week alongside the central narrative strand, different stories concerning the legal team and the cases they were assigned were to be developed. Thus *Murder One* was envisaged as a sort of compilation experiment which combined elements from previous Bochco successes. Yet this was not how the series ended up. Perhaps the increasingly tortuous 'previously on *Murder One*' section at the front of the show signalled most dramatically the problems with the conception. The very format seemed designed to prevent the recruitment of new viewers to the plot – the labyrinthine set of red herrings and sub-plots became off-putting at the very least. Unlike the quirkier equivalent of *Twin Peaks* some years before, which used a similar structure, explicitly marked as surreal and incomprehensible, audiences apparently refused the formal premise of *Murder One*. As episodes were written and rewritten in the process, the focus of the series changed in ways that are interesting in terms of the limits of experimentation.[7]

The narrative of *Murder One* centred on the murder of a sexually active, white teenage girl, Jessica Costello. The investigation of the crime and the arrest and trial of 'up-and-coming' movie star Neil Avedon evokes wealth and glamour through the showbiz world of Los Angeles which provides the backdrop. As with the novels of Patricia Cornwell, there is an element of voyeuristic pleasure in exposing the forensic – the gradual revelation of the corpse and the murder

scenario in the credit sequence of *Murder One* and, later, in the episodes themselves add to the notion that it is Jessica's sexuality, expressed in the posing of her
corpse, that is the central enigma. Indeed this corpse only appears in images
within images – the red/black of the credit sequence which gradually revealed
'more' to the viewer and the final vindicating video tape. The themes of
voyeurism and violent sex run throughout the series as an issue – with the pleasures and limits of sadomasochism an evidentiary point of debate in the trial. As
the series developed, not only does the corpse come centre stage along with the
figure of the promiscuous teenager, but other crude ideological figures are
brought into play. An opposition between public and private worlds is also
developed. The familiar figure of the supportive 'wife' (there in *Hill Street Blues*
with Frank and Joyce[8]) waiting at home with a glass of wine and a shoulder to
cry on, becomes dissatisfied and sues for divorce. Yet it is episode ten (of twenty
three) before she appears in the office: home and work are kept strictly apart.

The problem with *Murder One* became precisely the lack of a reasonable doubt,
in a terrain that sought to open up the workings of the law, both guilt and innocence are writ large. As the series stumbled on to its conclusion, it drew on a
whole series of crime fiction clichés, from the stereotypical invocation of a 'Latin'
temperament, to demonic, manipulative, self-destructive villain-with-AIDS
Richard Cross. When it is clear that the swan-murdering Neil Avedon is innocent
(Annie, the wife of chief lawyer Ted, includes him in their Christmas party) a fall-
guy must be found. Thus the idea of a focus on one crime as a way of opening up
the functioning of legal systems and exploring character becomes subsumed in
something else. This double tone had always haunted the narrative of *LA Law*, situating light comedy against stark tragedy and corruption. *LA Law* had personified
liberalism and concern in its 'ethnic' figures (primarily the Jimmy Smits character).
Among the bright, white legal team of affluent but liberal lawyers these questions
remain unspoken, reinforcing the notion that questions of 'race' have little to do
with whiteness, a problem in the context of the OJ Simpson trial to which *Murder
One* appealed (in the unfolding of a celebrity murder case and in the producers'
suggestions that the experiment in serial form which the show was offering was
catering to viewers who had become accustomed to watching the legal scenario
being played out). And yet issues of race and class as questions for the law, as concerns with which the legal system might be implicated, are marginalised here.
Vanessa Williams (later to star alongside Schwarzenegger as an executive with a
conscience in *Eraser*) as receptionist introduces a subplot to do with her boyfriend.
At another point the team defend a young gang member who has murdered: a cue
for much sage shaking of heads.

The cult to mainstream success story of *The X Files* offers a 1990s inflection
on the white buddy cop pairing. A combination of the police procedural/fantasy
genres the show builds on the quirky articulation of the FBI in David Lynch's
Twin Peaks, at the same time as it draws on a deep suspicion of any such government institution. Thus Dana Scully (Gillian Anderson) and Fox Mulder
(David Duchovny) work for the FBI, but in the basement. Their pairing is ini-

tially reluctant, but is quickly followed by the familiar mutual respect. Scully, a successful FBI agent and medical doctor, is assigned to work with Mulder in order to police and report on his activities. Scully's status as a (brilliant) woman positions her at just the right amount of distance from the organisation for which she works, allowing a little scepticism to prevent her from accepting help (to get off the detail, perceived as taking her career nowhere) from her FBI academy buddies, a group of suits from whom she becomes increasingly distanced. The show's 'twist' in terms of gender type is firstly to cast Scully as the voice of rationality and scientific knowledge against her partner's mysticism and belief in the supernatural. Mulder is driven by a personal quest, the search for his missing sister or for information about what may have happened to her. This translates in paranoid fashion into an anxiety around the State, fears of conspiracy, of 'the biggest lie of all'. In the first episode, Mulder presents Scully with a mystifying death (an 'X-file'). Their conversation sets the terms of their relationship, based on an intellectual opposition that also structures the series:

> Mulder: 'When convention and science offer us no answers might we finally turn to the fantastic as a possibility?'
> Scully: 'The girl obviously died of something. If it was natural causes it's plausible that there was something missed in the post-mortem. If she was murdered it's plausible that there was a sloppy investigation. What I find fantastic is any notion that there are answers beyond the realm of science. The answers are there. You just have to look'.

Yet, as regular viewers will know, there is as much agreement as conflict expressed here. Scully's last statement is one on which they both agree (there are 'answers'). Mulder comments, 'that's why they put the "eye" in FBI', a pun on the interchangeability of vision, knowledge and investigation which links both an empirical science and a 'keep watching the skies' paranoia.

There is a contradiction built into the show – or, more precisely, a tension, as Heidi Kaye has suggested, between the show's two identifying slogans: 'The truth is out there' and 'Trust no-one'.[9] Thus some 'supernatural' events are revealed to have 'scientific' explanations whilst others suggest the existence of phenomenon such as possession, the work of an alien intelligence or of government conspiracy. Scully's scepticism and Mulder's faith in supernatural phenomena are preserved by frequent recourse to a device whereby Scully does not see an action or event which Mulder (and the audience) does – a body floating off the ground in an episode entitled 'Shadows', for example.[10] There is a second 'twist' in relation to the conventional male/female pairing: the avoidance of any projected evolution of the pairing into a (hetero)sexual relationship. Thus Mulder and Scully might disagree but rarely engage in the kind of banter that signals, within popular representation, that sex/romance is just around the corner.[11] If *The X Files* articulates a platonic variant on the male/female buddy pairing, images surrounding and promoting the show insistently sexualise both actors and their relationship: the cover of *Rolling Stone* pictured the stars in bed together, and both have appeared semi-naked in such magazines as *Esquire*. The insistence on sexualising both stars in extra-textual representations surrounding *The X Files* is perhaps indicative of not only an increased production of the white male body as sexual spectacle, but a reluctance fully to allow a woman to signify supposedly asexual qualities of reason. Such a reluctance is reaffirmed in those fictions in which the female officer/investigator is more complexly involved with psycho-sexual dynamics, in which the female investigator allows an articulation of the law and a critique of the law.

Fetishistic fictions: Woman as investigator

As we have seen, the figure of the female officer working undercover as prostitute combines an articulation of investigator (cop), investigated (criminal) and victim (since she is subject to violence). Such fictions are suggestive in terms of the per-ception of a relationship between the terms of women, work and sexuality. In this context, Sondra Locke's *Impulse* (1990) offers an interesting articulation on the cop/prostitute theme. Theresa Russell plays Lottie Mason, an undercover 'vice' officer who becomes preoccupied with her prostitute persona/alter ego; the results of this preoccupation set the narrative in motion. The film's opening sequence reveals a city street at night, deserted but for the figure of a 'street-walker', clad in a tight gold dress and with long blonde hair. Initially introduced through a series of full figure and anonymous partial body shots that serve both to objectify and indicate her status as an available commodity (giving a driver's-eye point of view), Russell is then identified as she leans in the car window to talk to the driver. After agreeing to a sexual exchange, Lottie pushes the man aside when he attempts to 'take a little bite', the first indication that she intends some other exchange. Of course this type of scene works through disavowal, since the audi-ence already 'knows' that this is a police/crime narrative and that Russell is its star (but all the same, she is a prostitute). As the police move in, Lottie/Russell walks away (the camera moving with her), back to her 'station' on the street corner. This opening sequence is followed by a more sinister crime scene in which Tony Peron, a criminal under witness protection, kills both his associate and the drug-dealers they are negotiating with. As the film develops, Peron and Lottie will come together. Following an undercover operation that puts her in danger, Lottie goes into a bar for a drink, still wearing her costume. Here she meets Peron, gives in to her 'impulse', takes his money and goes home with him. At his house she has begun to have doubts and vows to leave, but Peron is shot and she is left with a case full of money. A second 'impulse' leads to her reporting the death anony-mously and stealing the cash so that she has in effect become her criminal alter ego. Meanwhile, Lottie becomes involved with the cop who is hunting Peron, Peron's killer and, ultimately, her so that she becomes the object of investigation on a variety of levels.

While the opening sequence reveals Lottie to be a cop rather than a prostitute, she exchanges no words with the other officers. The lack of cop camaraderie, so much a convention of the genre, is confirmed in subsequent scenes. The structure of disavowal bound up in the image of female cop as prostitute is echoed in the narrative structure which situates Lottie as both investigator and investigated. Lottie drives home in the morning to find her boss Morgan in her apartment. 'Your costume's affecting your manners', he grunts: a double-edged comment since she wears her 'streetwalker' gold dress with a blue denim jacket over the top, a mix of styles and of signifiers. His comment relates to her request for him to leave but also relates to a *wish* for her costume to affect her manner in another way – for her to be sexually available in return for money (her salary). He comments on her many bills and debts, that it would be a bad time to be unemployed and so on, leaving her to pick up the mail from the floor where he has thrown it. The hierarchical relation (male boss/female employee, standing/kneeling), together with the fact that the proposition takes place at her home further underlines her distance from the force. This distance is reinforced in the next sequence which features Lottie interviewed by a police psychiatrist/therapist. Wearing shades and smoking a cigarette, the interview confirms Lottie's status as 'enigmatic'. Cast next as a bedraggled low-life who buys drugs to entrap a dealer, the vindictive Morgan has Lottie arrested, processed and held in gaol to 'keep her cover'. Thus it is not until some twenty minutes into the movie that Lottie is seen in the police station *as a cop*. Although ultimately Lottie is reintegrated, giving back the cash and opting for coupledom at the end of the movie, at the same time she still manages to outwit her corrupt boss.

The reason for Lottie attending therapy is to certify her continuing 'stability' (she has shot a 'perp'), but the session also defines her single status in terms of an on-going pathology, a problem that she has. In response, Lottie speaks of her fascination with her undercover role: 'Sometimes, working vice. Strangers – the way they look at you . . . feel all that power over them – making them pay. It excites me. I just – I wonder what it would be like just to do it – lose, lose control'. Breaking away from her mirror image provided by the window when the psychiatrist comments that 'fantasies can be healthy', Lottie starts to toy with the books on the shelves and with the professional woman who seeks to understand her. With face averted she offers up a polished masochistic fantasy to the therapist, talking about her wish to be degraded before revealing that she is 'just joking'. The ability to manipulate the terms of psychiatry/therapy is similarly articulated in the perverse heroines of *Basic Instinct* and *Final Analysis* (the revelation in *Basic Instinct* that Catherine Trammel majored in English and Psychology leads to the comment that she has 'a degree in screwing people's heads'). Nick Curran (Michael Douglas) is also required to attend therapy in *Basic Instinct*, pleading with his therapist and ex-lover Beth to tell Internal Affairs that, 'I'm just your average, healthy, totally fucked-up cop and let me out of here – please'. With both male and female protagonists, images of cops in therapy serve to underline the extent to which they are maladjusted individuals and how uncertain their position is within the institutions of law enforcement (they rarely attend therapy sessions voluntarily).[12] If in other police narratives the cop as prostitute wants to transfer to another department (typically from vice to homicide, from dealing in sex to dealing in death: Cagney's 'We want off this cleavage detail'), Lottie resists any such move from her role as undercover cop, a job at which she is 'the best'.

The narrative of an uncertain identity and an identification with a more dangerous self that develops around Lottie combines the crime genre with elements of both the women's picture (self-discovery) and soft pornography or the erotic thriller. The two scenes with psychiatrist Dr Gardner (Lynn Thigmann) are a lead-in for the latter with the confession of fantasies of degradation which are then turned round as Lottie teasing the psychiatrist, playing to expectations. The soft-porn movie *Hard Evidence* (1996) declares its female protagonist to be 'torn between the tough world of police work and her secret world of striptease'. Here the female captain causes traffic pile-ups by masturbating on the freeway, her voice-over providing a cynical, world-weary commentary on the insatiable nature of her own desires. In making the comparison to soft pornography, I'm not arguing that *Impulse* is somehow 'for men' in any simplistic fashion. Rather I'm pointing to the use of a recurrent strand within pornographic narratives in which a (sexually) dissatisfied heroine experiments with different identities, costumes and practices to extend the limits of her existence (often 'finding herself' in the scenarios she enacts) involving a negotiation of conventional pleasure. In this way what for Linda Ruth Williams is a staple feature of the erotic thriller, 'the Beverley Hills housewife with an appetite for sexual danger', is related to the transformation through costume found in the women's picture (1993: 12).[13] Stan, the Assistant DA with whom Lottie becomes involved, and who offers her the chance to return the stolen money, is himself looking for a woman with what he terms 'curb appeal', a phrase that the *Variety* review read as a real estate reference, but which also clearly relates to Lottie's cop/prostitute persona.[14]

It is a cliché of Hollywood cinema, pulp fictions and psychoanalysis that tomboys or active heroines somehow identify with their fathers. In action films, the heroine is presented as either motivated by her maternal instincts or as taking over/inheriting her father's position. This suggests very little space for the heroine as articulating an identity for herself, one that is beyond the terms of the masculine, mother or Other. Indeed this is one of the reasons that these *sexualised* narratives of self-discovery, which might seem to be reductively fetishistic or objectifying, represent interesting textual spaces in which the female cop has been located. Moreover, the narrative of father-identified cops is not as straightforward as it might be assumed. Megan Turner in *Blue Steel* is framed by a problematic relationship with her violent father and victimised mother. Her parents don't attend her Police Academy graduation which opens the film. Megan's father is hostile to her role as cop. She in turn handcuffs him after a fight between her parents, and starts to drive him to the station (relenting part way there). If Christine Cagney speaks in the pilot film of having always wanted the blue suit and brass buttons worn by her father and brothers, *Cagney and Lacey* charted the problems posed by her alcoholic cop father Charlie. *Backstreet*

Justice offers a further twist on the daughter-of-a-good-cop scenario deployed in the film *China O'Brien* or the Warshawski novels. Linda Kozlowski plays Kerri Finnegan, a private investigator whose career is overshadowed by the memory of her corrupt cop father. The investigation with which the narrative is concerned involves clearing his name and finding out that her surrogate up-market, District Attorney father is actually the one who is corrupt. In each case the father haunts the narrative, but precisely what he signifies is uncertain.

Impulse and *Blue Steel* share central, ambiguously motivated, cop characters involved in situations which gradually move out of their control. The films also share a structure in which the heroine is insistently objectified by male colleagues and by the criminal men with which they become involved. The films also insistently foreground the (hetero)sexuality of the female officer, finding in the couple a resolution of sorts to the problem that she poses. Yet this is not to say that these two films are simply involved in display or objectification of the female characters/performers. Rather this indicates the problems involved in critically opposing social realism as good object to fantasy as bad object. While the 'daughter of a good cop' and the 'sexual fantasy' scenarios provide a sort of framing device through which to read the female investigator, the image also *exceeds* these frames, is not complete in terms of either one. Of course this raises a more general discussion about the relationship between image and narrative, one in which I am arguing that it is mistaken to assume a hierarchy through which narrative and dialogue necessarily predominate over the image. If, within Hollywood representations, it is women who seem to 'contaminate' the male workplace with their sexuality, we might also note that the films discussed here have a *noir*-like aspect to their presentation of the world of law enforcement, an imagery which triggers a different set of connotations. The evocation of psychological 'erotic thrillers' in which motivation, projection and fantasy investments in crime and criminal bodies are clearly at stake overlays the 'realist' terms of the crime fiction.

Bodily Harm, for example, is also situated in a *noir*-crime tradition, offering a sort of reversed role version of *Basic Instinct* in which a female cop becomes sexually involved with the prime suspect in a murder case, an involvement that allows an equation between investigation, desire and sexuality usually devolved around the male cop/private detective. Linda Fiorentino plays Rita Cates, a Las Vegas detective investigating a murder in which her former lover (and ex-cop), the wealthy Sam McKeon (Daniel Baldwin), is the prime suspect. As in *Impulse*, the film features scenes with Rita discussing her ambivalent feelings with a department therapist. She reveals that in her previous affair with Sam the riskier the sex had been, the more attraction the affair had held for her. We learn in a flashback that Rita's cop husband Michael had found the two in bed and shot himself in front of them, an image which once more juxtaposes sex and death, also serving to suggest the moral ambiguity of the central characters. For whilst it is a cliché of *male* cop dramas that the hero harbours feelings of loss/revenge for their dead/divorced wives or girlfriends, they are also typically portrayed as misunderstood. Cates' renewed involvement with Sam is conducted to the dismay and disbelief of her colleagues. An 'expert' judges from evidence left at crime scenes that anyone attracted to the killer 'would have to have a sick flirtation with self-destruction'. One of the couple's assignations takes place in a hotel above a casino, the camera-work emphasising a familiar movie-land Vegas setting and equating the danger of their affair with gambling. As Cates lies on top of him in bed, she and McKeon laugh when she reveals that the police have requested a court order for a fluid sample from him. 'Did you bring a receptacle?', he asks, with a lewd inference that underlines the extent to which work as sexual performance is written over the body of the female investigator. Her body is the receptacle for his semen/fluid sample. Following a later encounter, Rita finds crucial evidence in Sam's house which implicates her lover. She steals the evidence, a pair of latex gloves, return-ing the next day to replace/plant them with the knowledge and collusion of her boss and cop partner. Though the police close the case on a suitably deranged female suspect, Sam's guilt is suggested in the film's final image (another fairly bla-tant reference to *Basic Instinct*). Following Rita's refusal to continue the relationship (it is 'just not good' she tells him, before driving off smiling with her cop buddy), a knife identical to that used in the first murder is revealed in the glove-box of Sam's car (accompanied by a jarring burst of music which confirms the image).

Bodily Harm draws on the codes of erotic fantasy and *noir*-style thrillers to sit-uate its ambiguous female cop protagonist within a narrative which explores her desires in the context of a criminal investigation. Yet role reversal, as the action film also makes apparent, is not straightforward. Rita's partner JD, discovering that she has become sexually involved with Sam again, tells her 'if you were a man, I'd say it was your dick talking' – but she isn't and he is lost for words (or rather he cannot say the words, since they are unspeakable).[15] The movie clearly works to capitalise on Fiorentino's cable to big-screen success as the cold, tough, sexual Bridget in John Dahl's *The Last Seduction*. Her cop in *Bodily Harm* is super-cool, wearing linen suits and shades. Her police work is bound up with her sexual pre-occupations rather than a concern for the crimes (or the victims) themselves. The movie opens with establishing shots of Las Vegas at night and extended scenes of women dancing in a strip club. One of the strippers is seen enthusiasti-cally getting ready for a date, presumably with McKeon, before being murdered in the parking lot. The second woman murdered is McKeon's lover/therapist, Rebecca Lawrence. The third it is implied will be Cates. Another murder comes to light in the course of the film: some years before McKeon had shot his then girlfriend (a stripper) with the killing found to be accidental. The film explicitly puts forward an opposition between good and bad women, with Cates ambigu-ously positioned somewhere between these two categories. McKeon we are told 'prefers women that society would classify as bad' but feels guilt over this, finding redemption in 'women he perceives as more pure'. JD asks which category Rita sees herself in 'the good girl or the bad girl', a question she avoids but which underscores the parallel between the two. On a job to interview witnesses in a strip club, Cates is absorbed in watching the dancers herself, and has to be pulled away.

Sexuality and women's work are brought together not only in the figure of Cates and of the inevitable female shrink, a woman whose entire working life revolves around an exploration of sexuality it seems, but in the generalised sex industry backdrop that features in so many investigative narratives. Just as the erotic thriller narrative and the sex industry setting of *Bodily Harm* allow an exploration of desire and danger around the *female* investigator, they also combine to produce working women as working girls.

Investigation and identification

As *Bodily Harm* suggests, questions of desire and sexuality are foregrounded in those narratives which enact a process of investigation defined by a lack of distance between hunter and hunted. Whether this is in terms of a sexual involvement (*Basic Instinct, Bodily Harm*), or through an obsessive pursuit, the investigator is in danger of losing his/her identity. If such narratives have something of a surreal quality, as the central character becomes more involved in the world of the criminal(s) they pursue, narratives such as *The Silence of the Lambs* are also to some extent police procedurals. Their difference lies in an emphasis on an *intuition* which can be perceived as somehow uncanny. This may also work in reverse – the extent to which Catherine Trammell/Sharon Stone 'knows' Nick Curran/Michael Douglas serves to reinforce the suggestion of similarity between them and to signal that she is as involved with *his* story (which, after all, she is using as the basis for a novel) as he is to become with hers. Three quite different examples can serve here to highlight the implications of the play of identification and investigation in relation to the female investigator: *Black Widow, The Silence of the Lambs* and *Copycat*. In all three films the female investigator protagonists shift between or simultaneously inhabit more than one of the three positions of investigator, investigated and victim.

Bob Rafelson's *Black Widow* sits between genres, drawing on the conventions of *film noir*, the police procedural and the woman's film. Theresa Russell plays a *femme fatale*, a woman whose true name we never know as she moves through a series of aliases, marrying and murdering wealthy men. Debra Winger is Alex, the FBI data-analyst turned investigator who becomes obsessed with tracking her down. Catherine's/Russell's work is self-creation, again expressed as sexualised performance as labour. As 'Renee' she tells Alex/Jessica that 'I used to think of it as my job – making myself appealing. I was a professional'. In turn, Alex is rebuked by her boss, who alternately comes on to her and suggests she get a (sexual) life outside the office, for being over-invested in her work. Though 'Catherine' may be a 'temptress' who is involved with and then married to several men, sexual encounters are not particularly foregrounded within the film (in contrast to the more evidently visually *noir*-like *Body Heat* and *Body of Evidence*). The focus is instead placed on the developing relationship – one of antagonism and attraction – between Russell in her various guises and Debra Winger's investigator. Doubling and identification are regular features of crime narratives, generating uncertainty, ambiguity and suspense. The dissolution of the identity of the investigating officer is a cliché of the crime/thriller genre, from the parallels drawn between hero and villain in Michael Mann's *Heat* to the identity-swallowing Hannibal Lecter in *Manhunter* and *The Silence of the Lambs*. Less artful cop/villain mirroring is found in a variety of thrillers such as *Tightrope* or *In the Line of Fire*. The profiler, it is implied, is some form of method actor who immerses him/herself in the identity of the serial killer.

Judith Mayne describes a scene in *Black Widow* in which Alex projects a shifting series of images of Catherine onto her apartment wall, standing in front of them, situating herself in relation to this shape-shifter, as suffused 'at the very least with a sense of discovery of a heretofore unknown (or unacknowledged) fascination' (1990: 47). The fascination is with a female other, a fascination which prompts a lesbian reading of the film on the part of critics such as Cherry Smyth, but also a fascination with the possibilities of transformation.[16] For Smyth the slideshow, '[o]verplayed and extremely seductive', portrays 'a butch controlling the image of a femme in all her different masquerades' (Burston and Richardson 1995: 130). As in *Impulse* we see the process of self-discovery enacted through an identification with an other, an alternative space related to fantasy and perceived as both attractive but dangerous. Yet neither Smyth's nor Mayne's analysis suggest that identification and desire are somehow mutually exclusive terms, rather that in this sequence Alex is enveloped in 'the private fantasy of the transformative agency of desire' (ibid.: 132). Both identification and desire are mediated through the activities of investigation and transformation in which both women are engaged.

Though transformation, and pleasure in the possibilities that transformation offers, is at issue in all three films, *Black Widow* remains distinct in its articulation of two women in this central relationship. All three films play on the evident comparisons between investigator and investigated. *The Silence of the Lambs* constructs an extended analogy between Starling and Buffalo Bill. This is partially qualified by her understanding of and identification with the victims – for example, her instant recognition during the autopsy of the social location a female corpse once inhabited ('she's not local – her ears are pierced three times and there's glitter nail polish – looks like town to me'). Yet, as Elizabeth Young (1991) notes, both Bill and Starling seek transformation. And it is through her destruction of Bill that Starling's transformation is enabled: even down to the way in which the final pursuit through his darkened house re-enacts an earlier, brief training sequence in which Clarice had 'died' following her failure to check the corner for danger. In this 'replay' her reactions are correct, saving her life. The image of the butterfly, signifier of transformation throughout the film, and singled out by the camera as light bursts into the room where Bill lies dead through a window shattered by Starling's bullet, refers then to them both. *Copycat*'s Dr Helen Hudson (Sigourney Weaver), is a psychiatrist and writer who has achieved celebrity in writing about serial killers, but who is now confined by agoraphobia to her (luxurious) home following an attack by Darryll Lee Cullum (Harry Connick Jnr). She is confronted by a 'copycat' serial killer, Peter Foley. Both killer and doctor share a

106

detailed knowledge of their joint obsession: the history and repertoire of serial killers in America.[17] Peter Foley's re-enactment of notorious crimes is for Hudson's appreciation: the seemingly random manner in which the killer reconstructs past crimes is based on the ordering that Hudson herself has provided in the lecture that begins the film (attempts to murder her will also both begin and end the film). Hudson is also the privileged audience to the extent that the fraternity of serial killers (for whom she is a 'pin-up girl') aim to be written up by her. Her professional success is fuelled by the very type of killer who threatens her and the rather lurid public interest that is also part of the marketing for the film itself, the interest in the macabre off which it feeds.

Starling becomes an FBI agent over the corpse of Buffalo Bill. Alex Barnes/Jessica Bates achieves professional success, and escape from the routine that stifles her, on her triumph over 'Catherine': the media are present in force at the critical moment in both movies. Hudson, already a media celebrity, is victim to a private re-enactment of the attempt to kill her, a re-enactment in which she not only escapes, but escapes transformed, signified by her laughter as she faces Foley. These films are concerned not only with a dynamic of identification then, but with a process of transformation: movements that complement each other to the extent that we might understand the production of identities through identification. The theme is evident in crime films in which the heroine either takes on an active role or assumes a position of authority. I've already considered the motif of the 'undercover' operation, in terms of the cop/prostitute role, a motif which suggests a concern with disguise and exploration in crime fictions and underlines the instability or shifting nature of the female hero.[18] Standing in opposition to 'undercover' work in many American crime fictions is the 'uniform': typically from the lower ranks, 'uniforms' are defined by the explicit costumes they adopt which clearly mark their status. The opening sequence of *Blue Steel* links display with authority through the fragmented montage of Megan donning her uniform – yet it is also a 'rookie' uniform and Megan is only one among many, a face in the crowd. In a similar fashion Clarice Starling in *The Silence of the Lambs* is explicitly situated as 'fledgling'. For both characters, entering an agency of law enforcement is about a transformation which is linked to costume and which, it might be suggested, functions as a sort of cross-dressing. Starling is defined by her ethnic/class position (Lecter pinpoints her as emerging from 'poor white trash') and her desire to escape it. Both she and Alex Barnes in *Black Widow* are defined by a professional ambition as well as a personal involvement in the case. Identification and the understanding that it brings, produces identity in a double sense then, since it is through capture of the killer that these women will get something of the transformation that they desire: 'advancement' for Starling in Lecter's words, a way out of the office with 'green windows' for Alex Barnes, a way out of her imprisoning apartment for Helen Hudson.

Transformation involves a negotiation of positions across the sites of investigator, investigated and victim. For Young the process whereby Starling 'reveals her stories to Lecter's scrutiny', is one in which she 'is forced to relinquish the authority invested in her position as detective' (1991: 39). Crawford warns Starling against this before she first goes to the asylum: 'Believe me, you don't want Hannibal Lecter inside your head'.[19] Yet later it is precisely Starling's intuitive detective work in relation to her understanding of both Buffalo Bill's methodology and the character of the first victim, Frederica Bimmel, that enables her to track him down. The opening sequence of *Blue Steel* in which Megan is seen, through a series of close-ups putting on her uniform (and new cop identity) for a formal display shortly to be shattered, is visually matched by the scene in the hospital towards the end of the film. Positioned here as victim, attacked and raped, Megan spits out the sleeping pills she has been given, knocks out her guard and steals his uniform in order to track down Eugene for the final confrontation. From dress uniform (designed for display) to working uniform (designed for action), the slow montage of extreme close-ups charts Megan's (re)production as cop protagonist-cum-vigilante.[20]

Young argues that both the character Clarice Starling and the star persona of Jodie Foster 'consistently [refuse] to adhere to conventional gender boundaries' (1991: 11). The other films discussed in this chapter, particularly *Copycat*, but also *Impulse* and *Blue Steel*, make textual use of star images. Debra Winger, Sigourney Weaver, Holly Hunter, Theresa Russell, Jamie Lee Curtis: all are associated in differing ways with 'strong' roles. And even the rather different *Eye for an Eye* (1995), discussed further later in this chapter, makes use of aspects of Sally Field's star image, in both her 'Norma Rae'-like determination and the 'triumph through suffering', connotations derived from her performance in such melodramas as *Steel Magnolias. The Silence of the Lambs* and *Copycat* also use star images to sidestep the seemingly inexorable move towards the constitution of a heterosexual couple found in other crime films. As Clare Whatling observes, Jonathan Demme's *The Silence of the Lambs* completely departs from the 'unconvincing' conclusion of Harris' novel, in which the happily Oedipalised Clarice is in bed with a male entomologist. Whatling considers this in terms of the trajectory of the film as a whole, the Ardelia Mapp character and Foster's star persona, noting that: '[n]one of this makes Starling a lesbian of course. But it does make her a character who is never comfortably recuperable to a heterosexual paradigm' (Budge and Hamer 1994: 193). If the contribution of Jodie Foster's image to her films in general, and to *The Silence of the Lambs* in particular, has been the subject of critical comment, Signourney Weaver already signifies both an upper-middle class assurance (a quality exploited in her role as First Lady in *Dave* and as the self-assured bitch boss from hell in *Working Girl*) and a physical set of capabilities, heroic strength and determination derived from her role as Ripley in the *Alien* films. Lizzie Francke's review remarked that 'Weaver is forever Ripley – the viewer is somehow safe in the knowledge that she is immune from the dangers that threaten, however sadistic'.[21] In this way the articulation in *Copycat* of a transformation of her professional working woman persona around an axis of public/private is particularly pertinent. Her command of space in the opening sequence speaks confidence – a stature confirmed by the larger than life version of her own image projected on the screen behind her. Here she is confident enough to turn the camera around on the audience (in the lecture theatre) indicating light-heartedly which of them is likely to be a serial killer by age and ethnic group. The attack that follows, which will be re-enacted by the copycat at the climax of the film, sends Hudson into a private world. Just as her enhanced, projected image and Weaver's star image speak of her class and professional location, the splendid apartment to which she is confined signals a continued, if limited, command over space: one bought by wealth. And, crucially, Hudson has a command of technology, communicating with the world and, ultimately, with the killer, via her modem.

Copycat seems to suggest an alliance between two women, opposed along the familiar lines of the buddy movie: super-confident cop and brilliant but neurotic doctor. Hudson has an uncanny ability to describe a scene at which she is not present (directing them to notes and clues over the phone). Holly Hunter plays the investigating officer who involves Hudson, against the wishes of her superior. Yet the two stars are typically kept apart on screen. The pairing of Hunter and Weaver is effective nonetheless: Hunter exudes calm authority (she is clearly the superior in her partnership with young cop Ruben) against Weaver's regular attacks of panic and incessant consumption of alcohol and cigarettes. The narrative begins and ends with Hudson/Weaver in a position of authority, moving through a period of fear and isolation. Hudson's home is invaded, her (gay) male assistant dies and ultimately her own attempted murder is re-enacted. Symptomatically she wears the same red suit in both opening and closing sequences: though the copycat serial killer has dressed her up for the finale, she regains her oral authority. It is her laughter (and the contempt that it signifies) which produces and seals her victory. Within an elaborate expression of a public/private dichotomy, Hudson portrays a professional woman fixed in terms of a sexual role (the serial killer who wants her underwear for a trophy) that she confronts with hiding, cynicism and, finally, laughter.

Criminal women

Transformation is also central within a quite distinct group of crime narratives in which women move from the position of victim to that of aggressor/criminal, sometimes via the activity of investigation, more often through the motif of revenge. The phrase 'criminal women' serves to signal transgression in a literal sense (that of law breakers) and, potentially, in a more symbolic sense. The two are not necessarily linked. The cat burglar played by Kim Basinger in *The Real McCoy* (1993), for example. The film has the reluctant heroine battling a corrupt establishment in defence of her son and inept criminal toyboy, played by Val Kilmer. Barely a hair out of place, this is not a narrative of transgression or of bodily vulnerability. The most 'extreme', and perhaps the most familiar articulation of female criminality in this double sense comes in the form of the rape revenge movie, discussed at length by Carol Clover. Clover reads both *Thelma and Louise* and *Mortal Thoughts* (1991) as mainstream narratives that emerge from the possibilities established in low-budget films of the 1970s and 1980s and, in particular, from the persona of the 'boyish, knife-wielding victim-heroes of slasher films and the grim avengers of their own rapes in films like *Ms 45* and *I Spit on Your Grave*' (1992: 6). In the context of the action film and the emergent action heroine of the same period, the vulnerability of the female body is most often expressed through images of rape or sexual assault, images that perhaps, as Clover implies, work to literalise the sexual connotations of penetration by knife, bullet, arrow and the other weapons to which the male hero is perpetually subject in the genre. Involving a movement from victim to vigilante, the rape/revenge scenario foregrounds concerns of female sexuality, point of view and the law.

John Schlesinger's *Eye For an Eye* recasts the rape revenge movie around an avenging mother. Sally Field plays Karen McCann, a successful, confident professional (she works in the Media Museum) whose seventeen-year-old daughter Julie is brutally raped and murdered. This, in only the fourth scene of the film, signals a rapid move from family celebration (the youngest child Megan's birthday party) to the thriller/horror base. The film positions Karen as listener and the audience as viewer to the murder. Stuck in city traffic (the claustrophobia captured in an establishing shot from above with honking horns on the soundtrack), McCann is speaking on the phone to Julie, who is preparing the party for her sister Megan. Julie answers the door to her attacker. The violence of the soundtrack and of the images of assault is inter-cut with the mother's panic and horrified reaction shots. As the title of the film suggests, the narrative develops in relation to the well-worn path of the vigilante ('What do you do when justice fails?' asked the promotional slogan). However, the film conducts the movement to vigilante as a gradual process, explored at a slow pace as the narrative unfolds (moving from therapeutic scenes at a support group to self-defence training led by martial arts star Cynthia Rothrock, and shooting lessons). In the process, McKann also becomes an investigator, donning a military-style outfit, cap and shades to follow her prey. At the film's conclusion, McKann orchestrates a scenario in which she takes the role of victim and vigilante simultaneously, luring the killer (Keifer Sutherland) to her house in order to stage his murder as an act of self-defence.

The focus on the subjectivity of a (usually female) protagonist defines this scenario of rape/revenge. *Mortal Thoughts*, which is almost entirely told from the point of view of an unreliable narrator, is also an investigation of the lives of its female protagonists. The strength of the friendship between Cynthia (Demi Moore) and Joyce (Glenne Headly) structures the remembrance, as does the power of a man, Jimmy Urbanski (Bruce Willis) to come between them, even in death. Cynthia's story is told in flashback as she is interrogated in a police station, her words and image filmed for the record. Her story slowly falls apart under questioning. Finally she leaves and, sitting in her stationary car outside the police station, recalls in another flashback a quite different version of the events she has been recounting. Here it is revealed that it was Cynthia and not her friend Joyce

Urbanski who killed brutal husband Jimmy Urbanski during his attempt to rape her. Later, it is revealed, Joyce returns the favour, dispatching Cynthia's husband who is threatening to take her children from her. A strong sense of loss pervades the movie in which the rape revenge narrative does not lead to a triumphal killing. Distance and loss are conveyed through the framing device of the flashbacks, the unreliable narrator and by the credit sequence which dwells on photos of the two friends growing up together. The investigation produces heterosexuality as the site of violence and death. There is no small irony, observes Kathleen Murphy, when:

> Cyn tells her interrogator that she first noticed problems between Joyce and . . . Jimmy . . . at their *wedding*. A ritual celebration meant to civi-lize copulation becomes an occasion for symbolic rape, with the groom roughing up his wife to get at the gift money in her white satin purse.
>
> (1991: 27).

A portrayal of marriage as conflict and misunderstanding is framed by this investigative narrative in which the loss of friendship is more tragic than murder.

Point of view and remembrance is also at issue in *The Accused* (1988), for which Jodie Foster won her first Academy Award. Kaplan's film explores the ways in which rape cases involve judgements around both attacker and assailant. Sarah Tobias, a young, white working-class woman is subject to a brutal gang rape. The charge is reduced in a plea-bargain since Sarah's attorney feels that her overt sexuality would invalidate her testimony. Subsequently she is pursued and taunted by a lout who claims she is fair game since, as he tells lawyer Kathryn Murphy, 'she's a whore'. Here 'whore' suggests one who does not have the right to bargain for her body – who has no control over what she no longer owns (and sells). In relation to issues of ownership and consent, this language of abuse returns us to the image of the prostitute. And once more the relationship between imaging class and discourses of sexuality is made explicit. Sarah's spirit and independence mark her as strong: the film maps the way in which she also needs support. While *The Accused* represents a welcome discourse on the question of consent in legal discourse around rape for Clover, she sees as problematic the extent to which it accommodates to the mainstream in its valorisation of the law as site of solace or solution. At the same time, as she also notes, the conviction of the men who cheered while the rape took place (and therefore by admission the rapists themselves who will now serve the full term for their crime) is on an obscure offence. For Clover *The Accused* enacts an up-scale version of the rape-revenge narrative, one in which agency is taken from the victim and handed to the legal system that is shown in countless other movies as failing:

> When I see an Oscar-winning film like *The Accused* or the artful *Alien* and its blockbuster sequel *Aliens* or, more recently, *Sleeping with the Enemy* and *The Silence of the Lambs*, and even *Thelma and Louise*, I cannot help thinking of all the low-budget, often harsh and awkward but

111

sometimes deeply energetic films that preceded them by a decade or more – films that said it all, and in flatter terms, and on a shoestring.

(Clover 1992: 20)

In *The Accused* then, a legal drama with low-budget roots intersects with the social problem film and a characterisation familiar from television of the 'liberal crusading lawyer'.[22]

Clover has identified class and the terms of economic exploitation as central to the rape-revenge plot, articulated in terms of an opposition between country and city (or in *Ms 45* within and around a city economy: Thana's work in the sweatshop). *The Accused* charts the conflict and ultimate reconciliation of sorts between independent, working-class victim Sarah Tobias and middle-class lawyer Kathryn Murphy (Kelly McGillis) who at first lets her down and then returns to support her. Her sexuality marks Sarah Tobias as working class, defined as different from both Murphy and the college boys who are involved in the assault. Sarah's house is on the wrong side of the tracks: it is one of the elements she mentions in her harangue against Kathryn. Kathryn drops her off from the hospital in the dark and rain: we don't see the houses clearly, only Sarah running away in her borrowed clothes, picked out in the headlights. When Murphy drives up in the daylight a sweeping camera movement displays the semi-industrial wasteland in which Sarah's home is located (the bar where the attack happens is called The Mill). Subsequently, Murphy's change of heart follows two incidents. One in which Tobias angrily confronts Murphy, bursting into the lawyer's apartment, catching her in the throes of an elaborate dinner party that is viewed only from a distance. The second in which Tobias rams her car into that of one of the onlookers, ending up in hospital once more. Both scenarios inscribe Tobias as both aggressive and victimised, indicating the film's complex view of her character, but also challenging Murphy to examine her position (expressed in class terms). *The Accused* is unusual in focusing primarily on the character of Tobias rather than exclusively on the heroic investigator. It is Sarah Tobias who is contextualised, given a history. Whilst, as Clover suggests, the narrative turns to the law for a solution, Murphy's character remains strangely amorphous. We see Sarah trying to come to terms with what has happened to her – attempting to function and coming up against prejudice. Sarah is shown at home and at work, Katherine almost exclusively at work. My point here is not to argue against Clover in terms of her comparison between 'high' and 'low', mainstream and exploitation, but to signal that the articulation of women across the roles of victim, investigated and investigator in Kaplan's film involves an evocation of various generic roots which in turn are made subject to qualification.

In different ways scenarios of criminal women and of women as cops negotiate the developing position of women within the structures of crime narratives, and the (slowly) changing position of women in such institutions of authority. The production of female cops or investigators does not function straightforwardly to articulate some new female heroism, drawing as these scenarios so often do on a

112

range of generic sources. For Clover, slasher-film origins account for the characterisation of Clarice Starling as 'masculine in both manner and career, uninterested in sex or men, and dead serious about her career' (1992: 233). Other generic origins produce female investigators such as Rita Cates or Lottie Mason as ambivalent about their involvement in the institutions of law enforcement, as self-absorbed and implicated in structures of sexual fantasy. We might return here to *The X Files* in which voice of reason Dana Scully says, 'I saw the FBI as a place where I could distinguish myself'. This evocation of a progress narrative around a brilliant woman is framed by a narrative context of fantasy and paranoia within which her very lack of fit with authority (as a non-WASP woman in an institution peopled by men in suits) heightens the populist ambivalence towards such institutions that the show itself portrays.

5

'NEW HOLLYWOOD', NEW *FILM NOIR* AND THE *FEMME FATALE*

'Don't be surprised if I'm back in ten years to buy this place': Demi Moore as Merideth Johnson, Michael Douglas' predatory boss in *Disclosure*

'New *film noir*' or 'film *après noir*' are critical terms that attempt to describe a quite specific trend in the American cinema of the 1970s and since, an emulation of the style, tone, narratives and *mise en scène* of the *film noir* of the 1940s.[1] Yet the term may also be used to signal more broadly the extent to which 1940s' *film noir* has continued to register an influence in contemporary film-making. This chapter opens with some contextualising remarks that aim to situate new *film noir* in relation to 'new Hollywood', itself an uncertain term, before moving to a more specific focus on feminist perspectives and the figure of the *femme fatale* as indicative of *contemporary* anxieties around gender and sexuality. The figure of the *femme fatale*, showcased in 1940s' *film noir*, rearticulated in the 1970s and beyond, has preoccupied feminist film criticism as both an archetype which suggests an equation between female sexuality, death and danger, and simultaneously as a textual space within which women function as the vibrant centre of the narrative. How, we might ask, has this archetype, familiar from classical Hollywood, developed in a post-classical cinema that is also operating post-Production Code, is to an extent post-feminist and, more contentiously perhaps, postmodern?

By the 1970s, *film noir* had achieved a certain cachet within critical circles and among younger aspiring film-makers, such as Paul Schrader, who relished both the rich ambiguity of the *noir* style and the kudos that visual references to that moment of cinema history could bring. The establishment of what might be called an American 'art' cinema with its own *auteurs* can also be traced from this period. Film-makers who were to become *star* directors, such as Scorsese and Coppola, borrowed freely from both European art cinema traditions and from the genres and styles of classical Hollywood. Remakes of *noir* classics, both artful and artless, have appeared throughout the 1970s, into the 1980s and beyond. A number of film-makers have also made extensive and diverse use of *noir* imagery, *noir* plots and *noir* cinematography. Further, as Frank Krutnik argues, there is also a distinctive commercial logic involved in this process:

> The problematic identity of *film noir* serves to intensify its highly bankable and 'seductive' mystique: when a new film is labelled '*noir*' this

serves as a promise of quality, that the film in question is more than just
a thriller.

(Krutnick 1991: 16)

Marketing a new release with reference to *noir* elements and antecedents now
serves as industry shorthand for an arthouse 'quality', often combined with eroticism. Lawrence Kasdan's *Body Heat* (1980), a steamy drama of murder and fraud,
could be understood as an homage to, or as plagiarism of, various *The Postman
Always Rings Twice* derivatives including Billy Wilder's *Double Indemnity* (1944).
Contemporary reviews and those greeting its reissue in 1992 framed it precisely
in this way, with the opening of Richard Corliss' review ('It is 1946: It is 1981')
an indicative example.[2] Ridley Scott's 1982 science fiction film *Blade Runner* coupled anxieties about human identity in relation to technology (anxieties
characteristic of science fiction) with an imagined future Los Angeles visualised in
terms of the shadows and rain-lashed streets of 1940s' *noir*. Paul Schrader's
American Gigolo (1980), as well as making pointed gestures in the direction of
such American movies as Coppola's *The Conversation* (1974) in the Richard Gere
character's methodical destruction of his apartment, figured some of the visual
devices associated with *noir* (light falling through venetian blinds, for example),
coupled with a plot that had the hero spiralling downwards in a conspiratorial
world of secrets and sexuality.[3] And it was Schrader in his incarnation as critic who
had written, in a 1972 article published in *Film Comment*, of the richness of the
noir style for conveying the anxiety and paranoia of a particular cultural moment.
Referring in that context to the immediate post-war period, the particular con-
stellation of elements orchestrated in *American Gigolo* could be taken to signal
the uncertainties of masculine identity at the beginning of the decade.[4] And
though publicity stills emphasised the stylised quality associated with the *noir* style,
it can be argued that *Body Heat* nonetheless displays distinctly contemporary
concerns.

In its insistent, if eclectic reference to other films and other periods of cinema
history, new *film noir* is marked by a certain nostalgia, a nostalgia that for Fredric
Jameson marks the postmodern. As an exemplar of pastiche in 1980s' cinema,
Jameson cites Kasdan's *Body Heat*. Noel Carroll also commences his discussion
of 'allusion' in the cinema of the 1970s with a discussion of the same film, situating it alongside blockbuster exercises in pastiche such as *Star Wars* or *Raiders
of the Lost Ark* (which Kasdan also co-wrote) with their allusions to the cinema
of the past. Thus he argues that *Body Heat* does not 'merely rework an old plot'
but:

> tries to evoke the old films, films of the forties, that the plot was a part
> of. *Body Heat*'s costumes are contemporary, but of a nostalgic variety that
> lets us – no, asks us – to see the film as a shifting figure, shifting between
> the past and the present .
>
> (Carroll 1982: 51)

For Carroll, films such as *Body Heat* may be read as symptomatic not only in terms of a transparent allusion to other films and cinematic moments, but to the extent that little distinction is drawn in the process between the type or 'quality' of texts referred to.[5] *Star Wars*, for example, offers a pastiche of scenes from the Western, and the adventure serials of the 1930s combined with, notoriously, reference to Leni Riefensthal's *Triumph of the Will*. Yet, the precise *meaning* of such reference is more difficult to ascertain. In this sense, new *film noir*, in its nostalgia and cleverness, in its raiding of the cinematic past, could be seen as part of an American cinema reluctant to articulate the concerns of the present – eager to avoid a staging of the problems of contemporary America.[6] For Jameson such aesthetic strategies enact an erasure of history in which nostalgia and reference for its own sake is read as 'an elaborated symptom of the waning of our historicity' (1984: 68). He argues of *Body Heat* that it is:

> exceedingly symptomatic to find the very style of nostalgia films invading and colonizing even those movies today which have contemporary settings: as though, for some reason, we were unable to focus on our own present, as though we have become incapable of achieving aesthetic representations of our own current experience.
>
> (Jameson 1984: 117)

So it is the fact of reference to the past rather than what is being referred to that is significant. Approached through the issue of shifting gender roles and developing discourses of sexuality however, new *film noir* emerges as a rather different object, one in which a reference to and rearticulation of past images serve a distinct, narrative logic rather than functioning as a throwaway bid for arthouse status. This is not to invalidate, but to add to, the reading of new-*noir*-as-postmodern which I have outlined very briefly here. In effect it is to consider the historical specificity of new *film noir*, rather than to read these movies (only) as a sign or symptom of the loss of history.

Feminism, the *femme fatale* and the *film noir*

The 1970s, a period in which movies such as Polanski's *Chinatown* (1974) revisited the cynical landscape of an earlier age involving corruption, capitalism and incest, was also a time in which film studies was becoming established as an academic discipline, and in which *film noir* as a genre or style of film-making acquired increasing acclaim and interest. The 1970s was also a period in which a specifically *feminist* film criticism and theory had begun to establish itself. Feminist criticism had moved broadly from an initial emphasis on the identification, classification and cataloguing of stereotypes to an interest in alternative forms of film production and a fascination with seeking out cracks in the seamless world of classic Hollywood, through detailed and increasingly sophisticated textual explorations. The 1978 publication of a short BFI collection edited by Ann Kaplan, *Women in*

Film Noir, was emblematic of the strength and richness of feminist film criticism as well as indicating the strength of interest in *film noir* (in both its 1940s' and 1970s' manifestations since the collection is framed by two essays from Christine Gledhill examining *Klute*).[7] The essays in *Women in Film Noir* turned attention from what had been, in Jane Root's phrase, 'a masculine perspective' which concentrated 'on the existential dilemmas of the *noir* hero' to an exploration of the contradictory evocation of 'woman' as desirable but dangerous in the *film noir* (Cook 1985: 97). The vigour of the arguments presented in this collection matched the extent to which what was still widely termed the 'women's movement' was effecting change in American and British culture and society. Feminist criticism looked with interest to the *noir* of the 1940s partly in terms of the historical period that produced these fictions, with an eye to the wartime redefinition of women's roles and the ideological negotiations which that redefinition involved.[8] One of the features of *noir* that intrigued feminist critics, then, was its generation of strong images of women within a historical moment (the Second World War and its aftermath) in which women were being called on to perform roles associated primarily with men. Whether read as an anxious response or a performance of power, such images seemed particularly historically grounded. At another historical moment (the 1970s and 1980s) when feminism was developing a commentary on the representation of women found in *film noir*, critics examined the images of women in contemporary Hollywood and found them lacking. Janey Place picked up on the historical parallels, speculating on the appeal of *noir* narratives, with their 'regressive ideological function' for 1970s' audiences. Her primary concern is an exploration of the possible contradictions between narrative and visual style, with the 1940s a period 'in which women are deadly but sexy, exciting and strong' (Kaplan 1980: 54). Here then it is the sheer *energy* and *vitality* of the *femme fatale* that stands out.

The appeal of the *femme fatale* for feminism may lie in this particular confluence of elements. Drawing on a tradition of representation in which women are mysteriously seductive but evil, in which 'woman' is not only defined by her sexuality but also by the power that this generates. She is a transgressive figure who misleads the hero and who is punished for her pains. Though she is punished she has, as both Place and Sylvia Harvey point out, a life and vigour absent from the other women within the typical *noir* narrative – those who stay in their place (Kaplan 1980). The *femme fatale* in both her 1940s' and her 'new Hollywood' incarnations is defined by at least four significant aspects. First, her seductive sexuality. Second, the power and strength (over men) that this sexuality generates for the *femme fatale*. Third, the deceptions, disguises and confusion that surrounds her, producing her as an ambiguous figure for both the audience and the hero. Fourth, as a consequence the sense of woman as 'enigma', typically located within an investigative narrative structure which seeks to find 'truth' amidst the deception. This particular combination of elements, both inviting and dangerous, makes her threatening to the heterosexual male hero. Her appeal for feminist critics lies in her potentially transgressive refusal of patriarchal values. Generally constructed in opposition to a 'good' woman, whose nurturing qualities are evident in her behaviour towards the hero, she is the site of energy and power. The opposition of good and bad women was to some extent premised on the suppression of an explicit sexuality, relying instead on an implicit assertion of an aggressive sexuality signified through costume, posture and so on, all of which run counter to the comfortable familiarity of domesticity. Post the Production Code, however, the *femme fatale* appears a rather different figure: not least in relation to an increasingly explicit, though no less metaphoric, display of a body coded in terms of sexuality. Speaking of the *femme fatale* as a figure of modernity, Mary Anne Doane notes that:

> [h]er power is of a peculiar sort insofar as it is not usually subject to her conscious will, hence appearing to blur the distinction between passivity and activity. She is an ambivalent figure because she is not the subject of power but its carrier.
>
> (Doane 1991: 2)[9]

What then of the *femme fatale* within a post-classical/postmodern cinema? How distinct is the representation of deadly women who do know how to wield the power that they possess, as in *The Last Seduction*, or, quite differently, in *Bound*. Once again, work and status function as key signifiers here, signifiers which suggest an historically specific reading.

The 1970s saw the emergence of a new popular stereotype, that of the 'independent woman', figured in terms of a bright, advertising culture confidence and a narrative refusal to accept a submissive role within relationships or professionally. Jane Fonda's role as Bree Daniels in *Klute*, indeed Fonda's star image at this time, works within this type of the independent woman quite precisely.[10] In various examples of new *film noir* and in later films which, whilst sharing elements, cannot be said precisely to fit that category, the types of the independent woman and *femme fatale* have complexly informed each other, transmuting into a new version of the *femme fatale* which comes to situate her as a powerful woman whose threat quite overtly lies in the context of work. Janey Place evokes the figure of the 'dark lady, the spider woman, the evil seductress who tempts man and brings about his destruction' as an ancient theme in western 'art, literature, mythology and religion', a figure therefore who long pre-dates 1940s' *noir*, who is 'as old as Eve, and as current as today's movies, comic books and dime novels' (Kaplan 1980: 35). If these biblical and contemporary reference points suggest the longevity of the type, feminist film historians and theorists have produced fascinating work linking the image of the *femme fatale* of 1940s' noir to specific social, cultural and historical configurations (Kaplan 1980; Williams 1988). In this vein, Place argues that:

> [t]he tendency of popular culture to create narratives in which male fears are concretised in sexually aggressive women who must be destroyed is not specific to the forties to middle-fifties in the United

States, but is seen today to a degree that might help to account for the sudden popularity of these films on college campuses, television, and film retrospectives.

(Kaplan 1980)

This phenomenon must, she indicates, be set alongside the ambivalence of the *noir* text in which narrative and sensual impressions are to some extent opposed or in contradiction. My main concern in this chapter is not so much with how 1940s' versions were received in the 1970s, but the rearticulation of these themes within the cinema loosely termed 'new Hollywood'. How, does the new *film noir* present the opposition of good woman/*femme fatale* articulated in the earlier films to which they refer? In what senses might contemporary versions of this 'archetype' be said to have a *historical specificity*? Is this simply part of an empty reference to a critically venerated cinematic past on the part of status-hungry film-makers? Or is the articulation of powerful female sexuality in the context of 1970s', representation-conscious feminism (and of post-feminism) of a different order?

Allusionistic invocations of the 'strong' image of woman associated with 1940s' noir or the style of lighting and *mise en scène* more generally, generate no single, coherent group of meanings or connotations. In order to explore some aspects of this question we can consider how a range of movies have made very different use of such reference in terms of scope, scale and significance. I've already referred to the use of a self-conscious visual style influenced by *noir* to portray the city of the future in *Blade Runner*, a style that serves to underscore the sense of uncertainty surrounding the hero's identity. The film's female lead and romantic interest Rachel (Sean Young) first appears in 1940s' attire– a tailored suit, her hair up on her head in a sculpted style and a cigarette emphasising her painted red lips. She appears smoking, calm and sophisticated, a model of the self-confident heroine. Rachel's identity is also in question, a narrative device that once more presents woman as an enigma, a puzzle to be figured out by the hero. If her distance and ambiguity present her as a potentially threatening figure, we discover that this stems from a *failure* of identity – a lack which she seeks to fill by reinventing her-self, initially through a set of faked photographs of a simulated past and, ultimately, in a scenario of heterosexual romance. The harsh, cold look through which she initially presents herself to the world is transformed into a Pre-Raphaelite muse. Bigelow's *Strange Days* also borrows from this visual repertoire to portray a millennial, racially-divided Los Angeles with a hero, addicted to his own memories, whose identity is falling apart. The film deploys an opposition between good woman and bad woman, with the dissolute Faith (Juliette Lewis) opposed to the self-sufficient Mace (Angela Bassett). If Lewis is castrating, Mace is both phallic and nurturing (she is a mother) and the only character whose identity is stable (she resists the pleasures of playback).[11]

In *Trial By Jury* (1994), Joanne Whalley-Kilmer plays Valerie, a single mother running a small business who is called for jury duty and finds herself pressurised into arguing for mobster Rusty Pirone's innocence to defend her son. Pirone (Armand Assante) sees himself as an old-style movie gangster and Valerie as a woman with enough class to play alongside of him. He admires her beauty, seeing in her the glamour of old-style movie stars who lived at a time when, he elaborates, figures such as himself were respected. There is no little irony in the fact that her business involves selling period clothing, and that it is from her own stock that Pirone picks out a suitable dress for her to wear in the part he has picked for her.[12] Valerie's status as single mother, businesswoman and good citizen (she doesn't have to do jury service but feels it is her duty) is quite at odds with the vision Pirone has of her. Having argued the jury round to set Pirone free, and surviving an assassination attempt (she is saved by William Hurt's corrupted ex-cop character), Valerie visits Pirone dressed to suit his fantasy. Yet in her clutch bag she carries an ice pick, with which she kills him. Pirone's nostalgia for the glamour of the past blinds him to her independence, to a strength that she only discovers in herself through the course of the movie. Historical setting is a factor in the different uses these movies make of reference to *noir* images and plots. Finally, by contrast Carl Franklin's *Devil in a Blue Dress* is set in neither the present nor the future, but the past: a period reconstruction with fine attention to the details of the immediate post-war period. Franklin's film echoes Mosley's novel in its replay of a familiar style, the sparse yet eloquent description, interior monologue and dialogue. The marginal position of the private investigator in 1940s' *noir* is heightened and explored in the precarious position of Easy Rawlins (Denzel Washington) as a black American. Franklin's movie re-frames and draws our attention to the operation of both 'race' and gender in the *film noir*. While it isn't useful to conflate these different orders of reference (whether narrative, visual, setting, costume) they perhaps indicate something of the complex fashion in which individual film texts insert themselves into cinematic and other histories.

Bodies of evidence

New *film noir* can be situated in relation to 'new Hollywood' in terms of a defining visual nostalgia and an overt reference to other films, cinematic eras and movements (features that such films as *Chinatown* share with *Star Wars* and its ilk). But it can also be situated in relation to new Hollywood in a quite distinct fashion – that is in terms of changing patterns of regulation and censorship. The well-documented collapse of both post-war audiences and the industry's system of self-regulation in the form of the production code, the associated development of a ratings system, of fragmented audiences and niche marketing all contribute to the selling of certain films through the promise of an explicit portrayal of sexuality and/or violence. The development of segmented markets that both produced that challenge to the regulation system and was developed as a result of it (teenage, adult, cult), a movement accentuated by the relationship with television, has allowed the location of the *femme fatale* in 'adult' genres such as the erotic thriller, horror/crime, as well as new *film noir*. Consider *Body Heat*, already mentioned as a film that insistently signposts its references to a generic past. Kasdan's film was one of a group of ostentatious remakes of 'classics' which had themselves only relatively recently acquired classic status. When the film was first released in 1981 it was sold precisely in these terms. Yet marketing and publicity coupled the status of *noir* references with the promise of an explicit portrayal of sexuality ('Torrid Movie, Hot New Star' proclaimed *Time*). And, after all, since the *femme fatale* of the 1940s was associated primarily with 'B' movies, her re-inscription in a cinema of up-market erotic thrillers should come as no surprise.[13] Indeed Frank Krutnik's account of the production context of 1940s' noir, with smaller studios bidding for the 'quality' associations of an Expressionist style, indicates that:

> These stylistics seem to have functioned as a conventionalised means of upgrading the status of productions, operating as a language of stylistic differentiation which was as standardised in many ways as the classical norms.
>
> (Krutnik 1991: 21)

Carroll argues that '[e]ven [*Body Heat*'s] eroticism requires our explicit association of the female lead with certain movie myths – for example, the woman-as-devil/ temptress archetype – in order to be really forceful' (1982: 51). Yet the insistent focus on the body and scenes of heterosexual love-making is actually an aspect of the movie that marks it as quite distinct from the predecessors that it alludes to, an element not commented on by either Jameson or Carroll who perhaps regarded this as only a superficial difference. Reviewers, however, dwelt (with some relish) on the foregrounding of the visceral, drawing attention to images such as steam rising, the sweat on the lovers' bodies, and so on. Marketing movies through an association with explicit sex, transgressive sexualities or taboo topics has continued across a range of films which showcase the contemporary *femme fatale*. Publicity for *Fatal Attraction* (1987), for example, played heavily on an explicit treatment of adulterous sex with brief clips from scenes between Glenn Close and Michael Douglas in the lift and kitchen included in the trailer for the film. *Basic Instinct*, which featured Sharon Stone as a bisexual *femme fatale* (the role that effectively took her to star status), achieved controversy in terms of its politics and through Stone's flash of pussy in the leg-crossing scene. *Bound* (1996) has a butch/femme lesbian couple in a caper to rip off the mob. Madonna starred in *Body of Evidence* (1993), a film that exploited both the success of *Basic Instinct* and the then fashionable interest in sadomasochism (as had David Lynch's earlier 1986 *Blue Velvet*), tallying this with the star's reputation as a taboo-breaker.[14] And in *Disclosure*, Michael Douglas plays Tom Sanders, sexually harassed by Demi Moore's Meredith. Posters for *Disclosure* featured an image of the two stars entwined around each other. The accompanying slogan 'Sex is Power' suggesting little of the film's actual content which is, for the most part located in an office and in a quasi-legal setting.

An explicit representation of sexuality is not the only way in which the *femme fatale* has developed post-feminism and post-Production Code. The demise of the Production Code, together with the desire to build in a sequel if possible, has meant that the *femme fatale* can (sometimes) survive to the end of the narrative and be successful in her schemes, whether explicitly as in *Body Heat* or *Bound* or ambiguously as in *Basic Instinct*. The concluding scenes of *Body Heat* feature William Hurt's realisation that Kathleen Turner's *femme fatale* has not died in the boathouse explosion as the police think. And although he almost convinces his police buddy otherwise, there is no suggestion that she will be ultimately captured. We are left with a final image of Maddy/Kathleen Turner lying on a beach, looking at the blue sky to which the camera pans, a literalisation of the dream outlined in her high school year book (which Ned/William Hurt has been reading in prison) finally fulfilled. Interestingly, the *Daily Mirror* review (titled 'You'll like it hot') which speaks of '[t]he love scenes' as 'couplings of extraordinary eroticism which a few years ago would have had the censor reaching for his scissors', tells its readers that '[i]t doesn't matter if you don't understand the enigmatic ending. It's not all that important'.[15] Yet the ending is far from enigmatic and Maddy's duplicity is hardly unexpected by this point. The conclusion of *Basic Instinct* is more ambivalent. As Curran and Trammell share a bed, he happily contemplating the life they will have together, the camera which shows her consternation, tracks down to reveal an ice pick (the killer's weapon of choice) lodged within reach under the bed. In *Bound* the lesbian couple drive off in a new truck, unharmed, unconverted and with the blessing (or at least without arousing the suspicions) of the mob.

Of course, not all narratives showcasing the *femme fatale* in contemporary cinema offer her as a triumphant figure or reject the structures of heterosexual relationships as these films seem to do. *Fatal Attraction*, the subject of much critical comment, turns into a sort of horror movie in order to obliterate the strong woman as monster, ending up with a final lingering close-up of a family portrait which suggests that Douglas' adulterous character will be readmitted to the family.[16] Similarly, in *Body of Evidence* Madonna's *femme fatale* Rebecca overestimates her own power and ends up shot, falling back through a glass window and drowned in the water below. As Frank, the vacillating hero played by Willem Dafoe, contemplates the scene from Rebecca's balcony, cynical cop Garett (Joe Mantegna) mutters the usual clichés about 'karma' and how 'people usually get what they deserve'. The camera pans left and down to reveal a bagged body being wheeled away on a stretcher along the jetty, just as the figure of estranged wife Sharon appears, presumably to patch up the partnership. Corpse and wife cross paths and Sharon looks up to the balcony, a gesture that suggests a meeting of eyes. As the final credits roll, in a high angle shot we see Frank coming out to meet her. This low-key ending signals the relative status of the different characters: the interest has gone from the scene with the departure of Rebecca. Nonetheless she *has* been dispatched, just as Daphne Monet disappears from the scene at the conclusion of *Devil in a Blue Dress*.

It is to some extent the relocation of the threat posed by the deadly woman to the hero to the context of work that is one of the most significant products of the fusion between *femme fatale* and independent woman of the 1970s. For Christine Gledhill, the fact that Jane Fonda's performance in *Klute* is as a prostitute rather than as *femme fatale* involves a superficial engagement with 'modern' images of women (liberated and located within an urban culture) whilst actually operating to contain the 'mysterious and unknowable power of women' articulated in the stereotype of the *femme fatale* within the over-determined space of the prostitute which represents, 'a more defined sexual role, amenable to social control, and shorn of the earlier stereotype's fatality' (Kaplan 1980: 122). We might also read *Klute* not as the straightforward replacement of one stereotype with another, but as an early example of the collision and reformation of both types in a process that has continued on the contemporary screen. *Klute* works to articulate an opposition between two versions of femininity, one associated with domesticity, one with a dangerous rejection of such conventional roles. For Gledhill, Bree Daniels combines the role of 'victim and predator', just as she is caught between two men who represent 'two sides of the *noir* hero' (ibid.: 127). The film's two 'endings' match these different possibilities (the final scene shows Daniels and Klute seemingly leaving together, whilst her voice on the soundtrack indicates her doubt, the sense that she may well return to the city). Whilst Gledhill's reading is a powerful one which privileges the image (pointing to the way in which, for example, Bree's apartment is stripped of all its decor), *Klute*, like *Basic Instinct*, ultimately refuses to come down on either side. It is certainly a contradictory film, one in which the reinscription of the *femme fatale* as working girl involves some loss of mystery and of power. Yet it is also very much Fonda's film (her Oscar, her 'method' acting), one that draws upon and helped to redefine her evolving star image. There is some attempt to cast doubt on Daniels' motivation: she doesn't co-operate immediately with the investigation, her flight to the club seems self-destructive, her attack on Klute vicious, frenzied and suggestive of horror conventions. Yet Fonda the star connotes more of a dazzling directness and honesty, suggests something already different from the ambiguity of the *femme fatale*. The *femme fatale* is, like the vamp, (as the French phrasing suggests) implicitly un-American, evoking a stereotypical tradition which associates the evil temptress with an exoticism marked as foreign. *The Lady from Shanghai* (1948) for example, presented the all-American Rita Hayworth as a *femme fatale*, her otherness signified by an association with Shanghai, her facility with Cantonese and her familiarity with the chinatown that Polanski was later to invoke as some indeterminate sign of the unpredictable.[17]

Women, work and sexuality

If in the early 1970s the sexually independent, working woman heroine of new *noir* is figured as a working girl (that is as a prostitute), it is increasingly common in the 1990s to find her in a business suit. While prostitution foregrounds class, ownership of labour and so on, Daniels'/Fonda's very middle-class call-girl may be as far from the street as is possible. Indeed it was her business-like approach to sex that some found shocking in *Klute* (the scene in which she looks at her watch whilst faking sexual pleasure). This isn't to refute Gledhill's reading of the prostitute as stereotypical. However, the particular version offered in *Klute* is of interest for its use of images that were already clichés to some extent but which have become more so – the contrast between the dehumanising experience of auditions with her pleasure in the control she has as a prostitute. Moving away from *Klute* to consider new *noir* more widely, we find that the evolution of female stereotypes may be best understood – as Gledhill implies – in relation to shifts and evolution surrounding the male hero of *noir*. The instabilities of the *noir* hero have been pointed to by a range of critics and form the basis of Frank Krutnik's study, *In a Lonely Street*, in which he identifies 'an obsession with the non-correspondence between the desires of the individual male subject and the cultural regime of "masculine identification"' (1991: 85). As shifts in regulation make it at least *possible* for the *femme fatale* to profit by her crimes, the *noir* hero of such movies as *Body Heat* or even *Body of Evidence* in which the heroine is finally killed off, emerge as inept in, if possible, a more thorough-going way than their 1940s' predecessors. In this way we can consider the significance of Jameson's feeling that William Hurt 'has nothing of the distinctive style of the preceding generation of male superstars' (1984: 117). We might account for Jameson's sense of a 'faintly archaic feel' around Hurt's 'ambiguous' style of hero in terms of the way in which his character is constantly framed by images of an impending failure that an audience, clued in by the heavy-handed references, are probably already all too aware of. Ned doesn't have the authority of a voice-over, but we know he is doomed in any case. Consider his mistake in accosting Marianne – 'Hey lady, do you wanna fuck?' – and his subsequent embarrassment ('I am an *idiot*'). Or the sight of his distracted face when Maddy gives him a blow job. Or the scene in which Maddy presents him with a trilby so that he will look the part: she winds up the side windshield of the car so that her image is replaced by his own reflection – framed as he admires himself. His attempt to toss the hat onto the stand in his office fails. And yet more bizarrely in the run up to the murder, we see Ned about to get into his car when a clown in full make-up drives by, immediately followed by a shot that slowly pulls away from Ned's surprised face. While the 1940s' *noir* hero was perpetually losing consciousness/control, contemporary scenarios exaggerate this sense of his vulnerabilty. 'You're not too smart are you?' asks Maddy of Ned on their first meeting, adding 'I like that in a man'.

A contrast between two rather different films with a criminal/legal setting, *Presumed Innocent* and *Judicial Consent*, throws the success of the working girl as independent woman into relief. The latter film also serves to underline Carol Clover's comments on the different possibilities and potentialities explored, however crudely, outside the purview of movies with big league stars, prestige sources and significant advertising budgets. Both Clover (writing on the horror film) and Linda Ruth Williams (in a short essay on erotic thrillers) have suggested that themes addressed in a tentative or diluted manner in mainstream cinema are explored in much rawer and fresher fashion in the low-budget, straight-to-video sector.[18] If there is a possibility of taking risks in the independent and low-budget sectors which relates to finance and working practices, there is also a need to offer something different. What can't be delivered in special effects, for example, can be made up for in other ways. While *Presumed Innocent* is a prestige production, *Judicial Consent* is a medium-budget production released straight-to-video. Both centre around a successful professional woman in the law: one alive and one dead. *Presumed Innocent*, which involves an investigation of the life and death of Carolyn Polhemus (Greta Scacchi), a body whose state and meaning is narrated or explained by a variety of different voices, has been described by Amelia Jones as an example of 1990s' noir that draws on the conventions of the woman's picture, one of a group of films which 'narrativize the rise and fall of career women in contemporary American life and work to punish these deviant women or reinscribe them within traditional family structures' (1991: 297). Hero Rusty Sabich (Harrison Ford) finds himself implicated in Pulhemus' murder, suspected of killing a woman with whom he was involved and who he cannot forget. As Jones indicates, the film offers woman as both victim and villain in the twin figures of Polhemus and Barbara Sabich, the betrayed wife who has murdered her, orchestrating the scene in mimicry of a violent rape and leaving traces of her husband's semen. The twist, that the good woman is actually a murderer ensures that there can be no final return to a normality defined in terms of domesticity (the photo of the family that seeks to seal the ending of *Fatal Attraction*).

If *Presumed Innocent* works, as Jones suggests, to 'narrativize the rise and fall of career women in contemporary American life' through Sabich's investigation of Polhemus, *Judicial Consent* takes the story of Judge Gwen Warwick as its centre. Bonnie Bedelia's Warwick finds herself caught up in a similar scenario to Rusty Sabich in *Presumed Innocent* (in which Bedelia plays the 'guilty wife'), implicated in the case over which she presides. Gwen Warwick is building a successful legal career for herself. Having been a judge for eight years, she is about to be confirmed as a Justice for the State, but finds herself elaborately framed for the murder of a colleague. Warwick is frequently shown putting on and taking off her glasses, signifier of a sort of generalised intellect used by Signourney Weaver's Helen Hudson in *Copycat*.[19] Just as Rusty Sabich is assigned to investigate the crime for which he will later be arrested, Warwick finds herself selected as trial judge in a case which seems to rapidly, and inexplicably, accumulate evidence against her. It is Warwick's impulsive sexual liaison with a young man that is at the root of the mystery. Martin (Billy Wirth) functions as a sort of *homme fatal* – attractive but enigmatic and ultimately dangerous. Like *Impulse*, discussed in Chapter four, the film makes use of the narrative conventions of erotic fiction through the way in which Gwen Warwick is portrayed, from the start, as lonely and in a loveless marriage. Linda Ruth Williams describes the moment in *Indecent Proposal* when Demi Moore's husband rejects her advances as a clear generic clue to the audience: '[v]iewers in the know will spot this gesture as the first step on the slippery slope towards erotic thriller infidelity, and the perils as well as the pleasures of sex' (1993: 12). Warwick's affair is no surprise in this sense, since her husband is cast as a distant, unsupportive, even vaguely threatening figure. Their home is dark and austere, crammed with trophy cabinets.

The status of *Judicial Consent* as a mildly racy thriller is signalled in the opening sequence which features a naked heterosexual couple having passionate sex in the sleeper compartment of a moving train. The pair are disrupted when an unidentified killer bursts in on them. Of course this opening sequence functions not only to stake out the film's generic/thematic location (sex, crime, death) but reinforces a thriller cliché that sexual encounters bring danger. Thus when Gwen meets and becomes involved with Martin, the viewer has already been reminded of the 'perils as well as the pleasures' of illicit sexual encounters. The movie retains the tenor of soft pornography/erotic fiction for women in the sequences of courtship and passion between the two. He plays to her interest in poetry, seeming to know all her likes (he has researched the part). She follows him home in the rain, fascinated and desiring; she encounters him on the street where they have sex in the shadows. These dark, rain-soaked streets provide the backdrop for a narrative of temptation and desire. Yet Gwen's illicit activities in this space so far from the office inevitably lead back to work. The motivation for the frame-up stems not from her or her husband's infidelity, though her husband's involvement is implied and he certainly accuses her of infidelity (though he fixes on the wrong man), but from another, much older infidelity and the crime which followed. Gwen Warwick's first case as a judge, we learn, was a difficult one, passed to her as a test or trial of her stamina (and of how she would fare in a 'man's' role). It was the trial of the man who committed the murders we see in the opening sequence, that of his wife and her male lover. Warwick passed the death penalty, partly to prove that she wasn't, in her own words 'too soft'. The condemned man's son, to whom ironically she relates this past initiation into the role of judge, now seeks his revenge by seducing her as part of an elaborate plot to bring about her downfall.

There are suggestions of *Fatal Attraction* here in the device of the protagonist brought down by the consequences of a passionate affair. *Judicial Consent* makes explicit its horror origins in the final sequence, as does *Fatal Attraction* with the monstrous revival of Glenn Close's character. However, *Judicial Consent* has no equivalent to the (good wife) Anne Archer character: in defeating Martin, Gwen can only count on herself. No united family is provided to close the narrative. She has a good cop friend, Detective Tony Canfield, but a more general relationship of hostility with the police force, a hostility which contributes to their enthusiasm in linking her to the crime (again as in *Presumed Innocent*). In Pakula's film, Polhemus seduces Sabich at work (they have returned to the office after a case, late at night). Her power and energy is linked to and also expressed through her sexuality. Sex at work, and the extent to which Polhemus clearly *uses* sex to advance herself at work (an image or fantasy which returns in *Disclosure*, discussed later in this chapter) functions to reinforce the association between working women and sexual performance. In the context of the thriller such a performance is also defined by aggression, threatening to the male. There is an analogous scene in *Judicial Consent* (again late at night, after hours) in which Martin is crouched under Gwen's desk while she takes a call from her boss: in fact, the call assigning her with the case that will implicate her in murder. Though we see him remove her underwear (which he will later plant as evidence in the murder) the camera focuses on Gwen's face, her sexual pleasure and her attempts to remain 'business-like' in her conversation with her boss. The expression of sexuality in illicit places (at work, in public etc.) is a cliché of erotic fiction/film, evoking a sense of both transgression and spontaneity. Yet an association between the erotic fantasy that allows sex into the workplace, professional success (built, it is apparent, on a con-centration upon work above all else and at the cost of relationships) and, of course, betrayal pervades the film. The movie's title alludes to a sexualised artic-ulation of the law. The rumours that persist around Judge Warwick as a suspect in the murder and as suspected of an excess of sexuality (the two are presented as mutually exclusive) that somehow resides in the very fact of her existence as a working woman, an excess underlined as her underwear is paraded in her own courtroom as evidence.

Though she is only passing through town, Bridget (Linda Fiorentino), the *femme fatale* anti-heroine in *The Last Seduction*, secures herself a top managerial position at the local company almost as an afterthought. Her power-dressed glamour, her ease in doing business and stylised look (her costumes are all mono-chrome) offer a pastiche of the *femme fatale* situated within the context of a bleak, parodic narrative of seduction and betrayal. Alongside the anti-heroine's professional skills in *The Last Seduction*, her amorality is figured throughout the film with reference to an aggressive sexuality and an ability to manipulate men who, perhaps ironically, seem to want little more than to set up home and settle down with her. The opening sequence cuts between husband Clay (Bill Pullman) dealing in drugs at her behest and Bridget's humiliation of the men whose work she is supervising in a rip-off sales operation. Later she demonstrates to small-town Mike that anything can be sold over the phone, negotiating with a woman to have her husband killed. Though in part an admiring symphony that sings the praises of the bitch-goddess, the *femme fatale* as working woman also has an ironic status shared by the film as a whole. That ironic tone is underscored through sex scenes shot from a distance, presented clinically and clearly functioning as part of a manipulative scheme on the part of the *femme fatale*. Further, there is no mystery in Bridget's motivation (cynical greed) as we are party to the moves that she makes. The film's parodic flavour stems also then from the extent to which the audience is 'in on' Bridget's/Wendy's manipulations, though the revelation that Mike has mistakenly married a transvestite during his one sojourn out of town (in Buffalo), is held over to the end of the movie. In contrast to *Body Heat* or the more recent *Body of Evidence*, sex is not an explicit selling point, with sex scenes shot for comedy as much as for eroticism (the bizarre locations, Bridget's laugh-ter, Mike's incessant efforts to get her to 'commit'). Rather, *The Last Seduction* offers an arthouse twist on the obsession with remakes of *noir* scenes and types.

Here the *femme fatale* is cast as a knowing dominatrix completely identified with the urban at the expense of the small town: Bridget loves New York to the extent that she takes Wendy Kroy (the letters rearranged) as her assumed name. Her sophistication is set against her husband's failing city doctor whom she uses to raise money and, in a more thorough-going fashion, the small-town men we are explicitly encouraged to read as 'hicks'. As in *Disclosure*, Bridget/Wendy makes use of prejudices and received types – a stereotypical black male sexuality, small-town naïveté, the terms of equal opportunities at work, provincial racism and a woman-as-victim role. Like the mainstream movies that it ironises, *The Last Seduction* functions around an equation between the working woman and sexual performance.

The association between an aggressive sexuality, immorality and the working woman is central to *Disclosure*, a film that, despite blanket advertising, failed to be as controversial as the producers may have wished. The marketing sought to generate attention through tapping into a controversial (and sexualised) 'issue'.[20] The publicity slogan 'Sex is Power' managed to be both meaningful and meaningless at the same time: meaningful in evoking the debates regarding sexual harassment within which the film situated itself as 'controversial', meaningless in the context of a narrative in which it is clearly technology that is power. Though it is technology rather than sex that is power in the high-tech world of *Disclosure*, the film does its best to conflate the two, operating a gendering of technology in which the two forces are seemingly aligned to displace the 'average white male'. This conflation is literalised in the image of a virtual Meredith Johnson (Demi Moore) deleting files in cyberspace as Tom Sanders (Michael Douglas) looks on powerless, having been 'locked out' of the system. While Sanders is 'in' (but locked out from) the company's high-tech corridor, it is a mobilisation of less cutting edge technologies that 'saves' him: fax, e-mail, video, answerphone and mobile phone all come to his rescue. Whilst her talents lie in deal-making, Meredith's mistake is her cost-cutting at the *production* plant in Malaysia. The film makes little of the location of production outside the States, highlighting instead the rise of women professionals and new technologies as the defining features of a changing American capitalism that leaves Sanders vulnerable.

If Johnson has been fired at the end of *Disclosure*, she nonetheless tells hero Tom with some confidence: 'I've had calls from ten head-hunters with job offers in the last hour. Don't be surprised if I'm back in ten years to buy this place.' Johnson exemplifies both the power and the limitations of an evolving hybrid stereotype produced from a *femme fatale* defined by sexual power and an independent woman defined largely by professional success. Levinson's movie cannot decide whether or not she is competent in the world of work. It is implied, for example, that she has succeeded through exploiting her sexuality. Yet at the same time we hear of her previous successes in business. Similarly Bridget in *The Last Seduction*, whilst evidently competent, is rarely seen working *per se*; she is frequently pictured in her office talking on the phone. The sort of work we do see her doing is perverse. She is able to pressurise and manipulate through language:

from the opening tyrannical sequence to the murder by phone stunt or the exploitation of crude sex/race stereotypes in the scene with Bill Nunn (she distracts his attention by persuading him to unzip his pants causing him to crash). Like Meredith Johnson her skills are in communication rather than production (an arena retained for the masculine).

Disclosure is one of a group of films starring Michael Douglas in which an ordinary man finds himself subject to an aggressively sexual woman (*Fatal Attraction, Basic Instinct*) or the impossible pressures of a 'masculine' role as in *Falling Down*.[21] The recurrence of this persecuted figure serves to situate the awkward scene in *Disclosure* during which Sanders rants about his powerlessness. His wife has spoken of her own experiences at work, suggesting that he should just accept the sexual dimensions of office politics and learn to live with it. Paraphrasing the words of the harassment lawyer Catherine Alvarez, Tom tells Susan that 'sexual harassment is about *power. When* did I have the power? When?'. This as he stands in the middle of their luxurious home, having shouted at and intimidated the maid who appears only in this scene, kept to the sidelines (like the office cleaning woman who is the only witness to Tom's behaviour on the disputed night and who disappears from the scene). Of course, there is a certain irony to this moment, the *mise en scène* undercutting Tom's protestations of powerlessness. Similarly through the course of the legal mediation which airs the sexual harassment case, Tom learns that his secretary Cindy (Jacqueline Kim) finds his behaviour inappropriate. At odds with itself, *Disclosure* struggles to offer a variant of liberal feminism in which it is at pains to point out that Meredith Johnson is not the only woman in the firm and that she is atypical in her aggressive behaviour. In contrast to *Basic Instinct*, for example, the workplace includes 'good' as well as 'bad' women. Rather than oppose good women in the home to bad women at work, *Disclosure* opposes good, supportive women at work (Stephanie Kaplan/Rosemary Forsyth) with the aggressively sexual Meredith. The 'liberal' credentials to which the film aspires are also indicated through the final appointment of Stephanie Kaplan to the top job: a woman who is marked as Tom's 'friend' (the anonymous e-mailer who sends him advice, via her son at University no less), Stephanie is also a decidedly asexual figure (in Hollywood terms) and a 'team player'. Yet if her acceptance speech acknowledges his work and calls on him to act as her 'right hand', Tom ends the movie where he began: passed over for a promotion he had already begun to celebrate.

If there are 'good' (maternal, nurturing) women in *Disclosure*, work is nonetheless rendered a sexualised space through the course of the film. At the same time home becomes something of a sterile environment in which Tom needs to cover up to hide the scars inflicted on him by the aggressive Johnson (just as Willem Dafoe's character must cover his torso from his wife in *Body of Evidence*). The sexualisation of work is both threatening and exciting in such movies as *Presumed Innocent* and *Judicial Consent*. Exciting in the spontaneity and the danger of illicit sex in a space reserved for unpleasure. Threatening both in terms of a fear of discovery and a fear of male passivity. When Mike attempts to be friendly with

Bridget/Wendy at work in *The Last Seduction* she pushes him violently into the men's toilets to explain the score ('I work here now – don't fuck with my image') and later slaps him in the building's foyer. A recurrent theme of job insecurity, a fear of redundancy, is related to a sense of feminisation, of the male worker becoming vulnerable. In *Disclosure*, management, in particular, is signified as 'feminised' through an attention to dress (suits) and through, for example, the sinister Phil Blackburn (Dylan Baker) seen meticulously manicuring his nails as he plots. Here we can recall the sequence in *Working Girl* in which Trainer tells Tess of the 'good men' who have been made redundant through 'just one lost deal'. During his journey to work in the opening sequences of *Disclosure* (a journey undertaken by ferry which, like his shabby dress, underlines his distance from the priorities of work) we see Tom talking to an unemployed businessman who, he tells us, was with IBM for twenty-eight years until found 'surplus' ('if they wanted a euphemism they should have used sodomized' he mutters). A nuisance who he fobs off with his assistant's card ('call Cindy'), the man comes to underline Tom's own sense of insecurity as the film progresses.

There is a short but indicative dream sequence at the heart of *Disclosure* in which Sanders, dressed in a smart suit, walks into the office building where he works. His appearance in a suit is surprising since his scruffiness is his distinguishing feature, signalling both his confidence (he doesn't need to bother) and his distance from 'management', whilst simultaneously rendering him a little comical (the toothpaste on his tie in the opening scenes suggest he is low-rent, though it also demonstrates an involvement with his children). In the dream Tom steps into a lift with his well-groomed boss Garvin (Donald Sutherland) who compliments him on his clothes, feeling the fabric before repeating Demi Moore's words of power and seduction ('Now you have the power. You have something I want') and moving to kiss him. As Garvin's mouth moves towards Tom/us/the camera, Sanders wakes up in horror. Although this sequence doesn't suggest that the film's anxieties aren't really about women, it does reveal that they are not *solely* about women. The image expresses a fear that the hero might be produced as object of (homo)sexual (as well as heterosexual) attentions, situated within the specular. Being smartly dressed (dressed like the management) involves becoming an object of display and desire for men and women. The fashioning of a public humiliation for Meredith is surely significant in this regard, showing her up in the space where she performs best (Tom has tracked down video images of Meredith in Malaysia which he plays as she asserts that she had never even seen the production line). Sanders has earlier been humiliated because he unquestioningly repeated her casual words in the context of a meeting. His decline in status is underlined here when he is forced to occupy the only chair remaining, which just happens to put him on a lower level than the others around the table, a realisation greeted with a look of surprise/pique by Sanders (and laughter from the cinema audience). In a similar fashion *Body Heat* has Maddy exploit Ned's record of professional ineptitude – having researched a malpractice suit over a contested will from four years previously. As his police buddy observes, it is in Ned's nature to 'mess up', though not usually on such a grand scale. In an equally complex scheme, *Final Analysis* has its *femme fatale* (Kim Basinger) turn psychoanalyst hero Richard Gere's work against him. She rehearses her sister with a dream taken from psychoanalytic literature to involve him in their case, a deception he does not see through until he attends a public lecture given by a female professor who comments on the very same dream (with some scathing additions on the psychoanalytic perspective on 'woman').

Klute's new *noir* articulation of prostitute as independent woman can be juxtaposed with an equally famous image of 1970s' cinema, what Thomas Schatz terms the pervasive 'nostalgic quality, invoking the male ethos and patriarchal order of a bygone era', in Francis Ford Coppola's *The Godfather* (1973) with its defining family of strong men (Collins *et al.* 1993: 16). Or Paul Schrader's *American Gigolo* in which a male prostitute protagonist configures a distinct set of concerns to those suggested by the 'working girl'. The role of gigolo positions Julian Kay (Richard Gere) as passive, as does his narcissistic concern with appearance (both also mark his place within the upper-class milieu in which he circulates) and the insistent invocation and refusal of gay sexuality (the friends who term him 'Julie', his comment to Michelle that 'this is my apartment – women don't come here'). Julian is characterised by his attention to female pleasure and a narcissism expressed through an obsessive attention to costume and an awareness of being looked at, framed, purchased. His manner is quite distinct from a violent misogynist masculinity in which women's bodies are understood as grotesque site of sexuality ('slap that cunt' he's told by a man who pays to watch his wife beaten and for whom sex is clearly power).[22] Conversely, *Bound*'s Violet (Jennifer Tilly) tells Corky (Gina Gershon) who has, along with the audience, listened to the sounds of 'passion' through the thin apartment wall that separates the two women 'That wasn't sex – that was work'. In a film that actually maintains its lesbian relationship to the end, this serves to underscore a suggestion that rarely rises to the surface in Hollywood movies: that a performance of heterosexuality might be 'work' for women.

New *film noir* explores and exploits evolving discourses around both masculinities and femininities through the conflation of sex and work in the figures of a feminised/persecuted hero, an aggressive *femme fatale* and the independent career woman. Films such as *Disclosure* or *The Last Seduction* offer a parodic fantasy of women's professional achievements in America today – one that can be situated alongside those movies of the 1990s which cast men as caring, nurturing fathers in the home. There have been dramatic changes in American society in terms of patterns of work and employment for men and women. These patterns are familiar in other western economies, with the rapid expansion of new technologies, part-time female employment and a movement away from the notion of the male 'breadwinner' or a job for life. The development of a female professional middle class working in medicine, law and education is also a feature of this economic transformation. These features are characteristic of an era designated by the term postmodernity. The new *film noir* can be read as part of a dehistoricised postmodern aesthetic, one in which film-makers raid and mark reference to both popular culture and high art from seemingly incompatible historical periods with little rhyme or reason. In this and in an explicit portrayal of sexual themes, new *film noir* is very much a part of 'new Hollywood'. In its articulation of the vulnerable, persecuted hero of *film noir* and the sexually aggressive and independent figure of the *femme fatale* – now often cast as career woman – new *film noir* addresses contemporary culture in its own appropriate paranoid fashion. It is then both ahistorical and very precisely of its time.

6

FEMALE FRIENDSHIP

Melodrama, romance, feminism

Whoopi Goldberg, Mary Louise Parker and Drew Barrymore in *Boys on the Side*

'I am *not* going over a cliff for you two – so just forget it', announces Jane DeLuca (Whoopi Goldberg) as the three stars of *Boys on the Side* (1995) make their getaway from Holly's (Drew Barrymore) violent boyfriend Nick. The joke reference to the ending of *Thelma and Louise* foregrounds the movie's location in relation to a narrative trajectory of escape from domestic restrictions and a reper-toire of images of female bonding and transformation. A buddy/romance which rehearses the attraction of (same-sex) opposites, the movie follows musician Jane falling for 'the whitest woman on the face of the planet', Robin (Mary Louise Parker). *En route* to California they 'rescue' Holly from an abusive relationship, though they cannot save her from falling for an Arizona cop named Abe Lincoln (Matthew McConaughey). If the *inadvertent* death of a violent man and the lovesick pursuit of a cop invert the images of flight showcased in Scott's film, in which a uniformed police officer is the focus of first fear and then ridicule, and in which Louise quite consciously chooses to kill Thelma's assailant, the two movies nonetheless draw on shared generic terrain. In its montage sequences, in settings such as the shared house in the desert and the Country and Western bar in Tucson, in its scenes of intense emotion between women, generational conflict, and the awkward negotiations around desire between the two straight women and a lesbian given to crushes on (seemingly) unattainable heterosexual objects of desire, *Boys on the Side* also rearticulates a familiar set of movie themes concerning female companionship.

Across the majority of its genres, the popular American cinema has marginalised representations of female friendship, more often favouring glamorous stars seen to exist in spectacular isolation, supportive figures who exist almost exclusively in relation to the hero, or women set in competition with each other. The seemingly nostalgic appeal of *noir* imagery, discussed in relation to contemporary discourses of women, work and sexuality in Chapter five, is pertinent once more here. In *Klute*, a movie that invokes lesbianism at its margins, Bree Daniels is isolated from other women, she is one of several in a militarised line-up in an early 'audition', but rarely does she speak to the other women.[1] The *femme fatale* is almost by def-inition opposed to other female characters, though in Rafelson's *Black Widow* the structuring tension of attraction/repulsion between her and the investigator is that between two women. In both *Fatal Attraction* and *Presumed Innocent* women are pitted against each other, so that in Amelia Jones' words they 'work to *destroy each other*' (1991: 312). *Bound*, with its lesbian partners-in-crime protagonists, stands as almost the only new *film noir* not to represent women in terms of contrast and conflict. Similarly, with the exception of the mythicised Western setting, parodied in *Even Cowgirls Get the Blues* and exploited in *Bad Girls*, relationships between women have only rarely provided the central dynamic of recent action-based narratives. Though the elaborate description of sentimental, homoerotic relationships between men is commonplace in the popular cinema, the successful female partnerships of *Thelma and Louise* or the television police duo *Cagney and Lacey*, for example, have generated in their wake no new wave of female buddy movies or television series. Symptomatically in Bigelow's *Blue Steel*, Megan Turner loses her best friend Tracey (Elizabeth Pena), murdered in front of her eyes by her serial-killer lover, Eugene. Following their declarations of mutual love in the opening graduation sequence, Tracey tries to set Megan up with eligible men. The presage to her murder, however, is a shared meal and scenes of bonding in which Megan speaks warmly of Tracey's supportive husband and family, whilst laughingly insisting that her friend refrain from trying to pair her off. The movement of Curtis' character into a heterosexual relationship here is explicitly bound up with death and destruction. Though Detective Nick Mann (Clancy Brown) is on hand to offer a less disturbing articulation of the cost of heterosexuality, he winds up near death himself, leaving Megan to go out for revenge alone. *Blue Steel* thus enacts (writ large) a familiar narrative trajectory; across a range of genres, the cost of heterosexuality and of the narrative that enacts this as a journey, is the death of female friendship. To some extent then the negotiations of *Boys on the Side* are symptomatic of a persistent tension in the cinematic representation of female friendship: one that is also suggested by its title. The promotional slogan promises the viewer 'a hilarious, touching and totally unforgettable tale of loyalty and trust, safety in numbers, women on top and . . . *Boys on the Side*'. The women's alliance has to do with love, power and safety, but with the reassuring presence of boys on the side. It is with this combination of friendship, desire and power within the spaces of melodrama and romance that this chapter is concerned.

Though problematic for Hollywood to fully incorporate, both feminist discourses and an invocation of lesbianism frame the action and the dialogue of *Boys on the Side* and another recent 'feel good' friendship movie, *The First Wives Club* (1996). Lesbianism is construed as a space distanced from men (and therefore to be valued) and as akin to, yet different from, the intense bonds of female friendship. Bent on revenge, the 'first wives' (Goldie Hawn, Diane Keaton, Bette Midler) head to a lesbian bar to enlist the support of Annie's (Diane Keaton) daughter Chris. Following a series of bruising encounters (played for comedy) in which she finds herself cast as 'the mother' and sidelined in terms of her age, movie star Elise (Goldie Hawn) is delighted to find herself greeted by adoring fans (led by comic Lea DeLaria). Lesbianism is articulated here as supportive, as a space within which the female body is a source of pleasure. Yet it is also different from, if related to, the world of the 'first wives' (literally related, via Chris). In this way, as Andy Medhurst suggests, 'the overall political function of introducing lesbianism into the film is conservative, since making it evident also makes it distanced (the province of Them not Us)' (1996: 45). Yet both Elise's delight in being admired and the comic exchange in which Brenda (Bette Midler) shares her experience with a woman at the bar (dykes can be 'first wives' too) involve a certain closeness as well as the familiar distancing (the 'Them not Us'). A similar operation takes place in *Boys on the Side*, the location of which as a melodrama informed by feminist discourses is made explicit in the (rather understated) courtroom scenes in which a prosecutor attempts to undermine Jane's testimony in terms of her sexuality, suggesting that her lesbianism makes her somehow untrustworthy. Both Jane's and Robin's statements are given a credence that the (male) lawyer couldn't hope to have in the genre. Yet while Robin speaks in her matter-of-fact tone of something that goes on between women', a bond that unites them, this is juxtaposed with Holly's excessive dependence on new playmate Abe's somewhat questionable judgement. The couple play out a sort of parody of heterosexual courtship and romance: his single-minded devotion to both Holly and the law which leads to his decision to arrest her, her blind trust in his judgement, their shared passion and childish smiles. Thus the movie extols the virtues of female companionship, and the appeal of a sort of sexless lesbian desire alongside a parodic articulation of heterosex played out between fashionably raunchy Drew Barrymore and a motorcycle cop who looks like he has stepped out of a gay nightclub. That his love finds its ultimate expression in arresting her underlines the extent to which the articulation of an adult heterosexuality at all is problematic for the film.

Melodrama/genre/feminisms

It is in movies that emphasise the melodramatic aspects of American cinema, what Christine Gledhill terms 'gestural, visual and musical excess' (1987: 30), or those that deal in comedy, a rather different kind of excess, which offer the most explicit space for the articulation of female friendship and, at least potentially, romance. In turn, Hollywood melodrama and the woman's film have long provided a fruitful site for a feminist film criticism concerned to explore these issues. Feminist critics have written of the significance of the (atypical) space given to female protagonists as well as the form of address that this potentially yields for the female spectator. Melodramatic narratives and the woman's film can be understood as both foregrounding and testing the contradictions between desire and duty in mainstream definitions of femininity. For example, recurrent images of the home as prison, of maternal sacrifice and of the articulation and punishment of transgressive female desires suggest the complexities of a cinematic articulation of gender in terms of social and cultural constructions. Classical Hollywood films such as *Stella Dallas* (1937), *Blonde Venus* (1932), *Mildred Pierce* (1945), *Letter*

141

From an Unknown Woman (1948) or N*ow, Voyager* (1942), have provided a staple reference point for feminist arguments concerning the articulation of female desire and point of view. In turn those films of the 1970s which explicitly addressed feminism within a pseudo-documentary aesthetic have also been discussed by critics such as Charlotte Brunsdon, Christine Geraghty and Annette Kuhn (Brunsdon 1987). During the 1980s, feminist writers also turned to television to consider the soap opera, reading the genre as a form which speaks of and to family concerns that privilege the female spectator (Gledhill 1987).[2]

If more recent examples of the melodrama or the woman's film have attracted less sustained attention, Christine Gledhill has argued, citing three diverse examples, *Coma* (1978), *Witness* (1985) and *The Color Purple* (1985), that though contemporary melodramas may enact moral dilemmas in different terms than their progenitors, they are nonetheless linked 'in their drive to identify the good and the evil and in their scenarios of persecuted innocence' (1987: 32). While conflict is no longer credible in the terms of past, Gledhill suggests that 'modern melodrama draws on contemporary discourses for the apportioning of responsibility, guilt and innocence – psychoanalysis, marriage guidance, medical ethics, politics, even feminism'. Melodramatic rhetoric must be seen as evolving, operating in terms of key debates within contemporary society which themselves evolve. Her point is not only that it is a mistake to see melodrama as something equated with a (naive) past, opposed to contemporary realism, but that:

> Whether melodrama takes its categories from Victorian morality or modern psychology, its enactment of the continuing struggle of good and evil forces running through social, political and psychic life draws into a public arena desires, fears, values and identities which lie beneath the surface of the publicly acknowledged world.
>
> (Gledhill 1987: 33)

There is then no inherent tension between feminism and the melodrama. Within fictional worlds where relations with men are repeatedly the cause of narrative dilemmas for women, both feminism and the invocation of lesbianism (though one that is significantly sexless) inform the production of a moral system. In these terms both the extent to which feminist discourses have been incorporated into the melodramatic rhetoric of contemporary cinema, and the clear limits of that incorporation, is evident in films from *Boys on the Side* to *The First Wives Club* or *Waiting to Exhale* (1995) which extol and celebrate female strength and friendship. Such movies both deploy and reject aestheticised images of suffering, offering the pleasures of a good ('four hankie') wallow and a discourse of friendship which provides a solution that can either exist alongside or function as an alternative to heterosexual romance.

Thelma and Louise, the movie that Jane comically alludes to in *Boys on the Side*, has triggered a series of recent debates around popular genres, gendered representation, the body and transformation. Whether condemning the movie or praising it, most commentators have agreed that *Thelma and Louise* has at least *some* relationship to feminist discourses. Many have also commented on its hybrid generic location and its articulation of female friendship as potential lesbian relationship. Western, buddy movie, road movie, romance: *Thelma and Louise* has been widely read as an appropriation, termed by some superficial, by others complex, of those Hollywood genres through which masculinity is produced for men. Sharon Willis argues in this context that 'the process by which the film parades the take-over of these clichés' works to foreground 'the posturing involved'. For Willis there are two significant effects of this theft/take-over:

> It remobilizes for women viewers the pleasures of fantasmatic identifications with embodied agents of travel, speed, force, and aggression, pleasures that we have historically enjoyed in a cross-gender framework, but this time offering room for a different mix of desire with that identification. At the same time, the spectacle of women acting like men works to disrupt the apparent naturalness of certain postures when performed by a male body.
>
> (Collins *et al.* 1993: 125)

In Chapter two, I argue that the concept of a female Western is both as problematic and as useful as that of male melodrama. Gledhill highlights the extent to which *all* American cinema is melodramatic, elaborating her case in relation to the Western. What, she asks:

> is the justification confining melodramatic categorisation to films about domestic situations and 'feminine' conditions? Why are the shoot-out, the lone trek through the wilderness, the rituals of horse and gun, any less excessive than a family conflict?
>
> (Gledhill 1987: 12–13)

There is of course little justification beyond the presence of men (or women). Since Westerns are typically melodramatic narratives bound up with masculinities, the location of women in the genre has a distinct impact. The iconography of the Western at work in *Thelma and Louise* provides a context in which signifiers of freedom and power (of masculinity) can accrue to woman. Thus the generic work of movies like *Thelma and Louise* and *Boys on the Side* is not to somehow 'feminise' the road movie by transmuting it through the presence of women into melodrama, but to enact a story about masculine self-sufficiency in relation to women, a story that in the process happens to lay bear the melodramatic aspects of the road movie and the Western.[3] The camp-fire scene in *Bad Girls* makes sense in relation to both the Western and the melodrama then, partly because the Western itself (like the road movie) is so melodramatic. Melodramatic in terms of, for example, the importance of *mise en scène* to the expression of meaning and character development.

To some extent it was the low-culture associations with melodrama and the road movie, rather than the problematic question of its 'realism' or political credentials, which led to the negative response *Thelma and Louise* received from some critics. In their introduction to a debate on the film in *Cineaste*, Toni Kamins and Cynthia Lucia suggest that the film, 'a mildly revisionist Hollywood genre item', was controversial not as a result of its 'modest artistic achievements' but in terms of 'its success in stimulating widespread public debate over the relationships between men and women' (1991: 28). Thus the film's significance is certainly not as 'art', nor even as a movie articulating a central relationship *between women*, but as a stimulant to a public debate about relationships between men and women. Though some contributors to the *Cineaste* debate *do* comment on the relationship between Thelma and Louise, all are critical of the movie's compromise, understood as an inherent product of its mainstream status. For Alice Cross the whole package is 'just the same old story artfully disguised to look like something new' (ibid.: 34), whilst Roy Grundmann rejects the 'romantic outlaw scenario' as inappropriate for a film exploring themes of sexual abuse and violence, a strategy that points to the movie's culpability (and that of Hollywood more generally) in seeking to 'pass off its marketplace morals as a high-flown ethical debate' (ibid.: 35–6).

It is the case that the engagement with feminist discourses, to do with rape, independence and sexuality, that is evident in such movies as *Thelma and Louise* or *Mortal Thoughts*, is not intellectual; that is, not verbalised or argued in some recognisable way. These discourses inform a construction of narrative, character and setting that is largely *emotive*. It is also the product of an engagement with generic conventions and with popular traditions of cinematic representation. To argue that the transformation Thelma and Louise undergo is superficial (about little more than costume, unmotivated in terms of psychology or dialogue) is to miss the extent to which, within melodrama, and within popular cinema more generally, meaning is generated *through mise en scène* (through costume, setting and so on). The cultural and generic connotations of signifiers such as cars, guns, the road, denim, add a further dimension to this process of meaning production. The portrayal of friendship and working relationships between women in some recent films within a variety of generic locations is symptomatic of the popular cinema's typically oblique engagement with contemporary political discourses. Consider the invocation of friendship between women as a source of strength in movies from *Beaches* (1988) to *Waiting to Exhale* or *Thelma and Louise*, or as a source of magic in *Bagdad Café* (1987), for example; all draw on feminist discourses about women *and* on a range of generic sources including the women's film, buddy movie and road movie (even the art cinema) to articulate an emotive response to women's desires and the differences between women. None invalidates the others, but all are, to an extent reformulated in the process.

As both Sharon Willis and Cathy Griggers suggest, the narrative journeys undertaken in *Thelma and Louise*, or in the more evidently melodramatic *Boys on the Side*, involve an imagery of transformation and an eroticised friendship (Collins et. al.: 1993). Willis points to the centrality of the car in *Thelma and Louise*, both as a technology associated with masculinity and as an instrument of agency. On the one hand we have the concerns and structures of the melodrama: battles of good and evil constructed in terms of feminist discourses, the home as prison, a desire to escape (followed in *Boys on the Side* by a return to the domestic). On the other is the buddy/road movie with its themes of friendship, the attraction of opposites, extraordinary (often surreal) encounters, the dangers and excitements of the journey. Images of movement (and of change) are thus juxtaposed with the characteristic structures of repetition involved in melodrama, a structure which continually returns to the same. The ironic tone so characteristic of the road movie stems not only from surreal encounters, but from the extent to which characters may travel vast distances whilst remaining in the same place. The road movie both literalises and narrativises the difficulties and the costs of transformation. The first images of *Waiting to Exhale*, which introduces each of the four female characters (and their different dilemmas) in turn, are of Monument Valley, an empty road and then of Savannah (Whitney Houston) in shades and a head-scarf driving an open-top car. Her voice-over explains in a matter-of-fact tone: 'The deal is the men in Denver are dead. No wonder I'm changing towns again: it's gotta be better in Phoenix.' Inevitably the situation is no better in Phoenix; at least, not in terms of the men that Savannah encounters. She finds happiness in Phoenix through her friendships with women rather than through heterosexual romance. The film ends with another car drive: the four women drive off to spend New Year together rather than with any of the various men who give them grief/happiness. This in the Mercedes stationwagon that Bernadine (Angela Bassett) has been awarded as part of a substantial divorce settlement (after a solemn handshake with her former husband she and Savannah run from the courtroom, arms around each other, screeching with laughter). The four toast the arrival of New Year and embrace by a campfire against a night sky that provides a convenient display of fireworks. This image closes a drama in which they have managed to get out of the cycles in which they are enmeshed, an escape effected through their encounters with and support for each other.

The title of Edward Zwick's *Leaving Normal* (1992) makes explicit the affiliation between the road movie's narrative of transformation and a transgression of gender roles understood as social norms (the movie has its oddball female couple driving together out of a small town called Normal). A clinical hyper-normality is further literalised in the suburban home of Marianne's (Meg Tilly) sister. Tempted momentarily to stay, Marianne instead opts to continue on her journey with Darly (Christine Lahti). The film takes the protagonists to Alaska, a space that, like the desert, signifies frontier/outpost/wilderness. Entranced by the Northern Lights, Marianne sets about building the home that Darly left unfinished when she abandoned her daughter eighteen years before, persuading the reluctant Darly to stay. Darly actually owns the land (part Eskimo, we are told, she took advantage of a government offer to buy cheap) but does not feel it to be her home until the end of the movie when Marianne has helped to turn the shell into a house.

Indeed the movie is as much about settling down as it is about travelling: Darly determines to look for her daughter; Marianne's movement from the pre-credit childhood sequence which situates her as a part of a fractured family that is constantly on the move to her new-found stability within an alternative family. Here again the cyclical structure associated with melodrama is juxtaposed with a linear journey and a trajectory of self-discovery associated with both the road movie and the woman's film. Marianne does discover heterosexual romance – in the form of a truck driver who writes (bad) poetry and vows to return when his delivery route allows – but domesticity is with Darly.

The friendships at the centre of *Leaving Normal* and *Thelma and Louise*, like the groups of women who are portrayed in *Waiting to Exhale* and *Steel Magnolias*, facilitate a process of transformation in which women become strong and gain independence through each other. They may gain in strength *against* men (whose inadequacies provide a recurrent talking point) but rarely achieve it through heterosexual romance. *Mystic Pizza* (like *Leaving Normal*) begins with images of childhood in a credit sequence montage of photographs charting the growth of three girls into the young women who form the centre of the movie. Such an accumulation of images also opens both *Mortal Thoughts* and *Now and Then*, drawing attention to the process of growing-up (as befits narratives of self-discovery) and the developing difference between the protagonists. At the same time these sequences foreground the peculiar nature of the photographic image. The sense of transience captured by photographs is also used in *Thelma and Louise*, when a snapshot taken at the beginning of their journey is blown from the back of the car in the final sequence. Photographs are also foregrounded in *Beaches* (the youthful friendship of C.C. and Hilary signified by the photo-booth image of the two together as much as in the letters they write to each other), in Penny Marshall's *A League of Their Own* (the hall of fame sequence at the end of the film where the women look in amazement at the assembled images, some life-size, of their younger selves) and in *Boys on the Side* (in both Robin's attempts to rediscover the past in the photograph album and in the polaroid of Holly grinning beside a bound and gagged Nick that comes back to haunt her in court). *Mystic Pizza* cuts from the montage of photographs to a church wedding (past to present). The bride looks dazed; we see her point of view, blurred through a veil as she walks up the aisle. Following the priest's words, comically stern on the binding commitment that marriage represents, Jojo (Lili Taylor) collapses at the altar. In the pizza parlour where she works with sisters Daisy (Julia Roberts) and Kat (Annabeth Gish), she explains her horrific vision of herself ten years on, 'fat and ugly' and surrounded by children. Jojo wants boyfriend Bill (Vincent D'Onofrio) for sex, but is afraid of the commitment and conformity that marriage represents. Meanwhile Kat, due to depart to study astronomy at Yale (an intellectual, romantic, stargazer), falls for a married man for whom she babysits while Daisy hooks up with a layabout WASP. While Jojo ultimately does marry Bill, lecturing him on her need for independence, the movie ends not with this image but with the reception at the pizza parlour and the three together on the steps drinking champagne and declaring their love for each other. If Jojo's apprehensions about marriage frame the film, it is friendships between women that form the centre. Thus the final image functions as an assurance that marriage does not necessarily equal the end of friendship.

Set during the Second World War, Penny Marshall's *A League of Their Own* takes as its focus the All American Girls Baseball League which developed in the absence of male players. Comedy and drama provide the generic location for the evocation of a female group, whilst the wartime scenario allows the absence of men that, it is suggested, makes the group possible. In this of course the film touches on a subject which has been explored by feminist historians: the opportunities and challenges for women in America that the war generated and the range of responses it produced.[4] Though comic in tone, the film explicitly foregrounds images and develops a narrative that seeks to some extent to reconstruct the history of professional baseball (which is, of course, a contentious, political, i.e. 'serious' history). An explicit commentary on this history is provided largely by the emotional present-day sequences which frame the film, involving a reunion and a belated admission of the women into the hall of fame. A comic commentary is produced in the main body of the film itself which asks audiences not to laugh at teams with such names as the 'Rockford Peaches', but to find comedy in the peculiar situations in which the women find themselves. In response to the 'feared masculinization of female players' the women are, for example, issued with 'impractical, scanty uniforms which clearly signpost the unmistakable femininity of their bodies', are given lessons in deportment and are involved in a host of media stunts to attract audiences to the games (Taylor 1995: 167). The film also maintains a family base, focusing on the rivalry between two sisters, Dottie Hinson (Geena Davis) and Kit (Lori Petty) as a framework for the group narrative, with its various characters and subplots. The movie begins with an older (widowed) Dottie reluctant to attend the reunion, who is persuaded/cajoled by her daughter, perplexed that her mother fails to understand how important the team had been. Arriving at the field, Dottie's remembrance frames the movie of wartime women's baseball. Her decision to leave the baseball team, of which she is the star, when her husband returns from war (albeit to briefly return to it) both enacts and frames the film's articulation of 'conventional' behaviour. Dottie's departure after only one season is explicitly flagged in terms of the pursuit of a feminine career as wife and mother: 'we want to have children' she tells Kit. Taking her leave of baseball she also tells her that she will miss her and 'the girls'.

Like *A League of Their Own*, *Now and Then* uses an evocation of the past to construct a community of women (or girls, in this case) in the 'absence' of men. A sort of 1970s' *Stand By Me* for girls, *Now and Then* looks to an adolescence in which boys play little or no part. The film tells the story of four twelve-year-old girls in the summer of 1970, framed by their reunion in the present day to be present at the birth of Chrissy's (Rita Wilson) baby, delivered by Roberta (Rosie O'Donnell) with Samantha (Demi Moore) and Tina (Melanie Griffith), the ones who have left the small town behind, as bystanders. Indeed we see more of the estate, the 'Gaslight Addition', than the town itself. The narrative of their younger selves is set against a background of families falling apart or families that never quite functioned in the first place. Roberta is dealing with the grief caused by the loss of her mother in a car accident, whilst Samantha's father has left and her parents are divorcing. It is only Chrissy, who is marked as excessively femme (frilly and phobic about dirt) who we see in adult life as married. Roberta, whose first romance is portrayed, lives with a man who remains unseen, whilst Tina and Samantha have progressed through a series of relationships. The choices the adults have made are prefigured in the main body of the film, focusing on the younger selves. Roberta's (Christina Ricci) first kiss is intercut with the image of Sam (Gaby Hoffman) and Tina (Thora Birch) sitting on a rooftop, a vast drive-in movie screen playing *Love Story* between them in the background, dividing the image. They share divided families and a desire to escape both small-town and conventional living. Narratives that revolve around groups of women in this way function to contextualise heterosexuality/domesticity which becomes a possibility rather than an inevitable conclusion to the narrative. The two sisters in *A League of Their Own* are not only juxtaposed in their choices, but set against the other women in the group (Mae/Madonna's overt sexuality or her 'butch' pal, Doris Murphy, played by Rosie O'Donnell). Eileen's decision to set up house with farmer William Tucker at the end of *Bad Girls* (and to reject Lilly) operates in terms of a conventional narrative movement towards heterosexuality but also, as we've seen in Chapter two, functions in terms of her excessive 'femme' persona and is juxtaposed with the image of the three remaining women riding off into the sunset together.

The four protagonists of *Waiting to Exhale* are initially all defined in terms of their relationships to men. Savannah moves to Phoenix in search of something ill-defined. 'A long time ago', her voice-over tells us over images of her making elaborate preparations to go out, 'I asked God to send me a decent man . . . I got Robert, Cedric, Daryl and Kenny: God's got some serious explaining to do'. Though her opening words suggest that she is motivated by the search for love, she reveals to Bernadine (Angela Bassett) that she has also taken a new job in this new town, taking a pay cut so as to pursue her career as a producer. Through most of the film she is involved with Kenneth (Dennis Haysbert), a married man who produces a series of unconvincing promises to leave his wife and excuses for not doing so. Bernadine is devastated when her husband leaves her after eleven years of marriage in which she has supported his business. Robin (Lela Rochon) is involved with men who are by turns irresponsible, insincere and exploitative. Gloria (Loretta Devine) is raising her son Tarik alone and is reluctant to let him go, feeling isolated. By the end of the film, the four women are defined primarily in terms of their relationships with each other. Savannah rejects Kenneth, telling her mother that she values her career and her friends. Bernadine gets a divorce settlement and her children. Robin is pregnant and defiantly single, rejecting the father, she sits back with a copy of 'Childbirth Choices'. Gloria, meanwhile, lets go of her son and finds romance with neighbour Gregory Hines.

The women come together at key points in a narrative framed by two New Years' celebrations, the first in which they are alone, the second in which they are together. The value of friendship is contrasted to the insincerity and the failure to communicate that characterises many of the film's male/female relationships. Thus while relationships with men are central, they are also repeatedly sidelined, partly through the manipulation and juxtaposition of sound and image. Encounters destined not to last feature the cynical thoughts of Savannah and Robin on the soundtrack, their disappointment and unspoken desires an ironic commentary on the image. A contrast is provided by images such as that of Bernie sitting with Savannah outside her spectacular home; surrounded by candles they hold hands and talk together. Such scenes are matched by the genuine intensity between Bernadine and an uncredited Wesley Snipes, who tells of his dying wife and his love for her (again, there is no voice-over here, but direct speech). The manipulation of voice-over, with its insistent suggestion of secret thoughts and things left unsaid is gradually removed towards the end of the film so that direct communication replaces artifice. An early scene in which Savannah and Robin talk on the phone uses split-screen to suggest the distance between them, the image of Robin in her apartment framed like a mirror. Later the two speak directly poolside, Robin recounting her past experience with a married man (pregnancy, rejection, abortion) as if it were the story of someone she had heard on a talk show. It is her experience that persuades Savannah to finally leave Kenneth behind and which gives a context to her pleasure in her pregnancy. Again the group narrative used here frames the different choices of the female protagonists.

Steel Magnolias (1989), another ensemble star vehicle (Julia Roberts was the only relative newcomer of the female leads), focuses on a group of women in a small Louisiana town, across several generations. Though it features many of the narrative events so typical of the family melodrama (generational tension, marriage and death), *Steel Magnolias* is not located exclusively within the sphere of the family, with the central family narrative told through the perspective of the group of female friends. Reviewers of both the stage and the screen production tended to identify a distinction (for some an awkward contradiction) between the comic wit that informs the dialogue and the groundswell emotion of the melodrama.[5] While the negative judgements might be the result of little more than the usual disdain for the excesses of the Hollywood women's film, the combination of emotions and comedy is distinctive ('laughter through tears is my favourite emotion' proclaims Truvy). The use of voice-over as an ironic counterpoint in *Waiting to Exhale* produces a similar contradictory tone, inviting the audience to view events from a distance, or rather from the distanced point of view that the protagonists take on events in which they are involved. In *Steel Magnolias* the relationship between Shelby (Roberts) and her mother M'Lynn (Sally Field) frames the film, with gatherings at the beginning and near the end of the film occasioned by Shelby's wedding and funeral. M'Lynn is primarily defined as a mother within both film and stage play, emphasising her overprotective relationship to the vibrant but fragile Shelby. Though in Robert Harling's play M'Lynn is described as a 'career woman', in neither version is she seen within the context of work. The relationship between M'Lynn and Shelby is echoed in that between Truvy (Dolly Parton) and her young assistant Annelle (Daryl Hannah), who she terms her 'semi-daughter'. The relationship is a source of both satisfaction and frustration for Truvy (as Annelle moves from shy to 'flighty', before adopting a stern form of Christianity, a series of guises that are a source of comedy).

Just as they sidestep an insistence on compulsory heterosexuality through the intensity of female friendship portrayed, group movies allow the articulation of alternatives among and across a range of characters. In *Steel Magnolias*, for example, the mother/daughter narrative of suffering and sacrifice is rearticulated by its location within the film's other concern: the relations between a group of women across class and generation. Shelby announces her pregnancy, which she is going ahead with against the doctor's (and her mother's) advice, at a family gathering. The friends see M'Lynn's distress and gather round her, clasping hands to signify their support. Mother/child relationships are also important in *Waiting to Exhale*. In a rare scene of Savannah at work, her mother phones to find out why she has left Kenny, a good man. Savannah talks about the other things in her life, her work and her friends; they argue and make up, agreeing to differ on the territory of what it is a woman should do and how she might best be happy. This mother/daughter relationship is set against the bond between Gloria and her son, Bernadine and her children, Robin and her baby-to-be; the positions of both mother and daughter, which generate conflicts of expectation, frustration and disappointment for numerous melodramatic narratives, are framed by the stories generated by friendship.

If friendships between women in the movies (and on television) take place in the absence of men, this doesn't necessarily mean that men are not involved in the narrative. The marginalisation of men implied by the title of *Boys on the Side* is taken up by Robin's mother who comments that contemporary women treat men as men used to treat women, as something 'on the side', an extra to be taken when wanted. Men provide a constant point of reference in Harling's *Steel Magnolias* stage play, though it is an ensemble piece for an all-female cast. Whilst various men are mentioned by the other characters they never appear on stage. The sound of Drum Eatenton's gun is heard off-stage, a disruption commented on but unseen. The inclusion of male characters stems from the film's opening up of the stage production from the confines of the beauty parlour setting to a range of domestic and exterior locations. Yet even in this expanded version, they are accorded little agency and very little screen time. This despite the use of well-known actors Tom Skerritt and Sam Shepard. M'Lynn's sons are briefly glimpsed at the wedding, before the operation and at the funeral, though they hardly speak. The screen version offers a more explicit sense of *both* the alienation and the reconciliation in relationships between men and women in the tortuous relationships of Annelle and Sam, Truvy and Spud, Ouiser and Owen. Yet, paradoxically, the inclusion of men as characters, functions if anything to emphasise their marginality. Men are the cause of narrative problems which we watch women dealing with in these movies, an inversion of the countless narratives in which women bring chaos into men's worlds.

Female friendship/lesbian chic

In narratives of heterosexual romance, female friendship is something to be left behind and, implicitly, to be grown out of. For Barbara Creed this accounts for the production and containment of the 'tomboy' within an Oedipal trajectory (a movement towards heterosexuality) which seeks to allay the lesbian connotations of her image. She also draws attention to a convention whereby 'female friendship films with lesbian undertones' including *Single White Female* (1992), *Fried Green Tomatoes at the Whistle Stop Café* (1991), *Beaches*, and *Outrageous Fortune* (1987) all involve the death of one of the women. Drawing on Babuscio, she casts this as a variant on the male buddy movie where 'the death of one or both friends has become a narrative convention' that:

> works to suppress questions of homosexual desire at a point where the narrative has run its course and the audience is wondering what these men will do next. The buddies have rejected both society and hetero-sexual domesticity – will they declare their love for each other?
>
> (Creed 1995: 98)

The threesome of *Boys on the Side* sidesteps some of the tensions around lesbianism posed by the female friendship movie – the 'threat' or instability posed by the developing love between Robin and Jane set against Drew Barrymore's bubbly airhead. And even if the women in *Boys on the Side* don't go over a cliff, love culminates in either heterosexuality or death all the same. Thus by the time Robin and Jane have revealed that they love each other, Robin is dying and Jane is cast in the chaste role of her carer. An equation between *heterosexuality* and death (the death of friendship) is literalised at the beginning of *The First Wives Club* when images of the four women as young graduating students, full of hope for the future, are followed by Cynthia's present-day suicide. Cynthia's death serves to bring the three friends back together (her letters to each of them bemoan the fact that they have drifted apart and warn of the dangers of isolation within marriage), thus inverting the equation to some extent.

If the cost of heterosexuality is so often female friendship, a process that suggests an opposition between the two, a concomitant sense that friendship between women is not only a source of strength but at least potentially lesbian in character frequently emerges in the popular cinema. Consider Paul Verhoeven's *Showgirls* (1995) in which Nomi (Elizabeth Berkley) arriving penniless in Las Vegas is befriended by Molly (Gina Ravera). 'Are you hitting on me?' she asks when Molly buys her a meal and invites her to stay. Molly, in turn asks Nomi: 'Are you a hooker?'. Having established that the two are neither lesbians nor prostitutes, the movie pursues an insistent equation between women's work and sexuality (the working girl once more) as well as equating female strength with an aggressive lesbianism. Thus chief showgirl Cristal Connors (Gina Gershon) pursues Nomi as much as an expression of her power as of her desire. While friendship between women is a source of strength in contemporary movies, the question of the closeness of that friendship to lesbian desire is in constant negotiation. For Cathy Griggers, *Thelma and Louise* enacts a transformation through which the acquisition of female independence can be termed 'lesbian'. 'For Thelma and Louise' she asserts:

> becoming butch – a psycho-social and virtually bodily process visually documented in the film – is as much an outcome of a material and social condition as a sexual preference. . . . Thelma and Louise, as prototypes of the mainstreaming of the new butch-femme, don't become butch because they're lesbians; they become lesbian because they've already become too butch to survive. And surviving in this context means staying alive while escaping the traps of the dependent housewife, the bad marriage, the innocent victim, and the single-working woman who's going it alone and not getting enough.
>
> (Collins *et al.* 1993: 140)

Griggers' theme here underlines the extent to which femininity is a concept produced through categories of class and 'race' within institutions of heterosexuality, that gender is inseparable from labour. Her comments also recall Creed's observation that all female bodies 'represent the threat or potential – depending on how you see it – of lesbianism'(1995: 87). It was not only the kiss and clasped hands with which the women go over the cliff, or even the strength of the friendship and the signifiers of music and costume, that affirmed the film as about becoming lesbian for many viewers and reviewers. The Hollywood cinema typically keeps the representation of strong, independent women distinct from narratives of female friendship; when they collide in a narrative that does not explicitly position 'the lesbian' as 'Them not Us', the lack of distinction between the signifiers of female strength and of lesbianism becomes apparent.

In *The Accused*, *Thelma and Louise*, *Mortal Thoughts* and even *Showgirls*, heterosexual men are a narrative 'problem', expressed in terms of sexual violence and exploitation of women (rape, marriage, or the sex industry). Men also cause a different order of trouble in such movies as *Waiting to Exhale*, *Steel Magnolias*, *Beaches* and *Mystic Pizza*. They provide many of the narrative problems against which women react and which their friendships help them to survive. In this sense, it is not only the closeness between women but the insistent presentation of heterosexuality *as a problem* that provides a context in which a movie like *Beaches* can be read in terms of lesbian subtext. Eliane Meyer, for example, describes the Australian hit *Muriel's Wedding* (1994) as a narrative of self-discovery in which conformity as marriage is 'first desired then denied then achieved, reassessed, found wanting and finally outgrown'. Hogan's movie addresses conventional notions of how women should behave and appear. Muriel's (Toni Collette) quirky fashion sense and her size set her apart from the 'beautiful' (thin, conformist) crowd who are then made to seem ridiculous. Female friendship is redemptive in a narrative that constructs marriage as an obsessive fantasy bound up in performance for Muriel (the spectacle of the wedding). As Meyer notes, music is used to underscore the camp elements of the drama, to undercut the seriousness of the wedding and the institutions of marriage/heterosexuality to which it is aligned and to draw an association between Muriel's and Rhonda's (Rachel Griffiths) life together and (male) gay culture (the use of ABBA songs). While, she notes, the first few bars of 'Dancing Queen' are 'played over and over again, then interrupted' the whole song ' is only heard at the end of the film when Muriel and Rhonda leave together'.[6]

It is not the case that the portrayal of female friendship *necessarily* involves the suggestion of lesbianism. Nonetheless , both women's friendships and cinematic portrayals of lesbianism operate in a shared terrain which involves female characters acting in a space not defined by male characters or by a narrative progress towards heterosexuality. When C.C. Bloom (Midler) toys with marriage to a doctor in *Beaches*, this is explicitly presented in terms of a comic image of conformity (her pastel suit and old-fashioned hat). Such conformity is rejected in favour of first, her career and second, her friendship with Hillary (to whom she delegates the task of telling her fiancé that she is leaving). The embrace of work and the refusal of heterosexuality are used again and again in Hollywood films to signify women's desire for something different, whether that something is specified or not. Clare Whatling discusses the possibilities of a lesbian reading of *The Accused* in terms of both the Jodie Foster persona and the centrality of the relationship between the two women on the screen. For Whatling it is *spectators* who work to lesbianise the image in a Hollywood cinema shy of lesbian content. Criticism of the 'closetry' of movies such as *Fried Green Tomatoes* misses the point, she argues, since:

> such films can also serve as seductive icons to the knowing observer, who reinstates lesbian desire in the face of platonic same-sex representations. One of the chief delights of these films is that they allow free scope for, indeed even depend on, the viewer's imagination, teasing her to make the connections and fill in the silences. There is a very particular pleasure in piecing together the lingering looks, smiles and moments of fingertips barely touching which form the covert lesbian subtext of such films.
>
> (Budge and Hamer 1994: 186)

In a related article, Christine Holmlund points out how responses to *Personal Best* demonstrate 'how skilled lesbians can be at raiding basically heterosexual texts for their own purposes' (1991: 154). Both then point to the work of the spectator in relation to Hollywood texts that prefer silence to naming.

The issues at stake in reading movies from *Thelma and Louise* to *Beaches* as lesbian frame the ambiguity of the naming of lesbianism, discussed earlier, in such movies as *The First Wives Club*. Lesbianism functions as a sort of cipher here, suggesting the development of a relationship between the three women that is clearly apart from heterosexuality without being clear in itself (the final scene has the three singing and dancing into the distance together in an evocation of the musical). An alternative space in which lesbianism is named, and in quite different ways, is that of the art cinema. '[I]f lesbianism hadn't already existed', suggests Mandy Merck, 'art cinema might have invented it'. Lesbianism provides the art cinema with 'a sufficient degree of difference from dominant cinematic representations of sex and sexuality' whilst allowing it to maintain an equation between women and sexuality (Brunsdon 1987:166). Merck frames the foregrounding of sex and spectatorship in John Sayles' *Lianna* and Diane Kurys' *Coup de Foudre* (1983) in this context, films that for Holmlund are symptomatic of the 'mainstream femme film'. Hollywood lesbianism is constructed, quite differently, in terms of female friendship. As Stacey suggests, 'female admiration and solidarity are the acceptable face of lesbianism on the Hollywood screen' in *The Color Purple* and *Fried Green Tomatoes* (Wilton 1995: 93). *The Color Purple* has Shug singing to Goldberg's Celie, performing for her on a public stage (she sings that they are 'sisters' and 'two of a kind') followed by a seduction scene of dressing up, dance, talk, kisses and a coy pan to windchimes. Holmlund points to a mainstreaming of the femme in the cinema of the 1980s, with such films as *Personal Best* 'merging female friendship and lesbian sexuality in a skilful cinematic adaptation of what Adrienne Rich has called the 'lesbian continuum' (1991: 145). This ambiguity is echoed in the way in which lesbian (and gay) characters have been deployed within American situation comedy in recent years. The 'lesbian wedding' episode of twenty-something sitcom *Friends* has Rachel's/Jennifer Aniston's mom announcing that she is thinking of leaving her husband. She gushes at having three women eye her up at the wedding since 'it's nice to know I have options'. Ironically it seems, one result of the sexless eroticism through which lesbianism is portrayed in (non-pornographic) popular film is a blurring between a repertoire of images signalling female friendship and those signalling lesbian. There is a sense then in which *all* female friendship occupies an ambiguous, eroticised territory.

Female friendship, class, ethnicity and 'race'

'I'm your only ethnic friend', C.C. Bloom/Bette Midler points out to the ultra-WASP Hillary (Barbara Hershey) in one of her unanswered letters, read on the soundtrack in *Beaches*, in which she pleads and harangues for a reunion after the two have fallen out. A t*our de force* of sentiment and showbiz, *Beaches* charts the close friendship, often conducted via correspondence, between these two different women. C.C.'s comment makes explicit that she is the 'other', the excitement, the locus of energy and glamour in Hillary's life. And of course Midler as C.C. is the star of the film which provides a showcase for her singing and her trademark independent but neurotic persona. This is the only point when ethnicity is mentioned: for the most part the movie subsumes it into class so that the friendship/'romance' of opposites is conducted in terms of an opposition between taste and vulgarity. Writing of her new review which will make her a 'huge star', to Hillary (who has given up her own career to support that of her husband), C.C. says with some glee: 'It's vulgar, it's gross, it's dirty'. Which it is; we see C.C. performing on stage an innuendo-packed number about the invention of the 'brassière', intercut with Hillary and her husband watching with evident distaste. As a child, Hillary had functioned as C.C.'s ideal, adoring spectator for a rendition of 'The Glory of Love'. At the end of the movie C.C., now surrogate mother to Hillary's daughter who watches from the wings, sings the same number in a 'classier' version. If C.C. is mother-identified, Hillary is associated with her father. Though C.C. ultimately becomes a sort of carer, she remains a star. A working out of difference is central to the conventions of the buddy movie of course. The buddy narrative typically moves towards a reconciliation of terms, so that the different characteristics of each partner come to complement each other (the two versions of 'The Glory of Love').

Explicit references to class, ethnicity or 'race' are uncommon in friendship movies, although they may bring together women from different social classes, ages and backgrounds or with very different tastes. Or rather it is precisely through references to taste, culture, costume and so on that these differences are articulated. The inscription of difference within the male buddy movie in terms of 'race' is primarily through initially antagonistic, typically hierarchical pairings of white and black men.[7] Within the buddy/friendship narrative both race and ethnicity are mapped into a series of oppositions which the couple (platonic or romantic) will come to terms with. In *Boys on the Side* the difference between Jane and Robin is constructed in relation to a series of terms including black/white, lesbian/straight, creative/business-oriented. On their first meeting, Jane terms Robin 'the whitest woman on the face of the planet', yet the tensions that develop between them stem from sexuality. Jane it seems is always getting crushes on straight women, causing herself pain in pursuit of unattainable objects of desire. The film has them fall in love anyway, through the conventions of the buddy movie which allow that opposites attract as much as romance fiction (Robin relaxes, Jane sings a Carpenters number), though not without a fatal illness that ensures they will not live happily ever after. In Chapter three, I look at the inscription of the format in *Strange Days* and *The Long Kiss Goodnight*. If female friendship is marginalised within Hollywood representation, and the connotations of same-sex desire are both invoked and repressed in such representations, how have differences between women in terms of class, ethnicity and 'race' been deployed? *Strange Days* atypically situates its longstanding friendship and developing romance between a white man and a black woman within a narrative that foregrounds the complexity of 'race', culture and identity as political issues. Of those feminist discourses on which the Hollywood cinema draws (a concern with women's independence and autonomy, self-respect and rights over the body, for example) an engagement with the political implications of the *differences* between women across the terms of class, 'race' and sexuality are not foregrounded.

Claire Monk observes in her review of *Moonlight and Valentino* (1995) that, despite the calibre of the performances in this tale of loss, love and female bonding, Whoopi Goldberg 'as often, is short-changed in a role where her very presence is supposed to signify eccentric colour-blind bohemianism'. This within a film that shows little sign that 'the film-makers have noticed she is black'.[8] Writing about another Goldberg movie, *Ghost* (for which she won an Oscar), Judith Mayne observes that:

> With Oda Mae [Goldberg] virtually the only character in the film who speaks of race, a central tenet of racial ideology is confirmed, i.e., that white people only have a race when a black person walks in the room, and that (in *Ghost*) it is blacks who have a race, and who are conscious of race, not whites.
>
> (Mayne 1993: 152)

On one side movies in which Goldberg is the site of 'race', the one who speaks it, draws attention to difference. On the other side, movies in which difference is (rigorously) left unspoken but nonetheless articulated.[9] Several critics have pointed to the fact that Goldberg's award-winning performance as Oda Mae in *Ghost* is an achievement, but one that involved negotiating, talking and performing her way around longstanding stereotypes which cast black women as maternal or nurturing (Bogle 1994; Mayne 1993). As Jane in *Boys on the Side*, Goldberg also ends up as carer in a film that finally allows the two women to acknowledge their love for each other only when Robin is about to die. The esoteric, character-driven *Bagdad Café* (1988), which paired C.C.H. Pounder as Brenda and Marianne Sagebrecht as Jasmin, is a rare exception with its use of surreal images such as the magic show scenes. (The short-lived television series that followed starred Goldberg in the Pounder role.) The development of respect and friendship stems from the familiar clash of opposites, transposed to a distanced, arthouse style that produces a different take on the conventions of the mismatched friendship theme. Typically, Hollywood cinema's friendships between black and white women, whether eroticised or not, are haunted by a history of representation in which black women are marginalised characters, primarily constructed as carers in relation to white women.

At the 'exploitation' end of the popular, consider *Showgirls*. Clearly, this is not a film we are invited to 'take seriously' (despite comments to the contrary from scriptwriter Joe Eszterhas). Yet perhaps because it is a film we are not invited to take seriously, the terms of its central friendship between a white woman and a black woman is indicative. Nomi arrives in Las Vegas and is immediately ripped off, her suitcase is stolen and she is left stranded. Molly befriends her, taking her in and looking out for her (after, as we've seen, the film establishes they are not a couple). Molly works backstage at the Stardust on a show called 'Goddess' which stars Cristal Connors, thus providing Nomi's and the audience's entrée into the world of the backstage musical. As a dresser, Molly is the only female character to keep her clothes on. Nomi gets hired, becomes Cristal's understudy, trips up the star and takes over. *Showgirls* displays its soft-porn roots in its fantasy (predatory) articulation of lesbianism; Nomi's and Cristal's relationship is based on exploitation and identification, the latter resignedly handing over power to the new star in the end. The friendship shared between Nomi and Molly is portrayed as girlish – giggling, sharing clothes and make-up (they even *skip* at one point). Yet as Nomi runs on stage for her first night in 'Goddess' she pauses to tell Molly 'I love you', and it is through Molly's eyes, standing in the wings, that we see the show. What seems like an age of blown kisses and whispered endearments later, Molly rejects her friend for having become part of the sleazy world. Yet ultimately Molly is herself positioned as victim, her brutal rape at Nomi's opening night party intercut with Nomi slow-dancing with Zack (Kyle MacLachlan). While the film produces heterosexuality as sleazy, violent and exploitative, it also contrasts an eroticised relationship between two women (Nomi and Cristal) in terms of conflict and competition with another (Nomi and Molly) constituted in terms of a sexless, protective hierarchy. At the end of the movie Nomi visits Molly's assailant and 'kicks shit out of him' before leaving for Los Angeles to (we are left to assume) conquer the world of the movies. Molly is doubly disempowered then, unable to enact her own revenge and abandoned by Nomi.

With its pairing of the emotionally independent, physically dependent (former) soap queen, May-Alice (Mary McDonnell) with a quietly sardonic nurse, Chantelle (Alfre Woodard), John Sayles' *Passion Fish* (1992) seems set to pursue a familiar pattern of foes to friends within a hierarchical relationship in which a black woman enables a white woman to regenerate, discovering herself through an other. This is how Donald Bogle reads the film, suggesting that while *Passion Fish* was 'one of the few movies to reflect on the lives of women' it 'did not venture far from traditional images of African Americans'. Why, he asks 'does such a fantasy – black women as nurturing marvels at helping poor white women untangle the knots in their lives – linger on, even in the mind of a contemporary independent film-maker?' (1994: 358–9). While *Passion Fish* evokes this fantasy of regeneration it also works to some extent to question it through the elaboration and juxtaposition of the two women's stories and through the use of the Louisiana setting within which differences of class and culture are foregrounded. The 'exotic' location, with its swamps, distinctive food and music produces a space within which both women experience narratives of transformation and regeneration. May-Alice had left Louisiana, a world in which she was perceived as 'different', years before as a young woman; we learn of the money she has spent trying to rid herself of her accent. Chantelle is also an outsider who comes from the North (Chicago), and it is mainly through her eyes that the audience views the Louisiana setting. Though May-Alice and Chantelle act on each other, their transformation is also located within a landscape in which they are both outsiders.

If *Passion Fish* evokes or enacts stereotypical narratives of transformation and regeneration via the unfamiliar, it also foregrounds the work of fantasy and of images of fantasy. Rennie (David Strathairn) takes the two women out into the swamp where he makes some of his living as a guide for tourists. May-Alice tells Chantelle how exciting and different Rennie and his father had seemed to her and her friends as young girls. She asks him later how she had treated him, realising that, just as she had found herself positioned as 'different' by her friends, she had regarded Rennie as something 'other', a site of fantasy rather than an individual. Meanwhile, Chantelle becomes friendly with Sugar (Vondie Curtis-Hall), who she terms on first meeting a 'French-talking Louisiana cowboy'. May-Alice's developing preoccupation with photography is set against her initial (listless) fascination with the soap operas of which she had been a star. The film's opening image of her waking in hospital, confused and paralysed, is accompanied by the television image of herself telling Dawn/'Rhona' (Angela Bassett) of her loss of memory. In turn, if this seems to imply a straightforward opposition between (active) production and (passive) consumption, the scenes in which her soap opera friends visit emphasise the work of the actor and the pleasure they take in their work whilst acknowledging its more bizarre aspects. While *Passion Fish* inhabits the well-worn territory of a developing relationship, the film does not equate a relation of employer/employee with one of friendship. Some of May-Alice's white visitors make assumptions about Chantelle's role, reading her as servant, as maid. A counterpoint to this comes in a short scene between Chantelle and Dawn, one of May-Alice's soap opera friends, in which they discover they both come from Chicago and are able to pinpoint each other's backgrounds from the neighbourhoods in which they lived. May-Alice later confesses that she doesn't know how to describe Chantelle's role or their relationship herself. To May-Alice's 'you're not my servant, you're not my babysitter or my housekeeper', a list to which Chantelle adds dispassionately, 'I'm not your friend' (also observing, 'It's a job, it's supposed to be boring'). The film is similarly haunted by a history of representation that it evokes and seeks to sidestep or re-frame. Ultimately at the end of the film the two are, in Chantelle's words 'stuck with each other', a term for their relationship still not agreed on. The film closes undecided, the two women sitting on a still boat in the middle of the lake.

In *Boys on the Side*, *Beaches* and *Steel Magnolias*, a genteel femininity is aligned with white women who gradually fade away and die.[10] It is interesting in this context to note just how regularly images and accents which evoke the 'South' recur in movies that elaborate narratives of female friendship. In part the South functions simply to designate 'otherness', a kind of exoticised or fantasy space akin to the desert or to Alaska in *Leaving Normal*. The magical qualities attributed to the sky and the stars in *Leaving Normal* or in *Mystic Pizza* where Kat is set to study astronomy at Yale suggest the metaphoric function of these spaces. The desert as an empty space for the protagonists of *Boys on the Side* is also marked (like *Passion Fish*) as tourist space (Robin taking snaps with her camera, posing her friends in a recreation of a childhood memory). The (cinematic) South generates a contradictory set of signifiers producing a white femininity defined as fragile and a repertoire of images of 'strong women', both white and black (though in different terms). *Thelma and Louise* and *The Silence of the Lambs* situate their independent women in part through accent. Starling's white working-class origins are detected by Lecter through her West Virginia accent. Waitress turned vigilante Louise Sawyer hails, we learn, from Texas. In this context, the title of *Steel Magnolias* refers to women's strength and seeming fragility, but also more specifically to white Southern women. Images of the South also evoke an oppressively genteel femininity that, somehow, it is *appropriate* (necessary even) for white women to rebel against. An articulation of women as 'ladylike' in a fashion so extreme that, despite the nostalgia that often accompanies its representation, it becomes absurd.

Attending classes designed to help keep her marriage special, Evelyn Couch (Kathy Bates), protagonist of *Fried Green Tomatoes at the Whistle Stop Café*, seems listless. A friend tells her that what they really need is 'an assertiveness class for Southern women – but that's a contradiction in terms', adding that Evelyn is still living in the 'Dark Ages'. The film meshes together the contemporary story of Evelyn's growing confidence via her friendship with the elderly Ninnie Threadgoode (Jessica Tandy), who she encounters in a nursing home, and the stories of the 1930s that the latter tells her at length. These stories of the past, which entrance Evelyn, revolve primarily around the relationship between Idgie Threadgoode (Mary Stuart Masterson) and Ruth Jamison (Mary Louise Parker). If Evelyn is described as living in the Dark Ages, it is in these women's past that she finds self-discovery and strength. The film thus elaborates a discourse between past and present, dependence and independence, in which relationships between women are a source of strength. Idgie as 'tomboy' and Ruth as 'good mother' are involved in the kind of unstated, sexless lesbian, butch/femme relationship beloved of the Hollywood cinema. Ruth's marriage is further portrayed as brutal and violent, a scenario that necessitates her departure with Idgie. Idgie's male dress is matched by her card-playing, drinking and night-time redistribution of food from trains passing through town. Their unconventional behaviour also chimes with an iconography of (white) eccentricity located in the South: the kind drawn on in Shirley MacLaine's role in *Steel Magnolias* or the 'literary' (i.e. gay) cousin played by Leo Burmester in *Passion Fish*.

If Whistle Stop is portrayed as a liberal town as far as white lesbians go, the point at which the couple's behaviour is marked as unacceptable is their relationship to the town's black residents, to whom they serve food in the back of the café. Idgie and Ruth are familiar types in Hollywood movies located in the South which produce unconventional whites who resist racial prejudice. Such archetypes typically work to reassure liberal white audiences ('Them not Us' again) whilst producing fictions 'about' racism which marginalise or objectify black characters produced as dignified, noble but with little agency. In *Fried Green Tomatoes* the story of Idgie and Ruth is underpinned by that of Sipsey (Cicely Tyson) and her son Big George (Stan Shaw) who work for them, cast in Bogle's words as 'almost shockingly familiar pliant noble servants' (1994: 327). When Idgie was young and in mourning for her brother Buddy, it was Big George who, we are told, took care of her as she lived 'wild' in the woods. It is Sipsey who kills Frank (Ruth's husband) and Big George who turns him into barbecue for the café. The articulation of the heroic protagonists as a lesbian couple represents a twist on the more usual scenario. Yet while Evelyn gains independence and a sense of purpose through her friendship with Ninny and an identification with the transgressive couple, the politics of 'race' and racism are barely raised in the present day segments of the film. Fannie Flagg's book makes it more explicit that Evelyn's self-discovery, which also revives her *marriage*, is not only through an identification with a lesbian couple in the 1930s, but through an identification with a present-day (Christian) black America.[11] As Whatling argues, such movies are contradictory texts which are available for lesbian spectatorship. The more general construction of lesbianism through an iconography of female friendship which draws on the buddy movie works to produce a potential eroticism in many other friendship movies. At the same time though, there are other dynamics and differences at work in these movies.

7

ACTING FUNNY
Comedy and authority

The sound of music: Whoopi Goldberg plays a lounge singer masquerading as a nun in *Sister Act*

Almost all comedic forms – from jokes to gags to slapstick routines to the most complex narrative structures – attempt a
liberation from authority. Like carnival, comedy levels the lofty
and erases distinctions, replacing the exalted hero of tragedy
with one reduced to the level of Everyman, or lower.

(Rowe 1990: 44)

If comedy has been seen as inherently 'subversive' because it
involves breaking aesthetic and ideological conventions, it has
also been seen as reactionary, because it involves the use of cultural stereotypes, and because the breaking of conventions is
itself a conventional generic requirement.

(Neale and Krutnik 1990: 82)

Comedy is not inherently 'reactionary' or 'progressive' of course, whether
our concern lies with the manipulation of form or more direct questions of
an overt 'political' content. Yet comedy, as Kathleen Rowe suggests in the opening to this chapter, does have a particular relationship to authority and to the
transgression of social convention; comedy provides a space in which taboos can
be addressed, made visible and also contained, negotiated. This makes the position
of women in comedy films and as comic performers an interesting one. The two
are quite distinct; female roles in comic films are not necessarily taken by comic
performers, for example (think of spoof movies such as *The Naked Gun* (1988)
and *Hot Shots* (1991)). In his analysis of Hollywood comedian-comedy Frank
Krutnik argues that the genre is male-centred, producing movies that marginalise
female performers. The eccentricity of the (male) comedian is defined partly in
terms of his refusal of a conformity that is projected onto women and thence dis-
owned and devalued. Thus the form 'repeatedly offers controlled assaults upon,
or inversions of, the conformist options of male identity, sexuality and responsibility'. This within a narrative context in which 'women tend to signify the
demands of integration and responsibility for the male' (Karnick and Jenkins

163

1995: 37). Some recent successful Hollywood comedies seem to affirm this trajectory. The hit movie *Dumb and Dumber* (1994), for example, casts Jim Carrey and Jeff Daniels as male partners who, while they are tempted by and drawn to women (the narrative is triggered, after all, by Carrey's mistaken plan to return a suitcase of money to Mary/Lauren Holly), are patently too childish to engage in adult relationships.[1] Such male comedy couples, like that of Jerry Lewis and Dean Martin or Laurel and Hardy discussed by Krutnik, operate in terms of a refusal of heterosexuality as conformity within an Oedipal framework that in turn constructs them as childish.

Female comic couples, a relatively recent phenomenon in any case, have rarely operated in terms of such a raucous refusal of heterosexuality. The BBC television series *Absolutely Fabulous* represents one of the few sustained variants of this formula for women.[2] Its central pairing of Jennifer Saunders as Edina and Joanna Lumley as Patsy is of two women who are determined to refuse adulthood and the responsibilities associated with it, celebrating instead the pleasures of excessive consumption: drugs, drink, cigarettes, sex and shopping. Over its run the show featured these comic characters in a series of grotesque scenarios forged out of the everyday difficulties of characters dedicated to consumption but unable to organise themselves effectively. Oscillating between contempt for others and extremes of self-loathing, Edina's and Patsy's egocentric excess and lack of bounded behaviour is played off against Edina's strait-laced daughter Saffy (Julia Sawalha) and her mother, played by sitcom veteran June Whitfield. Yet *Absolutely Fabulous* does not operate as a strict (or simple) role reversal of those infantile male comic couples. Male characters do not come to represent 'responsibility', though they are the cause for mirth, particularly in the shape of Edina's ex-husbands. Instead it is Saffy who is the personification of 'responsibility': with her political awareness, studious behaviour and conservative clothes played off against her mother's superficiality and desire to be up-to-the-minute, seemingly fixed in adolescence. Thus it is motherhood that signifies the responsibility from which Edina is in perpetual (and comic) flight, pulling faces in response to Saffy's rebukes, cajoling her when she wants a favour, flouncing off when she gets her way. In the episode 'New Best Friend', Edina's ultra-trendy 1960s' friends (all clean lines and calm) have had their lives turned upside down by parenthood. The elaborate preparations for Bettina's and Max's visit (which involves clearing everything away) are undercut by their arrival with seemingly the entire contents of Mothercare spilling into the hallway. An episode titled 'Death' in which Edina's father has died, has the comic pair consoling each other for not being the centre of attention and getting so drunk that they fall into a freshly dug grave at the cemetery. Edina decides that the coffin, laid out in the sitting room, clashes with her newly acquired art. As this might suggest there is a definite cynicism about a culture of consumption, a cynicism underlined by the elaborate ineffectiveness of both Edina and Patsy in the sphere of work. Although both have specific jobs, they spend little time actually 'at work' and are shown to be horribly incompetent when attempting work-related activity, in contrast to the super-efficient if callous magazine editor played by Kathy Burke.[3]

In the contemporary women's film, men, the institutions of heterosexuality and the family generate problems which female characters spend time talking over with each other and responding to. Within comic films that centre around women, conventions of the 'feminine', of male behaviour and of the heterosexual family also produce targets for humour. And since, as we've seen, the feminine is a term that is both produced and defined in relation to white middle-class women, the mobilisation of comedy by women who find themselves outside these terms operates not only in terms of the content of the comedy (gags, for example) but in the fact of performance itself. Commenting on the contested media images surrounding stand-up, television and film comedian Roseanne Barr, Sian Mile suggests that 'women are not expected to attempt humor, nor are they expected to succeed at it' (Barecca 1992: 43). If women are not expected to be funny, in conventional terms, they are expected to be beautiful. Or at least to be focused on and concerned with appearance; part of the pleasure of *Absolutely Fabulous* lies in its simultaneous humour at Edina and Patsy dressing-up like adolescents, its celebration of drag queen style and its send-up of beauty culture, as the protagonists work their way through various (disastrous) miracle cures and diets, including a facelift which goes horribly wrong for Patsy who is preparing for an interview for *Hello* magazine. *Muriel's Wedding* constructs and explores an opposition between the heroine's desire for a wedding, but not for marriage, within the comic context of a grotesque family. Though the set-piece of the film, its title and its publicity images are to do with Muriel's wedding, this staged moment is not constructed as the expression of romance (the wedding is precisely staged) though it is clearly the expression of fantasy, celebrated (and replayed) by Muriel as image and as spectacle. Dressing up for a wedding is juxtaposed with dressing up for an exuberant karaoke performance of 'Waterloo' which celebrates Muriel's and Rhonda's new-found friendship. Muriel's family are represented through a black comedy which renders them both awful and sympathetic. The 'beautiful' girls of her home town, Porpoise Spit, are rendered comically ugly, finally supplanted by Muriel's friendship with Rhonda, the image of which provides the final gag of the film as the pair drive off together to the tune of 'Dancing Queen'.

Like *Muriel's Wedding*, Gurinder Chadha's *Bhaji on the Beach* (1994) combines drama and comedy, rather than operating as a showcase for comic performance. Weaving together images of popular culture and practices with the lives of a group of Asian women from different backgrounds and generations, *Bhaji on the Beach* is a road movie that centres on a daytrip to Blackpool (the film's title evokes and juxtaposes the Indian food that has redefined 'British' cuisine, and the seaside holiday, staple of white, working-class British culture). A minibus transports the group (complete with tensions and problems) to the illuminations with both the journey and the scenes in Blackpool functioning as a setting for comic clashes of viewpoint and for emotion, romance and drama. For director Chadha 'just making *Bhaji* is a massive political statement for me' (Hussain 1992: 24). Written by actor and writer Meera Syal, the movie combines quite different tones, moving between, in Andrea Stuart's words, 'high drama and slapstick comedy'

(1994: 26). Comedy stems from the interplay of different generations (the gig-gling teenage girls, Madhu and Ladhu, who always seem to say the wrong thing, for example) and from the fantasy/dream sequences through which Asha (Lalita Ahmed) rehearses the events of the film in stylised form. The movie also makes much of the kitsch appeal of Blackpool (its games machines, karaoke, the elderly people clapping along to the 'Birdie Song', soggy chips and male strippers) whilst offering a fantasy of Blackpool as both Bombay and Bollywood: stepping onto the Golden Mile, Rekha (Souad Faress) exclaims with delight and/or surprise 'Bombay!', whilst Asha, sitting in the formal gardens, imagines herself in a movie romance. Drama stems from the crises of adolescence, from within relationships, from within communities and from tensions between communities (the tensions of an inter-racial romance; an unplanned pregnancy; a violent marriage; white racism).

It may seem that the dramatic aspects of *Bhaji on the Beach* are most explicitly concerned with questions of cultural and of gendered identity: the kinds of con-cerns that are discussed by the characters, on appropriate behaviour for young women, for example. Comedy is produced through ironic juxtapositions and through both visual and verbal gags. The use of humour in the movie also func-tions as a counterpoint to perceptions of Asian women and to the significance that *Bhaji on the Beach* has as the first feature film to be directed by an Asian woman in Britain. Chadha observed that with *Bhaji*:

> For the first time on British screens we'll be seeing ten Asian women who are strong, articulate and well-rounded characters who have their low-points and their high-points. We're showing them as multi-dimensional people rather than just as shopkeepers.
>
> (Hussain 1992)

If this emphasises the dramatic aspects of the film, the different stories of the women and the ways in which they come together, Andrea Stuart terms humour 'Chadha's secret weapon' quoting her thus:

> Whenever anyone describes one of my plots as 'A group of Asian women . . .' they think they have my number. So all my films have comedy in them to wrong foot people, to disrupt their expectations and to make them think about things in a different way.
>
> (Stuart 1994: 26)

Here comedy functions to 'wrong foot' an audience willing to make assumptions about Asian women. Since, as Mile suggests, comic performance is considered 'unfeminine', inappropriate for women, its use in *Bhaji on the Beach* works not only to undermine expectations about women and femininity *per se*, but at a more particular level to subvert the passive (i.e. excessively 'feminine') stereotypes of Asian women that persist in British culture. The humour also functions to locate the film, and the characters in it, as both English/British and Asian, picking up on British cinema's comic tradition and, in touches such as the Punjabi rendition of 'Summer Holiday', articulating the specificity of an English/British-Asian culture. In its groundbreaking role as a film about British-Asian women, and in its evocation of British-Asian culture, *Bhaji on the Beach* represents both an intervention in and contribution to the comic traditions which are so central to British cinema.[4]

The body, comedy, performance

As *comic performers*, particularly in stand-up, women frequently present themselves as cynical survivors of heterosexuality, rather than as enjoying the infantile pleasures identified by Krutnik in comedian-comedy or played out by Edina and Patsy in *Absolutely Fabulous*. The comedy associated with this cynicism tends to be verbal as much as physical, relying on wit rather than falling down or mugging. The world-weary tone of the British Jo Brand or American Roseanne Barr, at least in their stand-up routines, takes this cynical perspective to an extreme. Here humour stems from a knowing commentary on the shortcomings of conventional behaviours and structures juxtaposed with a celebration of the pleasures of indulgence. Within the different formats of Brand's stand-up/sketch show and Barr's long-running sitcom *Roseanne*, the two extract humour from conventional expectations and perceptions of the 'feminine' as well as exploiting the distance between the everyday experience of the world (of the body, of relationships) and the idealised images of women found in forms such as advertising. Both Brand and Barr deadpan one-liners and monologues on such 'taboo' topics as menstruation. Jill Marshall terms this 'an insistence on telling people things they don't want to hear', citing one of Jo Brand's gags:

> There's lots of these funny sayings: 'I'm on the plug', 'I've got the decorators coming', 'Arsenal are playing at home'; I prefer 'I've got copious quantities of blood spurting out of my fanny'.[5]

The gag underlines and mocks the extent to which the female body (as excess) is contained within a culture that only alludes to menstruation (those 'funny sayings'; the mystifying use of blue liquid to represent blood in advertising), or indeed to a female sexuality that Brand presents as both comic and voracious.

Roseanne Barr the performer and 'Roseanne' the performance are both framed by images of excess, images that relentlessly return to her body as sign. The lead in to John Lahr's 1995 profile of her is exemplary: 'Everything about Roseanne Barr is excessive,' we are told ,'her bulk, her ego, her wealth'.[6] Roseanne signifies an excess which is allied to the body but is not exhausted by the physical. Rather Roseanne's body becomes the overdetermined site and symptom of her status as a transgressive icon, of her refusal (or inability) to fit. 'Roseanne' is located as 'working class' in her series which portrays a blue collar family. Her body and her alignment with physical excess and vulgarity (visceral qualities), like the fact of performance itself (taking up space), do not fit with prevalent ideas or imagery of the 'lady'. Lahr suggests that 'her very presence was a provocation', that 'her body and her unladylike talk made her America's bourgeois nightmare come to comic life'. Roseanne has generated loathing within a culture that rejects and marginalises fat women, where, as Jill Marshall writes, fatness 'is experienced as a constantly walked line between unwanted street visibility and social dismissability'. Feminist-informed discourses of women's magazines and daytime television ask women to value themselves rather than the body. Yet they simultaneously retain normative notions of the body, as in the 'I'm OK but look at the new me' of chat-show host Oprah Winfrey or Ricki Lake, a doubleness which expresses something of the ambivalence through which women's bodies are discursively produced and experienced.[7] In a related fashion, Meyer notes how publicity surrounding the release of *Muriel's Wedding* worked to reassure audiences that Toni Collette was 'really' thin, juxtaposing images from the film with shots of the actor after shedding the weight that she had gained to play Muriel.

It may seem ironic that Roseanne is also criticised for *claiming* an authenticity to do with her body and working-class identity that she cannot sustain – for being vulgar, for being fat, for having plastic surgery, for flaunting all these things. A short article in the *Independent* concludes that Roseanne 'as a concept, is simply a fraud', juxtaposing a series of 'myths' with the 'truth' about the star in a mock tabloid style:

> Myth: Roseanne has come to terms with her weight. 'I'm fat and proud of it,' she says. 'If someone asks me how my diet is going, I say, Fine, how was your lobotomy?'
>
> Truth: Roseanne has had treatment for 'food addiction', which she ascribes to an unhappy childhood. At her heaviest , she weighed 16-and-a-half stone, but recently she shed five of them. At one stage she agreed to promote the Slimfast diet plan, but her contract was cancelled when she gained 40 pounds. She reportedly sends her children to WeightWatchers, 'so they don't end up fat like me'.[8]

The same article asserts that despite the construction of Roseanne's TV family as working class, they obviously have money, adding tartly that '[t]hey certainly spend enough on food'. For others, the mere fact of Roseanne's fame and success negates any commentary her comedy might make about class or gender. 'Whine as she might about her role as the voice of the working-class woman,' writes one journalist, 'Roseanne has a maid, a Mercedes, a brand new Hollywood husband and a reputation for temperament that would not exactly be tolerated on the assembly line.'[9] The implication is that her temperament shouldn't be tolerated in the television industry either, or perhaps that she should accept success 'gracefully'. Of course, in the context of comic performance, the female body is already at issue, out of place. In her analysis of Roseanne as spectacle, Kathleen Rowe writes that fat women are seen to somehow 'appropriate too much space' and that 'femininity is gauged by how little space women take up' (1990: 413). In turn, Marshall suggests that laughter:

> is one of the few replies fat women have of upsetting the dominant order, however temporarily and however easily laughter is used against them. Being funny may be a survival strategy but it gives fat women some cultural visibility and force.[10]

Both Rowe and Marshall emphasise performance then. Performance mediates and articulates the contradictory images, social experiences and cultural expectations which provide the material with which such female comics work. Similarly, for Sian Mile, Roseanne:

> succeeds in defining the female self as both public *and* as capable of creating the laugh – as capable of being the location of laughter. The credits at the start of *Roseanne* actually fade-out to the sound of her laughter.
>
> (Barecca 1992 : 43)

Yet Mile also points to the contested nature of Roseanne's image in the supermarket tabloids as an attempt to contain the female comic, to put her back in her place. The headlines 'suggest that she is a bad mother, an intolerable wife, a lesbian 'sympathizer' and an obese monstrosity' (ibid: 44). Of course, this process of framing and re-framing ever-multiplying images, gossip and tall-tales is also the territory of star images. Performance operates as a space of signification that is framed by but also exceeds the production of 'Roseanne', for example, as manufactured persona, television star and tabloid monster.

Television/stand-up: Performance and multiple personalities

It is no surprise that Roseanne Barr came to prominence as, and has largely remained, a television star, despite the occasional foray into cinema and television movies.[11] Though Frank Krutnik points to the marginal position of women in the 'classical' comedian-comedy tradition, he also makes some indicative comments on the position of women as comic performers within a post-classical cinema that is constructed in terms of a redefined relationship to television. Television, he suggests, has 'contributed to the widespread redefinition of the role and character of comedy in mainstream cinema' since its focus is not the contained narrative, whether centred around an individual performer or not. Television comedy which centres on performance is instead characterised by 'the sketch, the stand-up routine, the short sitcom or variety show'. And, though American network television is notoriously conservative, driven by advertising and sponsorship, Krutnik suggests that the medium:

has also provided more widespread exposure for comic performers long marginalized in the cinema – for women like Lucille Ball, Goldie Hawn and Roseanne Barr, for black comedians like Eddie Murphy, Bill Cosby and Britain's Lenny Henry.

(Karnick and Jenkins 1995: 352)

Comedy duo Dawn French and Jennifer Saunders occupy prime-time slots on British television, with the less mainstream BBC2 and Channel 4 broadcasting shows such as Jo Brand's *Through the Cakehole*, the Saunders hit *Absolutely Fabulous* (which subsequently moved to the major channel BBC1) and the sketch-based show *The Real McCoy*, featuring underused black and Asian-British comedians including Meera Syal, writer of *Bhaji on the Beach*.[12] Lesbian and gay comics have also had (limited) air-time via British television, usually in the form of broadcasts of live performance or by tapping into the existing camp/queer traditions of British comedy, with Julian Clary the best-known example. I am not suggesting that television is somehow a 'progressive' medium/industry. Rather, following Krutnik, we can note that the kinds of performance which television facilitates (short sketches and cameos, for example) has enabled the more confrontational performers and styles developed in live performance to feed into the mainstream, in turn redefining it.

French and Saunders have developed trademark spoofs of movies and music videos which have fun at the expense of the conventions of these forms, casting the two as male or female, slipping in and out of character to comment on how good their accents are, and so on. Spoofs of adverts and crime shows ('Drudge Squad'), among other popular forms, feature in Jo Brand's *Through the Cakehole*, along with the stand-up scenes and comic sketches. One episode, 'Crime and Punish Men', ends with a village hall, amateur dramatics production recreating the climax of *Reservoir Dogs*, with the parts all performed by primly-dressed, white, middle-aged women. The characteristics of what has become a cult film, with its articulation of tough guys falling apart and textured use of obscenity, is rendered ridiculous by its relocation. Within the mainstream of American television comedy such strategies are also used, as in the sitcom *Cybill* which stars Cybill Shepherd as Cybill Sheridan and sidekick Christine Baranski as Marianne, the vengeful ex-wife of Doctor Dick, a plastic surgeon who she pursues and torments.[13] Episodes typically start and end with a scenario related to whatever advert, TV series or low-budget movie Cybill is auditioning for or appearing in, skits that highlight the sleazy/comic aspects of the entertainment business. These scenarios involve either slapstick or a foregrounding of the female body and a cynical commentary on the exploitation involved, a commentary conducted via Cybill's acerbic discussions with Marianne, and our/her awareness of the star's age and the lack of fit this produces with Hollywood norms of beauty. Whether explicitly 'political' or not, comedy operates partly through an inversion of cultural assumptions which render them absurd, a foregrounding and transgression of conventions. Lesbian comic Suzanne Westenhoffer's jokes about heterosexuals – 'I like straight people – I do. I just don't want them teaching our

170

kids' – invert tried and tested bigotry. Joseph Bristow reads Julian Clary as simultaneously self-parodic and, with an image 'based in popular telly', a send-up of the conventions of mainstream comedy and culture (1989: 48).[14]

If comedy has a particular relationship to authority (which it typically subverts) it also emphasises performance: facial expression, intonation, delivery and body language. Roseanne developed her act, with its defining parodic persona of housewife as 'domestic goddess' in live comedy. Stand-up traditionally involves an aggressive style of performance, working with and against 'hardened' comedy audiences. And it is performance that, as we've seen, enables actors to negotiate their way around the most unpromising material. Comic performance frequently involves the performer working across multiple roles, whether as carefully defined characters or in the sort of short sketches used in television shows. Lily Tomlin, Roseanne Barr, Whoopi Goldberg and Sandra Bernhard have all worked with acts developed from carefully-crafted stage personas. With the exception of Roseanne, these performers have produced and shifted between multiple roles in their stage work. Pamela Noel's 1985 *Ebony* profile termed Goldberg an 'onstage chameleon'. Her Broadway one-woman show[15] revolved around six diverse characters, described thus:

> The hip-walking, slick-talking Fontaine . . . a White surfer girl who botches an abortion; a handicapped woman who talks about being in love; a Jamaican woman who inherits a fortune; an aging Black tap dancer who hasn't lost his timing, and a little Black girl who wants to be White with long luxurious blond hair so she can go on the *Love Boat*.
> (Noel 1985: 28)

The transition between these different personas, across categories of race, age, nationality, class and gender exemplifies both the performance involved in live comedy and the refusal of bodily/biological boundaries. The multiple personalities of this kind of performance comment on each other, foregrounding diverse social and cultural identities. In the same feature, Goldberg is quoted as saying that 'Richard [Pryor] does his thing as himself and I do *nothing* as myself'.

Goldberg's characters generated two made-for-cable concert films. *Fontaine – why am I straight?* (1988) frames Fontaine/Goldberg with an opening film sequence in which s/he leaves the Betty Ford clinic. Fontaine's monologue consists of amazed reflections on the world as he 'straightens up' to Reagan's America: 'looking at America through clean eyes – what a fucking deal'. The running gag, as Fontaine comments on cultural and political questions of the day, is the rhetorical question 'Maybe it's me? Maybe it's cos I just straightened up?', a repeated insistence on the peculiarities of the world described. Goldberg's obscenity-laden, cross-dressing performance (with ripped jeans and braids) sends up targets such as the Christian right and policies over AIDS ('you can't stop kids fucking – it feels good: it *does*, and if it doesn't get a new partner'). Andrea Stuart describes Fontaine as 'a treat: tough, over-the-top, lost' adding that:

Such comic characters are Goldberg's strength, and it is when she is allowed to develop this on film, as in *Ghost* or the glorious tampax routine in *The Player*, that her talent most clearly emerges.

(Stuart 1993: 13)

And while she has repeatedly insisted that she is not a comedian or a stand-up performer, but an actor who has worked in comedy and stand-up, Goldberg has had success with comic roles in the cinema. Two observations regularly made in relation to Goldberg's movie career are that she doesn't get the parts she deserves, and that her performances make something out of otherwise limited material. In her action/thriller films she exploits her abilities to assume different personas, as in the undercover sequences of *Fatal Beauty* or the opening scenes of *Burglar* (1987) which has her disguised as an elderly woman to break into a house. Elsewhere, as in *Sister Act* for example, an emphasis on performance frames her on-screen persona.

Like Roseanne, descriptions of Goldberg and journalistic comment, emphasise an appearance perceived as troubling. Since Goldberg is one of the few black women to have any sustained career in Hollywood this might be comprehensible in terms of the sign of 'race'. Yet whilst it is certainly the case that a black female star generates problems within a Hollywood economy that functions to keep black performers in marginal roles, the extent to which Goldberg has troubled is not simply about to this. A 1992 *Guardian* profile observed that Goldberg 'is known as a combative and (by Hollywood standards) unglamorous woman in an industry notoriously unreceptive to the same'. *The Voice* cites Goldberg herself on her role in *Fatal Beauty*, written for Cher and rejected by Tina Turner, that the 'film was written with a beautiful woman in mind. When they couldn't find one, they had to pay an ugly woman's price – $1.5 million'. This wry designation of herself as 'ugly', spoken in the same breath as her price tag offers an ironic commentary on her situation. In Goldberg's films, argues Andrea Stuart 'her outlandish appearance effectively de-sexes her' (1993: 13). Stuart suggests that hostile responses to Goldberg have been generated not only by some poor films but through her dress:

> The sartorial has been one of the few mechanisms for negotiating social hierarchies within black communities, so it is no surprise that the person who has appeared on the list of America's worst-dressed women more times than virtually any other actor should provoke her community's ire.
>
> (Stuart 1993: 13)

Goldberg's 'unconventional looks' and dress, as well as the roles she has played, are taken to position her as an outsider within a Hollywood defined by 'glamour', against an 'independent' (largely male) black American cinema (Spike Lee's critical comments, for example) and against the kind of mainstream cultural visibility black Americans have achieved through popular cultural forms including style, fashion, dance and music.[16] If, as Stuart and others argue, Hollywood

172

has difficulty perceiving Goldberg as a woman, this may relate not only to the evident reluctance to cast a black star in romantic roles with her white co-stars, but to her success as a 'man' (in her stage show) and in 'masculine' roles (her action films, her pool champion in *Kiss Shot*, her Hollywood 'butch' in *Boys on the Side*, her sports fan in the 1996 *Eddie*).

While Roseanne Barr's stand-up routine and hit TV show were built fairly directly around her persona as 'domestic goddess', 'Roseanne' is also situated rather differently in the two movies in which she has starred. Both, however, relate to and engage with the extra-textual construction of 'Roseanne', framed (in different ways to Goldberg) by her 'unconventional looks'. The opening of Susan Seidelman's under-rated *She-Devil* (1989) involves an explicit discourse on female beauty. Ruth/Roseanne's voice-over talks of women who can achieve 'beauty' naturally, others who have to spend a lot of time on it and those 'who need all the help they can get – like me'. On this line we see her face for the first time: sporting a large mole (which will later disappear without explanation), she signifies a body excluded from the codes of femininity that surround her. We see her struggling to get into a dress and sitting through various treatments whilst watching a television screen that shows a romantic scene from a Mary Fisher novel, followed by a parodic, sugary profile of the author (Meryl Streep) whose home and life, it is suggested, are just like her books. The establishment of Ruth's character runs through a series of popular feminist clichés about women, the body and low self-esteem: her perceived need for 'help' with her looks; her interest in romantic fiction; food as an antidote to sexual frustration. When husband Bob (Ed Begley) leaves her for Mary Fisher, Ruth methodically destroys his life and creates her own business empire out of an employment agency for marginalised women. Yet these 'signs' also make sense within the 'Roseanne' persona which involves a complex articulation of discourses around the female body, conventional beauty and self-worth. Ruth's organisation of a rebellion at the nursing home where she temporarily works, encouraging the elderly women to refuse their marginalisation, operates as both slapstick and satire. Within a film that parodies Mary Fisher's arch (and artificial) femininity, charting her evolution into feminist author at the end of the movie, Roseanne's persona is used to signal an 'unconventional' woman through comic performance rather than comic spectacle.[17]

Roseanne's second starring role was in a television movie, *Backfield in Motion* (1991). As (widowed) single mom Nancy, she moves from LA to Deerview, a pristine suburb in which all the wives bring tuna casseroles to welcome them, sharing what Nancy terms a 'game show contestant glow'. Nancy initiates and organises a small-town rebellion to demand a mothers and sons football game instead of the traditional fathers and sons match. Her insistence on equality (over something relatively contained) inspires 'housewife' rebellion (her three neighbours reveal that they 'hate baking') followed by fast-motion comedy sequences of the women training. The star quarterback is discovered as she throws breadrolls to her son. The television movie format allows an explicit play with the Roseanne persona. Co-star and romantic lead Tom Arnold was then Roseanne's husband, a further framing of the movie in terms of 'Roseanne'. The 'Deerview Devils' cheerleaders even have 'She Devil' written on their shirts. At the start of the final football game there is a close-up of Roseanne saying to camera 'Me? Sing the national anthem? I don't think so', a reference to her notorious rendition at a baseball game in 1990 in which she grabbed her crotch and spat after singing the national anthem, a juxtaposition of 'manly' and unpatriotic behaviour that, according to Mile, 'George Bush felt moved to call "disgraceful"' (Barecca 1992: 40). Under the headline 'WORST BARR NONE', *The Sun* linked this excess to her obscenity, her appetite for food and sex, suggesting she was 'on the verge of a nervous breakdown' and an unfit mother.[18] It is worth noting that Goldberg's concert film has Fontaine first come on stage singing a version of the national anthem which is punctuated by a series of comic 'motherfucking' and 'goddamns', a rendition that prefaces his/her 'state of the nation'-style monologue.

Comic performance: A 'pretty lady'

Questions of physical attractiveness are repeatedly raised in relation to female star bodies which are defined by the presence or absence of beauty defined along fairly strict lines. Like Roseanne Barr and Whoopi Goldberg, Sandra Bernhard is framed as unconventional. Yet she is also described as beautiful: an 'unconventional beauty'. A 1983 profile, following her successful performance as the manic Masha in Scorsese's *King of Comedy*, describes the tension and doubleness of one of her scenes in the film, before moving on to link this to Bernhard's appearance:

> And her face contributes to the schizoid mood: Straight on, it's almost pretty; in profile, with the protruding chin and lips, scrunched up in twitchy, aggressive intensity, it's pure terror; in repose, it's the sort of face that fates a woman to comedy. It's not a face you forget.[19]

Almost pretty. Rather than seeking to escape such designations, Bernhard's act involves a complex discourse on her status as a 'lady', as beautiful, as 'almost' pretty. Her book is titled *Confessions of a Pretty Lady*, while the introduction to the film version of *Without You I'm Nothing* has her sat before a mirror, as if preparing for the show. Absorbed by her own image, she abruptly turns to camera and speaks of her own beauty and glamour. Her frequent references in *Without You I'm Nothing* to her glamorous life and her 'smash-hit one woman show' function ironically, a performance in which she both inhabits and parodies her own success before a disinterested audience. Since her appearance in Scorsese's film, Bernhard has developed a career defined by a tangential relationship to a mainstream that she has been involved in (her role as Nancy on *Roseanne*, posing for *Playboy*) but also satirises. Her act suggests a total involvement in popular and consumer culture that is simultaneously produced as delightful and artificial.

Bernhard's pleasure in transgressing culturally constructed and lived categories of gender, ethnicity, 'race' and sexuality is mapped in profiles onto the sense of doubleness evoked by that 1983 article: almost pretty/pure terror. The use of multiple personas, allusions to popular culture, to celebrities and autobiographical material suggests a sort of unbounded persona. The same profile describes her stand-up routine, with its abrupt transition of tones, not so much jokes as 'long, almost musical commentary – often in a mocking fashion-show narrator's voice that turns abruptly mean. Too mean, maybe':

> 'I feel good tonight. I feel very good,' she says, sweet as Brooke Shields endorsing Calvins. 'I just moved in with new boyfriend, Burt Bacharach. I'm having a *wonderful* time, cooking, cleaning house. That's right, Burt Bacharach. I murdered his wife.' A small shock wave hits the audience, they gasp, and before they've quite recovered, she's singing 'Do You Know the Way to San Jose'. It's impossible to know whether she's serious or spoofing the song.
>
> (Wadler, *New York Times*, 21.2.83)

Too mean maybe? A face which 'fates' Bernhard to comedy, which is terrifying and almost pretty. Scorsese describes her as 'frightening', as 'tough, almost hostile'. Frequently the doubleness of Bernhard's performance returns to the territory of her body and how to define and/or describe it. Is Bernhard's a feminine body? a lesbian body? a white body? Her problematic location in relation to femininity is enacted through the frequent references to herself as a 'lady' and her aggressive, unladylike persona. Similarly her refusal to be a lesbian in the 'positive image' sense of the term, indeed her evident identification with male gay culture and drag queens, produces her as an ambivalent sexual figure. Her racial instability is enacted in terms of an identification with blackness, her imitation of black performers and a discourse on a white appropriation of black culture. Her Jewishness is enacted through an elaborate confessional tale of a childhood fantasy, 'the romance of being gentile', describing a family Christmas awful in its wholesomeness.

Bernhard has angered commentators by her reluctance to play the part, her refusal to make statements about her sexuality combined with an upfront acknowledgement of her lesbianism.[20] Like Madonna, with whom she was very publicly pictured for a while, Bernhard's act is much more to do with a male gay sensibility around 'camp' than a lesbian popular culture, though her rendition of 'Me and Mrs Jones' and her more recent role in the Australian film *Dallas Doll* (1993) could be framed in terms of 'lesbian camp'. Bernhard's homage to drag-disco-diva Sylvester is more typical, foregrounding the terms of authenticity/artifice/disguise that define her act. Camille Paglia enthuses:

> Fragments of ads, brand names, movies, TV, and celebrity gossip float through Bernhard's routines. But her technique is not the tiresome sterile irony of postmodernist 'appropriation'. On the contrary, she daringly explores a raw, stormy emotionalism, sudden tantrums that repel or terrify.
>
> (Paglia 1994: 139)

Terror again: Paglia's rejection of the postmodern is telling here. The satire, the abrupt meanness, the simultaneous delight in and mockery of the popular is resonant of camp rather than the distanced irony of an apolitical postmodernism. Andy Medhurst argues that camp, which he contrasts with postmodernism, 'comes from a sensibility that is too bruised, too bitter, too knowing to trust the credulous openness of sincerity' (1990: 19).[21]

Identifying herself with Blackness, Bernhard's musical performance expresses an ambivalent relationship to the appropriation of black musical culture by a white mainstream. According to Paglia:

> Bernhard has rejoined stand-up to its origins in vaudeville, where music and comedy were brassily interwoven. All musical styles of the past quarter century are evoked in Bernhard's shows: jazz, Broadway, country, rock, soul, Motown, disco, as ingeniously reinterpreted by a Jewish rapper.
>
> (ibid.)

Yet her serio-comic enactment of these styles also produces a commentary on these traditions. Her first number in the film *Without You I'm Nothing* is a rendition of Nina Simone's 'Four Women': dressed in African-style costume, turban and hoop earrings, the song's opening line ('My skin is black') underlines Bernhard's impersonation. Z. Isiling Nataf cites an interview titled 'Sandra's Blackness', which draws attention to her 'pumped up' hair and 'full' lips, 'signs usually read as racial signifiers of blackness' (Burston and Richardson 1995: 73). The film's staging of her performance not as a live concert off Broadway (that is, as a reproduction of her 'smash-hit one woman show') but for a bored, black LA audience, heightens the ambivalence of her appropriation/impersonation. Bernhard's reminiscences on fame, glamour and her childhood are greeted with silence rather than laughter as are her songs. Early on she declares they will start with some Israeli folk songs, exhorting her audience to join in, her enthusiasm unchecked by the lack of response. The lack of engagement on the part of the audience foregrounds the narcissism of the performance. The figure of black model Cynthia Bailey who, in Nataf's words, 'enigmatically haunts the margins of the film' extends this distance, only appearing in the club at the end of the film, when the rest of the audience has left. Still silent, she writes 'Fuck Sandra Bernhard' on a tablecloth before leaving the room. While the image refuses to 'reflect Sandra Bernhard back to herself as the alienated ideal', Bailey remains a figure of fantasy (Burston and Richardson 1995: 76–7). The defining doubleness of Bernhard's performance remains: an audience of one on screen, another audience in the cinema. Bernhard, draped in a Stars and Stripes cloak (another evocation of the nation) says 'without *you* I'm nothing', promising to speak the truth, remaining self-absorbed. And, of course, narcissism is both the defining feature of Bernhard's persona and the target of her comedy.

8

MUSIC, VIDEO, CINEMA

Singers and movie stars

Whitney Houston plays Rachel Marron, an Oscar-nominated actress and pop star in *The Bodyguard*

S tar images are elaborate constructions, characterised by their inclusion of diverse and potentially contradictory elements. In addition to, and indeed framing, any other specific performances, from movie roles or cameos, to public appearance and interviews, stars always 'perform' their star image. Through their performance stars constitute themselves in terms of particular identities, touching on and operating across social and cultural differences. All publicity feeds the star image, planned or unplanned; everything is ultimately managed, incorporated in some way. In his *Vanity Fair* profile of Dolly Parton, Kevin Sessums observes that the star 'has been so successful in packaging herself that now when we see her on-screen we do not see a character other than "Dolly Parton"'. Parton tells her interviewer, 'Look, I've always said that when I find something greater than "Dolly Parton", then I'll certainly play her'.[1] Her comment draws on, develops and confirms aspects of the Parton persona. Her pleasure in the role of 'Dolly Parton' and the *artifice* of that performance are simultaneously evoked. Her remarks are further framed by the peculiar combination of the artificial (constructed, marketed) and the direct 'simplicity' that characterises not only Parton, but country and western and even, to an extent, Hollywood itself. The foreword to her autobiography also addresses the reader in these terms:

> It is up to you to be the best . . . you can be. If I can help in any way, then I feel good about taking your money for this book. If I don't help, I still feel okay about taking your money because I think you will at least be entertained. Besides, I need the money. As I always say, 'It costs a lot to make a person look this cheap'.
>
> (Parton 1994: 2)

Parton's directness about her artifice reinforces a sense that she is 'actually' like the persona she performs, whilst simultaneously ridiculing any such interpretation; it is, after all, only an act. There is no referent, outside the world of the movies and entertainment, for her parodic authenticity, her performance of white (trash) womanhood.[2]

The star functions as commodity, as signifying system, as fetish object and, to some extent, as the space of a narcissistic identification on the part of audiences. Star bodies exceed the various texts that showcase them and the individual images that might otherwise contain them. This is in part related to a shared awareness of the fact of (an ongoing) performance. The star's body, worked out/on, transformed or preserved by surgery as it is, both offers and undermines a guarantee of authenticity, that of the 'naturalness' of the star herself (whether this is in terms of natural talent or natural beauty). Ultimately the body itself, the supposed ground of what it is to be sexed and raced, for example, a body which is only ever experienced by an audience as an image in any case, provides just one more layer to the star image, operating as another component that is worked over. Feminist criticism has long been aware of the ambiguity of the star, as Sue Thornham's summary of 1970s' feminist film criticism demonstrates. Of Marjorie Rosen's *Popcorn Venus* (1973) she writes:

> The star herself is seen to live out these contradictions. Identified with her roles, she is both a figure of male fantasy and a real woman forced to live out these fantasies and the contradictions they produce within her life, often in her relationships with the male directors of whose fantasies she is the literal embodiment.
>
> (Thornham 1997: 15)

The sense of a struggle within representation at work over the body of the (white) female star is evident in these writings. Whether theoretically 'sophisticated' or 'naive' in its understanding, both feminist criticism and theory share a sense of the fundamental ambiguity of the female star who speaks to desires for strength, sexual independence and self-reliance whilst she is simultaneously produced as spectacle. Christine Gledhill summarises this tension in terms of, on the one hand, economically powerful stars of the 1930s and 1940s who articulated 'independent female images' which 'overrode repressive narrative resolutions', whilst 'on the other hand, the female star who inevitably becomes a focus of visual pleasure for an apparently masculine spectator appears the epitome of the male fetish' (1990: xv). For Dyer a cultural analysis of stars centres on such contradictions, exploring 'the relationships . . . between stars and specific instabilities, ambiguities and contradictions in the culture' (Gledhill 1990: 58). As Dyer's work makes clear, the territory of the star image is also that of identity, of developing, testing and reformulating ways of being in the world.[3]

Stars are not unique to the cinema as a medium or to Hollywood as proponent of the movies. Neither do movie stars perform only in the cinema. Introducing her anthology on stardom, Gledhill comments in the context of 'new Hollywood' that:

> With the break up of the studio system and the emergence of the star as independent producer, freer to choose roles and focus on acting rather than image, the production of the bezass and gossip of stardom appears

to have passed from the cinema to the music industry or sports world.

(Gledhill 1990: xiii)

Yet, she continues, in relation to Kobena Mercer's analysis of pop star Michael Jackson, 'while other entertainment industries may manufacture stars, cinema still provides the ultimate confirmation of stardom' (1990: xiii). Mercer writes of Jackson that 'his image has attracted and maintained the kind of cultural fascination that makes him more *like a movie star* than a modern rhythm and blues artist' (ibid.: 314, my italics). Here Mercer suggests that the movie star represents a quite particular variant of stardom. Conversely musical performers have a quite distinctive place in relation to stardom, one which prizes the voice as much as (or often as well as) the body. The musical performer as movie star offers not necessarily a more extreme, but a specific instance of stardom, in part because they are already understood, and their images have been developed, in terms of an explicit and particular kind of performance. The body of the singer is defined through an elaborate and stylised performance that is often explicitly sexualised. She/he is also a figure of strength, controlling the image and compelling audiences with her/his voice. Writing of Michael Jackson's phenomenal success, Mercer points to the key elements of an enigmatic, elaborate star image and the centrality of the voice, citing Roland Barthes' observation that 'the grain is the body in the voice as it sings' (ibid.: 300). The relationship between body and voice, sexuality and emotion is bound up in the various conceptions of identity expressed in the star image (something that the term Diva attempts to designate).

While a redefined relationship between cinema and television is an important aspect of the post-war entertainment scene in North America, the development of music video in the 1980s as a way of marketing stars and their work, as well as feeding into star images, has had a significant effect on the relationship between musical and movie performance. Since the 1980s, directors and performers have increasingly moved between and across the different media of advertising, music video, television, live and recorded musical performance and movies.[4] Music video itself takes different forms, typically making use of rapid editing with sources such as still images, 'live' concert-style footage, dance, surreal scenes, and images that evoke seeming 'narrative' elements (suggestions of romance, for example). Writing about MTV, and therefore primarily of the rock/pop video, Kaplan argues that the advertising and video segments of the show use similar techniques so that 'desire is displaced onto the record that will embody the star's magnetism and fascination' (1987: 12). And for Michele Wallace the form is a 'hybrid of music performance documentaries and television ads' that functions to 'sell us what we expect to be free, namely our own private and unfulfillable desires' (1990: 77). Whilst advertising is clearly a source of imagery (and of personnel), Mercer's analysis of Michael Jackson's *Thriller* indicates that classical (and post-classical) Hollywood is also a reference point. Arguably, both advertising techniques and 'MTV aesthetics' can be said to have had an influence on movie-making, particularly but not exclusively in movies aimed at a 'youth' audience in recent years.[5] Ten years after Kaplan's

181

study was published, music videos are also marketed, alongside concert videos (and miscellaneous collections), as a product in their own right. 'Best of' collections such as Janet Jackson's *Design of a Decade* (1995) or Madonna's *The Immaculate Collection* (1990) are released in sound and video formats simultaneously (and are often grouped together in shops).

If music video evokes and suggests stories, it is not primarily a narrative form. Videos offer a proliferation of images of the star(s), an intensification of the layering associated with star images through which an individual image relates to a whole that is always evolving. While Bogle (1994: 291) reads the iconic use of Tina Turner as Auntie Entity, ruler of Bartertown in *Mad Max 3: Beyond Thunderdome* (1985) as 'exotic', the role also stems from her image as a strong woman and as a survivor, an image literalised in the post-apocalyptic world of the film. Turner's hit song from the movie, 'We Don't Need Another Hero', was emblematic. Music video has developed as a distinctive form involving strong images of women (often, though not always explicitly sexual), images that develop from a lengthy tradition of charismatic, controversial (eccentric even), popular female singers and performers. Whether the performance is of 'live' concert-type situations or a montage that complements the music, the music video involves the female singer in striking poses. Even within videos which tell a story or include framing narratives, this does not contain or explain (or even seek to do so) everything in the video. An imperative associated with narrative, the need to tie up loose ends, becomes subservient to an often intentional obscurity. Mainstream narratives need to explain away the active, masculinised female body with tomboy imagery, accounts of how she is stepping in for her father, or how she was raised with brothers. Music video, by contrast, thrives on a sexualised version of such images with little concern to 'explain' other than through the performance of the song itself. A performer's narcissistic or sexualised performance is not necessarily motivated by cutaways to a male viewer.

While the staging of female performance forms an important element of music video, with the concert or fashion/publicity/video shoot a recurrent setting, it is also typically a source of pleasure. Music videos feature numerous costume changes or elaborate costumes that can't be easily incorporated into the narrative world of mainstream cinema (outside the musical, that is). Dressing up, in both 'everyday' and surreal outfits, functions as a celebration of consumption, and of the performer's pleasure in costume and the body. Marjorie Garber suggests that Madonna's monocle and 'pinstriped suit strategically slashed to let her peach satin brassiere poke through', an ensemble used in the 1990 'Blond Ambition' tour which Garber terms a 'literalization of the "double-breasted suit"', functions to both mimic and mock 'effete male power' (Garber 1992: 155). If this costume evokes complex signifiers of femininity, masculinity and sexuality, it was also only one of many used in the tour (featured in the 1991 'documentary' *In Bed with Madonna*). The proliferation of signifiers suggest that music video is concerned not so much with narrative as with images, and with what can usefully be called *scenarios*, a term that emphasises the play of fantasy. Perhaps as a result, there is a certain tension between the evocative images produced by music/music video and the constraints of narrative as it has developed within the popular American cinema. Consider how the persona developed by Madonna during the 1980s and early 1990s changes when set within a narrative context. Her showcase scenes in *A League of Their Own* are those where she commands the dance floor in a roadhouse or teaches her friend to read via a racy novel: both scenes draw on the exuberant pleasure in physicality and sexuality that defines her image. The defiant, larger-than-life excess of, for example, the 'Justify My Love' video or the various video/stage renditions of 'Like a Virgin', are transposed into a somehow unsatisfactory *femme fatale* in *Body of Evidence*. Unsatisfactory since, in contrast to Madonna as 'vamp' in countless music videos or live performances, she is situated as manipulative and devious before being killed off. It is not so much that something is 'lost' in the transition between media, but that there is no easy fit or equivalence between the narrative cinema and the evocative 'narrative' images associated with the musical star. Think, for example, of how Kevin Costner's Frank Farmer in *The Bodyguard* (1992) is perpetually juxtaposed with, framed by or contemplating *images* of Whitney Houston's character, Rachel Marron. In a scene that indicates their increasing fascination with each other, Farmer watches a Marron video ('Run to You') whilst she looks down on him, watching him watch her image from her room. All the while, her voice on the soundtrack dominates the sequence so that the stylised image of voyeurism is framed by the conventions of music video.

Where performance is explicitly presented as 'objectifying', as in Tina Turner's 'Private Dancer' or Madonna's 'Open Your Heart', the juxtaposition of performance, orchestrated image and soundtrack works to produce a commentary on that 'narrative' of objectification. Lisa A. Lewis writes of Madonna's music video 'Borderline' (a title which already implies an uncertainty about location) that the presentation of the star as 'immersed in male street-corner culture' involves an appropriation of 'activities and spaces typically associated with male adolescence'. For Lewis:

> Such images confuse the iconography of the prostitute suggested by her street corner lingering and flirtation, and obviate the different social standards for male and female transgressions. Building a tension between the two implicitly raises questions about how the visual code of prostitution is elaborated and about how representations of female on the street might be revisioned.
>
> (Brown 1990: 92)

If the articulation of the street is discussed here by Lewis in terms of gender, the place of 'prostitute' that is being addressed, is also produced in terms of class and 'race'. In the video, the 'borderline' is also evoked in terms of age, class and ethnicity with the 'Madonna' character operating in two worlds, that of an older, wealthy white photographer who takes pictures of her spraying graffiti in a 'classical' setting (pillars, sculpture) and that of the street, with its young, working-class protagonists, its Italian-American star and evocation of Chicano culture. We might also bear in mind Madonna's appropriation of male gay culture and of black American music, her situation of herself as exoticised other through that appropriation and through the parody of fetishistic attitudes to the female body and female sexuality. She is an interesting figure to the extent that her appropriation does at times work to question assumptions. At other points she constructs hierarchies which seem content with the production of her as embodiment of white womanhood.[6]

Like popular music, music video and mainstream cinema are framed by both racial hierarchies and a relationship of appropriation to marginalised cultures. Jackson's success with his 'Thriller' video, notes Mercer, broke MTV's 'unspoken policy of excluding black artists' (Gledhill 1990: 302), whilst Kaplan points to MTV's marginalisation of black artists into specialist slots and draws attention to strategies of the mid-1980s such as black artists making videos with white artists, citing examples from Phil Collins/Phil Bailey to Aretha Franklin/Annie Lennox (1987: 16). Musical performance has long provided a visibility for strong black women that is rarely seen in the cinema. In turn, success in musical performance has been one (limited) route for black women to move into movie acting. Diana Ross made three movies in the 1970s, including *Lady Sings the Blues* (1972) for which she was nominated for an Academy Award.[7] In the 1980s Tina Turner appeared as Auntie Entity in the post-apocalyptic movie *Mad Max 3: Beyond Thunderdome*, before having her own autobiography turned into a hit film, *What's Love Got To Do With It* (1993), starring Angela Bassett and Laurence Fishburne. Whitney Houston moved into the movies with *The Bodyguard* and followed up with dramatic roles in *Waiting to Exhale* and Penny Marshall's *The Preacher's Wife*. In the 1990s both Janet Jackson and Queen Latifah have starred in Hollywood movies, Jackson in *Poetic Justice* (1993), discussed later in this chapter, and Queen Latifah in *Set It Off* (1997).[8] As some of these examples demonstrate, not all musical performers who go into movies end up in musical roles. Yet for Bette Midler in *The Rose* (1979), Ross in *Lady Sings the Blues* and Houston in *The Bodyguard*, starring roles for singers *as* singers have both showcased their talents and allowed a move into a new sphere of performance. The latter film has Houston's Rachel Marron, a pop star turned actress, win the Best Actress Oscar, with the movie's climax taking place at the Academy Awards ceremony. While black women have won Oscars for songs and supporting actress roles, Best Actress remains mainly an all-white affair.[9] Like the phenomenon of stardom itself, neither the opportunity for marginalised groups to succeed in spaces of performance or the prevalence of roles as showgirls, singers and actors are a product of the 'new Hollywood'. Performance has long been a Hollywood staple, allowing the production of both female flesh and women's work as sexual spectacle, whilst simultaneously evoking women's strength through the very power of the performance. And not only for black women, but for white women (usually via Broadway) who somehow do not fit the criteria of appearance found in Hollywood: Bette Midler or Barbra Streisand are two women who are framed as 'unconventional'.[10]

The relationship between music, music video and cinema performance is not unproblematic in these terms. Popular music and music video are both forums that are particularly charged in relation to discourses of 'race', precisely since the space of popular music *has* been one in which black women might find their image 'centre stage'. Judith Mayne suggests that for 'white audiences, one of the most stereotypical and therefore comfortable relationships between black and white is that of performer and onlooker' (1993: 154). The use of black women singers in the Hollywood film provides ample testimony to this. Recall in this context the image of Billie Holliday, cast as a maid, in *New Orleans* (1947) who 'just happens' to sing in a scene isolated from the rest of the narrative but in which she commands the screen.[11] This image encapsulates the ambivalence involved in such representations; Holliday is marginalised as a character within the narrative (in the role of maid) but dominates the movie during the (brief) space of her musical performance (rather than her performance as 'maid'). The use of black women's voices extends further than the play of margin and centre evoked by a confinement into performance pieces, but poses questions of the visibility of black women and the appropriation of their voices which are largely unaddressed within the Hollywood cinema, and which are re-posed in *Without You I'm Nothing*, discussed in Chapter seven.

Julie Dash's short independent film, *Illusions* (1982) explores the appropriation of black women's voices by a film industry structured in terms of racist hierarchies. Set in 1942, the film revolves around Mignon Dupree (Lornette McKee), an executive at 'National Studios' who has achieved a tenuous position of power because the draft has created opportunities for women. Dupree is not so much passing as invisible: 'they see me but they don't recognise me' she tells Ester Jeeter (Rosanne Katon), a singer called in to save a musical with her voice. Dash's movie articulates three levels of illusions, the first of which is an opposition between the 'real' stories that Dupree wants to tell (real in the sense of 'everyday' and in a socially inclusive sense) and the escapist product of the studio/classical Hollywood (the musical we see a segment of). The second level of illusion stems from the ironic juxtaposition of Ester singing in a darkened studio and, in Toni Cade Bambara's words, 'the larger-than-life, illuminated starlet on the silver screen' for whom she provides a voice. Both Mayne and Bambara note Dash's allusion to the Hollywood musical and to *Singin' in the Rain* (1952) in particular, with its climatic 'revelation' of Debbie Reynolds (standing behind the curtain) as the on-screen voice of Jean Hagan's character, whose harsh tones mark her as proletarian, against the chipper Reynolds, and thus unsuitable for the movies. The film, notes Bambara:

> provides Dash with a cinematic trope. Victoria Spivey, Blue Lu Barker, Lena Horne and other musicians contracted by Hollywood for on-screen and off-screen work provide the actual historical trope, for the Reynolds character image is false too. Behind that image, in the dark, behind a screen, in a booth, was a Black woman.
>
> (Diawara 1993: 141)

Ester is not only the singer but the cinematic spectator who, she tells Mignon, closes her eyes when watching a film, imagining herself on the screen. This sense of Ester as both producer and consumer leads to the third level of illusion, which revolves around Dupree's invisibility as a black woman within Hollywood and the work she wishes to do within the industry. She tells Ester that she has become an illusion herself. Yet this scene is followed by a confrontation with the flirtatious white Lieutenant working in the studio, and her defiant decision to carry on working within Hollywood to tell untold stories. After telling Ester that she 'wanted to be where history was made, where it is re-written on film', Dupree ultimately decides to create her own history. Dash's movie offers the pleasures of music and musical performance alongside its discourse about history, and its critique of the marginalisation of black women within Hollywood. In this way, Mayne argues, *Illusions* is an essay which explores an ambivalent relationship to a mainstream, one which is 'an affirmation of black women's cinema that acknowledges, simultaneously, the limitations of Hollywood representation' (1990: 67).

In a rather different context, and some years later, the video for Janet Jackson's 'Alright', directed by Julian Temple, also revisits classic Hollywood, constructing a pastiche of 1940s'/1950s' musicals which centres on a black woman in drag. Mock movie credits announce: 'Janet Jackson in "Alright", starring Cab Calloway, Cyd Charisse, Nicholas Brothers.' Jackson is flanked by two men. All are dressed 'guys and dolls'-style in pin-striped zoot suits. Together they dominate, indeed orchestrate, the vibrancy of the street. Cab Calloway's image begins and ends the 'narrative' in which the Nicholas Brothers dance outside a club and Jackson dances briefly with Cyd Charisse who emerges from a dress shop. Calloway and the Nicholas Brothers who appeared in musicals of the 1930s and 1940s as entertainment turns, are here incorporated in quite a different way in a different medium. Several of the videos in 'Design of a Decade' involve a scenario of sharing music with friends, both a narcissistic pleasure in the star body and a debunking of the 'star'. Elsewhere Jackson performs at the head of male and female group dancers. Think of the bleak industrial setting of Jackson's 'Rhythm Nation' (shot in black and white) in which an industrial/military iconography is utilised to produce an expression of unity/community. Michele Wallace contrasts the rough reception which greeted Michael Jackson's 'Bad' with Janet Jackson 'when she announced she was in 'Control' . . . in the process utilizing many of her brother's stylistic trademarks' (1990: 79).[12] In the spoken introduction, and the performance of the song 'Control', Jackson enacts freedom from or resistance to restraint (in the video, parental/male control). In another context, Wallace argues:

> Still, Janet Jackson's energetic performance in 'Control' should be read as a cautionary tale: in our culture, control doesn't proclaim itself. Here, the sign of the black woman draws upon its own peculiar malleability: it is doubly divested of meaning, and therefore particularly well suited to enigma without content.
>
> (Wallace 1990: 147)

What for Wallace is a cautionary tale offers another instance of the ambivalence involved in such images of strength; the assertion of control implies a need to assert it that is at odds with the sexual and racial hierarchies of western culture through which power is normalised, unstated. In 'Runaway' Jackson leaps across continents and jumps from buildings, flying/dancing through space. She runs across bridges, dances on an aeroplane wing, leaps from the top of the Sydney Opera House, the Tower of Pisa, and so on. The cultural appropriation of her wearing Asian-style dress and performing Asian-style dance-steps is echoed in her gleeful (visual) world domination in which she both is and isn't in 'control'.

John Singleton's *Poetic Justice* cast Janet Jackson in a dramatic role, though she did also provide a song for the soundtrack.[13] Singleton's follow-up to his successful debut as director, *Boyz N the Hood* (1991), and Jackson's movie debut also cast rapper Tupac Shakur as the romantic interest, Lucky. Jackson plays Justice, so named because her mother was pregnant with her whilst in law school, a beautician who writes poetry (written by Maya Angelou who also has a small cameo as Aunt June). The film has something of a surreal or introspective quality to it (what Bogle calls 'some oddly perceptive and moody sequences') generated in part by the reading of Justice's poems on the soundtrack (1994: 347). A sort of road movie, it begins with the title 'Once Upon a Time in South Central LA . . .', and pans across a city skyline at night, to the sound of Gershwin's 'Rhapsody in Blue', to reveal a wealthy couple (Lori Petty and Billy Zane) drinking wine in a luxurious apartment. As they embrace, a longer shot reveals the scene as a movie projected on a vast, drive-in screen; the sound of a helicopter and of contemporary music operating to underline the arcane image, contrasting the movie world with the world where movies are consumed, one from which they are far removed. The white couple and the stylised shooting on the screen (she empties a gun into him) is played against the black couple in a car, the murder of Justice's boyfriend and her horrified response seen in brutal close-up. The camera pans slowly from above the scene to face the bright light of the projector which in turn fades into the image of a notebook and the opening credits. We are then, firmly situated within a discourse on representation, sexuality and the violence of masculinity that formed the background to *Boyz N the Hood*.[14] This is a world in which justice is arbitrary rather than poetic.

Given Singleton's use of a road movie/romance format, there is heavy irony in the location of the opening, violent scene at a drive-in movie. Justice herself becomes detached from the world, uninterested in romance. She is quiet, introspective, but also assertive, a character whose thoughts we are given access to through the poems read on the soundtrack. There is an indicative sequence of Justice at home alone, before the journey to Oakland begins, which consists of a montage of images: Justice posing, making faces in front of the mirror, playing with her hair, a look of sadness on her face. Here the techniques of music video and the iconic image of Jackson, her strength and 'attitude', are evoked and developed within a narrative context. The film follows the development of her relationship with Lucky from initial antagonism to one of affection. Lucky first tries to talk to Justice in the beauty shop where she works, only to be publicly put down. Then, when she needs a ride to Oakland for a hair show, her friend Iesha (Regina King) offers to share her lift – which turns out to be in a mailvan driven by Lucky. In familiar road movie fashion, as the four share the journey they fall out, make up, fall out, encounter various characters (including Angelou's Aunt June at a vast family picnic) and find out about themselves. At the beginning of their journey, Justice stares straight ahead, barely speaking and with shades covering her eyes. After several attempts at conversation, Lucky sings to himself, 'I want a gangsta bitch'. Justice lectures him on his attitude towards women, asserting, 'I am a Black woman – I deserve respect'. The scenario however, is about communication and about earning respect. Justice and Lucky watch with unease the turbulent relationship between Iesha and Chicago, with Lucky finally leaving Chicago behind when he becomes violent. Justice also rebukes Iesha for her drinking, which brings unhappy memories. Sitting together by the ocean, Justice begins to open up, telling Lucky (and the audience) about her past. If this seems to suggest a trajectory in which the romantic couple is constituted at the expense of friendship, violence intervenes once more. Lucky pushes her away when, arriving at Oakland he discovers his cousin has been shot. The final scene of the movie has Lucky coming into the beauty shop with his daughter, apologising to Justice, who takes the little girl over to the mirror and talks to her about her hair, looking over at Lucky with a smile. Thus there is a circular end to the road movie romance, one in which the couple come together in the space where Justice first rejected Lucky. Like *Boyz N the Hood*, *Poetic Justice* explores questions of gender, relationships and communication against a background of violence and loss. In its narrative of romance/self-discovery that centres on a strong woman, the work of representation and creativity, as a way of dealing with loss, is foregrounded both through characterisation (Lucky inherits his cousin's musical equipment which he intends to use, Justice has her poetry) and through the two stars (as performers) themselves.

Poetic Justice is rare in the work of recent African-American directors in its focus on a black woman. Commenting on the opportunities available for black women in the cinema of the 1990s, Donald Bogle uses the phrase 'actresses in search of roles', noting the irony of the fact that 'the woman Hollywood believed might become a dramatic leading actress was not an actress at all: Whitney Houston' (1994: 356). Indeed, though Houston has certainly proved herself as an actress, she is constituted more as a movie star.[15] Whilst acknowledging the strength of Houston's debut performance as Rachel Marron, a singer and actress receiving death threats, in *The Bodyguard*, Bogle reads the film as 'an ideal white male fantasy' with Costner the wise protective hero and both Rachel and her sister Nicki (Michele Lamar Richards) 'competing for a wannabe white hunk'. For Bogle the film is basically deceptive in that though the film lured 'audiences into theaters with the idea of an interracial romance, race is a subject that is never discussed in the film. Neither it nor significant cultural differences seem to exist'. *The*

Bodyguard exemplifies the successful generic hybrid, combining two quite distinct modes or genres, one based on action and one on romance. It also owes a debt to music video and, to some extent, to the musical. The movie is put together so that action, drama, musical and romance sequences are alternated and juxtaposed. While many action narratives contain romantic interest, few spend time developing them. *The Bodyguard* thus fulfils the functions of a heterosexual 'date' movie, and offers a range of experiences and pleasures similar perhaps to the old programmes and double bills in which different genres of film were played together, largely for economic reasons.[16]

The Bodyguard rehearses a scenario of oppositions in which romance develops despite the evident differences between Rachel and Frank (Costner). Her voice and beauty/glamour are foregrounded, whilst he is both taciturn and soberly dressed, deliberately nondescript. She is surrounded by friends, family and hangers-on, whilst he is solitary. Inevitably, as they become attracted to each other, Rachel is revealed to be a private person as well as a public persona (she is deeper than her image). In turn, Frank is revealed to have a family and to be capable of expressing emotion. And of course, they have in common their dedication to work. To the extent that 'race' and cultural differences are signified in the movie at all, they are mediated through music. Houston had a huge hit with a version of Dolly Parton's 'I Will Always Love You' which she sings at the end of the movie. The song is first heard (sung by John Doe) when Rachel and Frank are on a date. He takes her to a movie, *The Seven Samurai*, a film that evokes the kinds of codes of honour associated with the Western, but which also operates as a signifier of 'art' rather than popular culture. They go on to a type of country and western bar where they dance to the tune ('Your kind of place? Your kind of *music*?' she quizzes him, with mocking emphasis on the second phrase). As they dance, Rachel laughs at the 'cowboy song': 'I mean it's so depressing – have you listened to the words?'. Her version, which closes the film, is a soulful rendition of the tune. From male voice to female voice, from country music that signifies white popular culture to Marron's/Houston's rendition which draws on the performer's fame as a singer and evokes quite different traditions of black popular music. During the scenes at Frank's father's isolated home (Herb Farmer is played by Ralph Waite of *The Waltons* no less) Nicki and Rachel sing 'Jesus Loves Me'. Herb comments on hearing 'church music' on a 'weekday'. The evocation of gospel here again draws on Houston's background but also on black American musical traditions. As we've seen, Frank is perpetually framed by Rachel's image, just as the film is interspersed with her singing. His fascination is expressed through the scene in which he watches one of her videos, she watching him from above. The closing song, 'I Will Always Love You', evokes their first date whilst allowing a fudge of the romance plot: the couple's embrace suggests reunion, coded as moment of romance (the mobile camera). Yet we cut from their embrace to a close-up of Marron/Houston performing the song (we don't see the audience for whom she is performing) followed by images of a Rotary Club dinner which reveals Frank, in the background, guarding a new

client. Thus the song, as a goodbye/love song, operates as a contradictory dec-
laration of love, one which alludes to the differences the film does not make
explicit.

Survivors and self-construction

While *Poetic Justice* cast a singer in a dramatic role, *What's Love Got to Do With It*
cast a dramatic actress in the role of musical star (Angela Bassett as Tina Turner).
The film draws on and contributes to Turner's star image, which involves tropes
of transformation and survival: Turner's comeback with a rock career in her mid-
forties, her strength and independence expressed in an aggressive stance and in the
power of her delivery. In turn, Angela Bassett's association with 'strong' dramatic
roles (whether emotional, physical, or intellectual) is drawn on and extended
through her performance. A biopic based on a rise-fall-rise structure (taken from
Turner's 1986 autobiography), the movie culminates in Turner's/Bassett's breakthrough solo performance of the title song, cutting to footage of Turner herself
performing live. Here the power of musical performance feeds into the story, itself
contributing to the mythology of Turner, and providing the film with its conclusion. Actor and 'star' explicitly overlap in this final sequence, but an interaction is
evident throughout. 'I act it, I don't sing it', observes Bassett.[17] While Turner's
voice is used for the songs, and while Bassett's performance as Turner precisely
catches her stance and expression, both are inflected by the film's narrative of
strength and survival. The film offers a specific story, but also a more generalised
one to do with dependence and independence, violence and love. A particular
story – Tina Turner's – provides a frame for the themes that the film, and the performances by Bassett and Fishburne (as Ike Turner), foregrounds.

The video of Turner's composition 'Nutbush City Limits', on her *Simply the
Best* video collection, is a montage of the present-day Turner in two settings, one
recording the song (with headphones and microphone), the second of her singing
and dancing in 'empty space'. These images are cut together with footage of her
past performances from the 1960s and 1970s and images of Nutbush, Tennessee
(her home town). 'Nutbush City Limits' is the only song on the collection to be
written by Turner and, not coincidentally perhaps, is very personal: the video
encourages us to see the song as somehow *about* Turner. In the movie, the
recording of 'Nutbush' turns into a disturbing scene of violence, a violence which
is overdetermined in relation to this song which is so much about Turner. The
recording studio is located in their home so that work and domesticity are co-
terminus (marriage and the act maintain Ike and Tina). Ike insists that she is not
singing the song correctly: Tina responds, 'I can remember the words – I wrote
it'. Ike is presented as jealous of Tina's popularity with audiences, retreating at one
point into the shadows at the back of the stage. Thus the violence of their fight
over this song, that she has written, comes to signify their struggle over creativity,
popularity and her independence. In their final confrontation (Ike enters her
dressing room as she is about to go on stage) Tina is unafraid, talking of the

190

people who have come to see her perform. The movie uses the 'Nutbush City Limits' sequence as pivotal in its narrative of the star's escape from, and survival after, an abusive relationship. The incident triggers an overdose; her friend Jackie (Vanessa Bell Calloway) visits her in hospital. When she returns home she visits Jackie, who introduces her to Buddhism which she then presents (in a TV interview) in terms of choice and self-determination. And if 'Nutbush City Limits' stands in for Turner (evoking her past), the film presents her new identity, or new found strength, in terms of music: Bassett/Turner telling her new manager she is interested in the energy of rock'n'roll rather than the 'blues'.[18]

Like Tina Turner, Cher's star image operates in terms of a refusal of dependence on a man and the determination not only to forge a career (as an actor) on her own terms but to refuse the conventional role assigned to women over forty years old in an industry that fetishises youth. In turn, observes Trish Winter, this 'has often been presented as a specifically female struggle, paralleling and standing for a more generalised female struggle for independence and recognition in the world of work'.[19] Cher's performance as Mrs Flax in *Mermaids* (1990) makes use of her strong, sexually assertive image ('A real woman is *never* too old' she tells her prurient daughter Charlotte). The film's 1960s setting evokes Cher's early career as 'Sonny and Cher', whilst the narrative explores concerns of transformation and transgression in relation to all central female characters, Mrs Flax and her two daughters, Charlotte (Winona Ryder) and Kate (Christina Ricci). Charlotte acts as narrator for this rites-of-passage tale: an eccentric herself, she identifies passionately with a series of 'others'. Immersing herself in the lives of the saints, idolising nuns whilst trying to resist her sexuality, running away from home and attempting to join a suburban family in New Haven ('perfect – like television'), dressing like her mother for an assignation, and, finally, developing a passion for Greek mythology. Meanwhile, Kate is a water-baby, an excellent swimmer who nearly drowns. Charlotte's identification with Christianity is both poignant and comic: Mrs Flax, after passing Charlotte's room while she is at her devotions, returns to make the observation, 'Charlotte, we're Jewish'. 'Mrs Flax', Charlotte tells us, 'doesn't believe in ritual or tradition': Charlotte believes in a whole succession of rituals and traditions. Mrs Flax's reluctance to eat a sit-down meal is offered as a symptom of her refusal to settle for domesticity: Charlotte observes that 'fun finger-foods is her main source book and that's all the woman cooks – anything more, she says, is too big a commitment'. Whilst *Mermaids* is a rites-of-passage tale, in which Charlotte discovers sex and her mother decides to stay in one place, this does not put a stop to their eccentricity or to Charlotte's fantasy identifications. The figure of Cher as self-produced, self-generating to some extent fixes this in place; the image of Cher/Mrs Flax dressed as a mermaid (a mythical creature) for a New Year's party expresses the extent, to which she crosses categories and boundaries. The film ends with mother and daughters fixing a meal, a sequence that is, perhaps unsurprisingly, orchestrated like a musical number.

Mermaids is not the only role to draw on Cher's star image as an unconventional, sexual woman. Marjorie Garber speculates that Cher's role in *Come Back to the Five and Dime, Jimmy Dean, Jimmy Dean* (1982), in which her character reveals the 'loss of her natural breasts', might be read as 'an intertextual reference to Cher's own constructedness, or relentless self-construction?' (1992: 117). Cher's supporting role in *Silkwood* (1983) cast her as a lesbian who dates a funeral home beautician employed in a mortuary, generating a bizarre scene in which the 'butch' Dolly/Cher is made up, her face deathly white (an equation of femininity, artifice and death). An early starring role in *Mask* (1985) cast her as a rebellious, independent, single mother, Rusty Dennis. Rusty hangs out with a motorcycle gang and does drugs. Her son Rocky (Eric Stoltz) is disfigured by a rare illness: together they are located in a community of outsiders, negotiating a space for themselves. Kathleen Rowe writes of *Moonstruck* (1987) that the characterisation of Loretta as 'a "woman on top" [is] enhanced by the unruly star persona Cher brings to the part' (Karnick and Jenkins 1995: 54). A performer whose roles have extended across music, television, stage, cinema and fitness videos, Cher's image is bound up with a contradictory refusal of convention (about gender or age, for example) and a celebration of artifice and self-construction (surgery, workouts, wigs). Her early 'bohemian' fashion (as part of the 'Sonny and Cher' duo) has been displaced by her adoption of typically fetishistic clothing that conceals and reveals her star body (lace, net, straps, leather) juxtaposed with a (male) rock star regalia of blue jeans, white T-shirt and black leather jacket.

The ambivalence which surrounds Cher as self-constructed is referenced in her brief cameo in Robert Altman's *Pret-a-Porter* (1994) in which the star appears as 'Cher', one of the guests at an expensive, glamorous party. She wears black leather trousers and waistcoat cut under her breasts, with a white T-shirt that reveals a tattoo. Interviewed by the hapless Kitty Potter (Kim Basinger) whose frustration with the pretentious world of (high) 'fashion' leads her to quit her job as a television presenter near the end of the movie, 'Cher' expresses her ambivalence about the fashion and beauty industries:

> Cher: 'I actually think the whole thing behind all of this . . . is about women trying to be beautiful. None of us are going to look like Naomi Campbell. None of us are going to look like Christy Turlington; so in a way I think it's kind of sad.'
> Basinger/Potter: 'Not many of us are going to look like you either, so . . .?'
> Cher: 'Well, yeah, I don't know. I'm a victim as a well as a perpetrator of this. I think it's not about what you put on your body. I think it's more about what you are on the inside.'
> Basinger/Potter (turns to camera, speechless): 'I *mean* this is *Cher*!'

Clothed in fetishistic but rebellious garb, Cher suggests something of the film's ambivalence towards the world it portrays: fascinating, sexy and artificial. Though Cher has constructed herself, she is also modelled as 'unconventional' in a way that musical performance particularly seems to facilitate (her aggressively sexual image, her refusal of 'age') which in turn informs her movies – the parts she is given and the performance she makes within them. Cher's 'unruly star persona' is showcased in her movies, but stems from her stage act and musical performances; spaces that allow the deployment of stylised, aggressive but non-narrative images of female sexuality. The cover-notes to her *Greatest Hits* collection (1992) point out with some pride that Cher's 'If I Could Turn Back Time' (a title that Trish Winter relates to her 'ageless', surgically-produced body) was 'the first video banned by MTV'.[20] Cher looks out from the cover of her 1995 album, *It's a Man's World*, with evidently artificial blue eyes. Wearing a green satin dress and clutching an apple, the star has a snake wrapped around her. This evocation of woman as temptress suggests an ironic commentary on the title song.

Music video and stage acts including Janet Jackson, Madonna and Tina Turner feature (usually female) backers who mimic and frame the star's performance. 'Cher Live at the Mirage', her 1992 Vegas show/concert film features a male dancer dressed in one of Cher's glamorous, revealing black costumes during a number in which Cher sings 'all my life I've been dreaming of perfection'. As the 'real' Cher comes on stage, dressed in sequinned versions of ripped blue jeans and white top, to confront her impersonator, 'she' stops singing: the two then 'perform' together as the 'fake' Cher poses, is photographed and pursued by dancers with an oversized contract. Cher seems to enjoy the joke, introducing her impersonator to the audience, along with the rest of the dancers and the band, towards the end of the show. Unique and cloned, female and male: Cher repeatedly comments on her own construction, on her search for perfection and on the performance of the female body.

9

PERFORMERS AND PRODUCERS

Barbra Streisand directs Mandy Patinkin and Amy Irving in *Yentl*

The analysis of female authorship in the cinema raises somewhat different questions than does the analysis of male authorship, not only for the obvious reason that women have not had the same relationship to the institutions of cinema as men have, but also because the articulation of female authorship threatens to upset the erasure of 'women' which is central to the articulation of 'woman' in the cinema.

(Mayne 1990: 97)

Chix Nix Prix' Flix
    (Bette Midler on the success of *The First Wives Club*)[1]

Theories of authorship have played something of a strategic role in the development of film studies, facilitating an academic and a popular understanding of film as 'art': an understanding which rapidly came to be organised around the figure of the male director and his oeuvre. Subsequent explorations of genre or of narrative, along with the work of cultural studies in opening up an investigation of popular entertainment, have also enabled an address to the mainstream cinema as a meaningful form of cultural production. Such models suggested that significant patterns, structures and repetitions might be discerned across the work of individuals or production teams, across genres and modes of production. If feminist critics have re-read the performances of classical Hollywood stars, exploring in detail the nuances of gendered representation in movies of the 1930s, 1940s and 1950s, Judith Mayne notes that '[s]urprisingly little . . . attention has been paid . . . to the function and position of the woman director' (1990: 98). Mayne attributes the neglect of female authorship in part to a critical determination to avoid essentialism. Since both essentialism and auteurism suggest a problematic understanding of both cinema and identity (one that is 'untheoretical', or perhaps simply using unfashionable theories) the topic of female authorship remains an awkward one. Constructions of authorship have a tendency to focus on the director, erasing the part played by other contributors to the textual and extra-textual production of meaning (not least, the work of audiences). Romantic constructions of authorship can equally fail to attend to the conventions of genre, the work of performers or the economic and other industrial pressures on the processes of film-making. Such factors have produced a tendency to examine the popular cinema in terms of its textual contradictions, or in terms of the range of responses it generates rather than in a search for some originary point. Yet, at the same time, women are now working in the American film industry as directors and producers, as well as in the more established roles of screenwriters and performers, on a scale unprecedented within classical Hollywood. What significance might this have, and how might feminist scholarship, reluctant in any case to take the popular too seriously, make sense of the developing visibility of women in the popular American cinema?

Writing histories that chart women's relationship to the institutions of film production, like studies of the articulation of gender in the cinema, involve a work of uncovering contributions which have not been spoken about, a process of re-reading texts, and challenging given assumptions. Models of authorship centred on the male director form one such given, one which can work, in Mayne's words, to 'repress or negate the significant ways in which female signatures do appear on film' (1990: 93). She points to the work of the 'often-forgotten, often-female' screenwriters who worked on movies throughout the studio era. Lizzie Francke's *Script Girls*, a study of the work of women as screenwriters in Hollywood, maps something of that untold history whilst operating as a commentary on the different levels of input made by different film-makers in different contexts. Francke's analysis takes as its starting point the diversity of women's contributions to the film industry and to screenwriting. Her accounts of such women and their work and her interviews with contemporary screenwriters emphasise that women have not only written 'women's' roles, working in Westerns, *noir* and gangster films, as well as indicating the complex effects of gendered hierarchies and assumptions. Francke cites Hilary Henkin's surprise at critical response to her work in the action genre, how *Rolling Stone* magazine found it 'problematic' that 'a woman had written *Road House*'.[2] The problem it seems stems from an assumption, also evident in responses to Kathryn Bigelow's films, that women will work best with emotionally led material. While Henkin emphasises that she has not 'had any trouble being accepted' as a woman screenwriter, Francke also records the indicative history of Henkin's original script for *Fatal Beauty*. What started out as a female version of Dirty Harry, a character written as 'driven, obsessive, violent and sexual' was turned into a comedy, with the character given maternal motivation for her personal war against drugs (Francke 1994: 120–2). Neither 'the Hollywood establishment' nor many of the actresses looking at such roles, it is suggested, are comfortable with the excess, the violence or the outlaw personas that Henkin is interested in: a combination of factors that, as Francke underlines, have a complex relationship to the set of cultural practices, assumption and ideologies designated but only tentatively opened up by the term 'essentialism'. Henkin's assertion that '[w]omen deal with violence all the time. The notion that women can't or

shouldn't write about violence is a total fallacy' both responds to and is structured by the cultural (and cinematic) production of gender.

Thelma and Louise, framed in terms of popular feminism, gender and violence,
exemplifies the work of such extra-textual factors. The situation of a female friendship scenario within the context of violence, the mobilisation of the iconography
of the Western and the evocation of the rape-revenge narrative, all suggest the
movie's peculiar status as a text that is both unconventional *and* generic. In this
context Francke traces Callie Khouri's script through Ridley Scott's direction, his
association with surface and spectacle, his decision 'to lighten the mood' and to
turn the film into a 'Hollywood extravanganza' (1994: 132). If Francke regards
Thelma and Louise as compromised by its budget and its director, by the mass culture machine which works to iron out contradictions and complexity, she indicates
in her discussion of *The Ballad of Little Jo* how writer-director Maggie Greenwald
' is convinced that her film would have been impossible to fund without the success of *Thelma and Louise*' (1994: 139). To the extent that it was controlled by
women, Francke regards Greenwald's film as a possible 'blueprint for the future'
(ibid. 141). The suggestion of an opposition between screenwriter and director
rehearses questions of multiple (and contested) authorship, with Francke looking
to the work of writer-directors such as Greenwald as a strategy. Of course, the
figure of writer-director is more familiar in the world of independent and 'art'
cinema production. Low-budget productions often depend on individuals taking
on several roles, while both independent and 'art' cinema use the figure of the
director as a central term for marketing the finished product. After the success of
Mira Nair's first feature, *Salaam Bombay!* (1988), which she produced and
directed, she worked on a 'studio' film *Mississippi Masala* (1992) which she also
developed, produced and directed. Independent film-maker Sally Potter moved
into what we might term the semi-mainstream of the international art cinema with
Orlando (1993), an adaptation of Virginia Woolf's novel for which Potter was
both director and screenwriter. Julie Dash operated as fundraiser, co-producer,
screenwriter and director for her acclaimed feature debut *Daughters of the Dust*
(1991). Rose Troche's *Go Fish*, co-produced and co-written by Troche and
Guinevere Turner is another example of low-budget film-making that crossed over
into mainstream success, largely through canny marketing and distribution. All
these films deal directly, and very differently, with questions of culture and identity. The film-makers all took time to develop their projects, with funding from
different sources accumulated over sometimes lengthy periods of time. The figure
of the director as either 'auteur' or as marketable is central to an independent distribution and festival circuit that has showcased such disparate work.[3]

Without suggesting that all women necessarily bring something distinct to
their work, it is the case that, as Mayne argues, women have had a different relationship from men to the institutions of film production and that the terms of that
different relationship may repay exploration. Andy Medhurst's insightful interrogation of authorship and *Brief Encounter* (1945) also commences with the
screenwriter (Noel Coward), juxtaposing a theoretical rejection of authorship

(the 'death of the author') with a search for gay authorship, and for 'that special thrill' of recognition. Both impulses are evoked by the figure of Roland Barthes, whom Medhurst terms 'that most rapturously polysemic and flirtatiously comic of writers' (1991: 198). Barthes' writings explored and exposed the 'special thrills' of cultural production: the peculiar, individual but also culturally located responses generated by particular images or sounds. Medhurst argues not only that *Brief Encounter* articulates a structure of feeling distinctive to gay men as 'a text which explores the pain and grief caused by having one's desires destroyed by the pressures of social convention', adding that 'it is this set of emotions which has sustained its reputations in gay subcultures', but that Coward's contribution has been erased from a (straight) critical history of the British cinema that focuses on the director (1991: 204).

Medhurst's critical intervention is to assert the importance of reading and of interpretation, for gay readers to find the traces of existences rarely articulated explicitly in popular culture. If the two impulses (a post-structuralist dispersal of meaning and a search for authorial intent) seem contradictory, we should also note that the death of the author was also the birth of the reader, and of the critic, for Barthes. Here the 'author' comes to stand for the unitary, critically agreed upon, meaning of the text. And it is precisely this kind of rigid interpretation that feminist, lesbian, gay and black cultural critics have resisted, seeing other things within the text. Focusing, for example, on marginal characters or particular moments that seem particularly redolent. If *Boys on the Side* doesn't let its lesbian love get off the ground, it does have Whoopi Goldberg perform a number with the Indigo Girls. None of this is to impose some alternative reading as 'the' reading of a text, or to suggest that somehow there are inevitably commonalities across the work of women film-makers, for example. There is also a particularity to the work of film-makers such as Nair, Dash or Potter, differences of 'race', ethnicity and sexuality which emphasise the essentialist assumptions within feminist discourses that recent critical work has attempted to open up.

Within the popular cinema meaning is produced through the work of performers, film-makers, audiences and through the history of generic conventions and images evoked, qualified and replayed. Thus, while *Thelma and Louise* may not be the original script, it finally functions both as a showcase for strong female characters and as a commentary on the genres and images that it makes use of and which contextualise it. Amy Heckerling, whose debut was *Fast Times at Ridgemont High* (1982) and is best known for the *Look Who's Talking* series, has regularly written, directed and produced mainstream movies, often comic but driven by clearly defined characters.[4] Her 1995 'teen' movie *Clueless* operates as comedy and satire without losing affection for its wheeler-dealing heroine, Cher (Alicia Silverstone) and her best friend Dionne (Stacey Dash). The film certainly isn't a political tract, not least since popular cinema doesn't tend to operate in that way. But it is an effective showcase for comic performances, and a girls' 'rites-of-passage' tale that finds humour in an affluent teen culture which it sends up without being condescending. Its reference points, like Penelope Spheeris' earlier spoof *Wayne's World* (1992), are the television series and the saccharine rites-of-passage conventions of 1980s' teen movies, tempered by the ironic tone of a movie like *Heathers* (1989). Or consider *Clueless* against the following year's *The Craft* (1996) in which the four teenage witches (dubbed 'the bitches of Eastwick') somehow just can't get on. Fairuza Balk plays the 'trailer trash' witch who gives her stepfather a heart attack and ends up institutionalised by the really powerful blonde witch. The landmarks that a film like *Clueless* works with are broadly popular cultural (a field that includes Jane Austen's *Emma* which it was widely flagged as re-working). It emerges from an inter-textual cultural context in which new media such as television and music video, for example, have had a significant impact on production, training and creative opportunities. It may come as no surprise that Alicia Silverstone first gained exposure in Aerosmith rock videos, before gaining two MTV awards for her movie debut.[5]

If there is little value in recasting a traditional model of authorship in terms of female directors in Hollywood, there is merit in considering how women inhabit and use popular forms – as performers, as producers and as audiences. Authorship is not simply equated with the figure of the director, but with an imagery of agency that the role suggests. The relationship of women as performers to male directors understood as the source of meaning (as the organising principle), has come to signify a world of film production (classical Hollywood) organised in terms of a hierarchical, gendered system. Yet as Judith Mayne suggests, citing the example of Bette Davis, 'the role of the actress does not always conform to common feminist wisdom about the controlling male gaze located in the persona of the male director' (1990: 93). Though the work of the performer may be particularly evident in comedy and musical forms, utilising as they so often do a doubling of performance, this book emphasises how cinematic performances more generally are produced within, and against, often constrained (stereotypical) roles and narrative situations. Women working in Hollywood (as performers, as film-makers) are defined by understandings of gender that they may attempt to negotiate or refuse: the conflation of work and sexuality that is encapsulated in the phrase 'working girls'. This formulation is most often expressed, explicitly at least, in relation to the body of the performer herself. Angela Bassett observes of this equation: 'I wouldn't mind making $12 million a picture, but you have to take your clothes off to do it' (she is alluding, of course, to Demi Moore's widely reported paycheque for *Striptease*).[6] A characteristic of star power in the post-war American cinema has been the move by performers into production, setting up their own companies largely in an attempt to generate roles. Demi Moore's partnership with Suzanne Todd as Moving Pictures has led to *Mortal Thoughts* (1991) and *Now and Then* (1995), in which the star plays only a framing role for the showcase performances by Christina Ricci and others. Bette Midler, in partnership with Bonnie Bruckheimer, formed All Girl productions in 1985. The name acts as a wry aside on its function: their motto they claim is 'we hold a grudge'.[7] Citing Midler's *For the Boys* (1991) and Cher in *Mermaids*, Lizzie Francke points to the emergence of new opportunities for female screenwriters in providing emotionally driven stories 'often with female protagonists, providing central roles for the roster of underused female stars' who in turn are actively seeking those roles via their own companies (1994: 100). Performance and production are here integrated in a quite particular way, generated by an industrial organisation which both forces and allows female stars to chase roles.

Perhaps particularly acute in this context is the number of women working in the industry who have shifted between the different roles of actor/performer to that of director as well as producer, writer and so on. Lizzie Francke outlines Callie Khouri's career in terms of an initial desire to act, a lack of satisfaction with the roles available and a subsequent desire, invested in the *Thelma and Louise* script, to 'do something outside' the terms of Hollywood stereotypes. But, as we've seen, the film itself is also shaped by and comments on those types in turn. Writer/performers like Meera Syal have also made this move, writing material for themselves to appear in.[8] Penny Marshall's comedy dramas such as *Jumpin' Jack Flash* (1986), *Big* (1988) and *A League of Their Own* followed her work as a performer in situation-comedy (where she also tried directing), features and television movies. Both Theresa Russell's star persona and Sondra Locke's experience as a performer feed into the discourses on identity, desire and gender in *Impulse* (1990), Locke's second feature as a director, following the more esoteric *Ratboy* (1986).[9] Russell is often associated with ambivalent, sexual characters. Following *Impulse*, she went on to play Liz in Ken Russell's minimalist *Whore* (1991), adapted by the director and Deborah Dalton from David Hines' play *Bondage*. Here prostitution is offered as an explicit metaphor for class exploitation with an alliance between Russell's white prostitute, a white educated lesbian and 'Rasta' (Antonio Fargas), a black man who finally comes to her rescue. This stagy adaptation (much of it given over to Liz/Theresa Russell speaking directly to camera) was marketed as a 'sexy' film, but operates in quite other terms as a discourse on the 'working girl'.

In her analysis of *Near Dark* and *Blue Steel*, Anna Powell suggests that auteurism 'has a particular resonance within feminism', concluding her discussion of family horror and transgression in these two Kathryn Bigelow movies with the assertion that they form 'significant and resonant contributions to a growing body of horror fantasy made by women, as new transmutations of feminist work enable its own repressed to return' (1994: 156). Bigelow currently occupies a unique position as a woman directing not only action pictures, but the kind of sophisticated generic hybrids that regularly accrue status for male directors. As I have noted elsewhere, both Bigelow herself and the central character of her 1990 movie *Blue Steel* are repeatedly asked why they have chosen to operate in what is supposedly a male space; as the director of action movies, as a fictional cop (Tasker 1993: 160). Jim Hillier also evokes a parallel between character and director, through rather differently, suggesting that the latter's description of Megan as 'a woman in an otherwise male-dominated world fighting for a voice' might apply rather better to Bigelow herself (1992: 128). A 1997 profile, which situates Bigelow as one of 'six uncommon women who play the Hollywood game by their own rules' (i.e. difficult to classify) indicates the extent to which Bigelow is still framed in these terms:

In *Blue Steel*, *Point Break* and *Strange Days*, she revels in exploiting the popular action formula, showing viewers who've paid for a wild ride the disturbing flip side of their fascination with violence. Her decidedly unladylike work has cast her as a maverick, a reputation that perplexes the fortyish director. 'I think it's because my films are difficult to categorize,' she says, musing over the label.[10]

Recall here John Lahr's comment made of Roseanne, with her 'unladylike talk': 'her very presence was a provocation'. If Bigelow's films are 'unladylike', perhaps this is why profiles of Bigelow are invariably accompanied by portraits that parade some of the signifiers of 'femininity' (for example, her long hair).[11] It is not only that Bigelow works with supposedly 'male' genres but that she has, since the early days of *The Loveless* and *Near Dark*, made big pictures with big budgets and big stars. She is a film-maker who develops her own projects, who inflects the genres that she works with, inhabiting them in complex ways.

In his search for 'progressive work by women in mainstream cinema' Robin Wood finds Streisand's *Yentl* wanting, contrasted to movies directed by Elaine May or Joan Micklin Silver among others. Though Streisand's film was 'directed, co-produced and co-written by a woman as her own cherished project', dwells on 'an explicitly feminist theme' and is neither awkward nor 'working against the grain' it is ultimately, Wood argues, little more than 'a generally agreeable entertainment with a few wonderful moments'. For Wood, *Yentl* 'offers no challenge to anyone', its feminist themes displaced onto 'a culture so remote from our own' that it can be viewed with complacency. Neither can the film be seen as a 'breakthrough for women directors, as its existence is entirely dependent on Streisand's status as Superstar' (1986: 210). Camille Paglia also finds the film anodyne, failing to fulfil its potential. Yet she situates her discussion of Streisand in terms of the star's persona: her political commitment, her 'aggressive ethnicity', signified by her refusal to alter her nose (1994: 142). Casting Streisand as 'all man and all woman' Paglia evokes the star as a figure who crosses conventional categories, just as for Marjorie Garber it is somehow appropriate that Streisand should choose a 'transvestite vehicle' for her first film as director. If *Yentl* is remote, as Wood suggests, it is also specifiable in terms of the star: as a defiantly Jewish film, as a musical, as a transvestite tale which eroticises the intellect.

Garber emphasises the image, the significance of Streisand as director and as director of this particular film, emblem of her 'manliness'. Does producing and directing make a woman 'manly', even to the extent that she might dress as a boy? Recall the comment made of *Yentl*, cited by Ally Acker: 'The film', writes Acker, 'was unfairly recognised as "Barbra's folly" – "the hubris of a forty-year-old actress/singer/producer/writer playing an eighteen-year-old-girl playing an eighteen-year-old-boy"' (1991: 87) Years later Streisand's *The Mirror Has Two Faces* (1996) was greeted by reviewers who seethed with indignation about her 'nerve' in casting Lauren Bacall as her mother. This in a film which revolves around a passionate, intellectual woman who is insecure about her appearance.

Popular media representations construct Streisand as both manly, aggressive, a 'ball-breaker' and as 'feminine', unnaturally obsessed with her appearance. In an article titled 'On *not* being manly' Stephen Maddison emphasises Streisand's appeal in terms of a lack of fit within the world of popular culture which she so successfully inhabits: both edgy and quirky in her choice of roles, unconventional in appearance and yet committed to glamour.[12]

What Paglia and Maddison both suggest is that cultural critics can and should be interested in the constructions that surround the star persona. And the director, as overdetermined symbol of 'authority' in the cinema, is as much framed by marketing (and the work of signification) as the performer. At the risk of seeming too literal, the construction of the 'director' as fiction is part of what 'we' read. Film critics and theorists have been interested for some time in the nuances that the work of the star image and the work of particular performers can bring to the popular cinema. The framing of women as film-makers seems equally intriguing, with high profile directors like Streisand or Bigelow particularly nuanced because they are *so* visible. Contrast the relative visibility of Gale Ann Hurd as producer, but also as co-writer on the cult classic *The Terminator* (1984). Independent directors are equally aware of the importance of image which is not (only) superficial but which evokes the usurping and the questioning of authority which is involved in both women's performance and their productions. Judith Mayne suggests that *Illusions*, in its articulation of both the production and the consumption of movies, 'dramatizes Julie Dash's own relationship, as a black woman, to the film medium' (1990: 61). One might also think of Mira Nair, casting herself as a gossip in *Mississippi Masala*. Or even of Jodie Foster directing herself in a film about a (male) child prodigy, *Little Man Tate* (1991). There is a negotiation of visibility at work here, one which is also a discourse on film production and on the production of identities. As performers and producers in contemporary cinema (as in classical Hollywood), women have not effected some dramatic impact, that sudden shift or breakthrough so beloved of biographers. The 'progressive' is not to be found in the popular or the independent cinema: images and narratives are more ambivalent and more evocative than that. Cultural production involves the work of characterisation and performance, the retelling and reworking of stories, the inflection and reproduction of generic conventions, even a process of making them strange. And, like critical re-readings, these representations are inevitably both discursive and political.

Linda Fiorentino in *The Last Seduction*

NOTES

INTRODUCTION: BAD GIRLS AND WORKING GIRLS IN THE 'NEW HOLLYWOOD'

1 In 1994 Goldberg became the first woman to host the Academy Awards ceremony solo, with the 1996 ceremony her second stint. Dennis McDougal predicted the star 'could bring some unexpected twists to Oscar night' ('Whoopi takes on Hollywood' *TV Guide*, 19 March 1994).

2 The ups and downs of Tyson's film career since her dramatic debut is testament to the difficulties faced by black women as dramatic actors. She recently had success and critical acclaim in the 1995 British TV series *Band of Gold*, again playing a prostitute. Here a strong script and strong performances locate her character in relation to other women (and as a mother) rather than exclusively functioning as cypher for the male characters' concerns. Of *Mona Lisa*, perhaps significantly it was co-star Bob Hoskins who was nominated for an Academy Award.

3 Goldberg's performances are discussed further in Chapter seven. See Andrea Stuart (1993) for a summary of the criticisms levelled at the star.

4 Christine Gledhill usefully discusses the composite of prostitute and *femme fatale* in *Klute* (Kaplan 1980).

5 'Whitney Lets Down Her Guard', interview with Anthony DeCurtis in *TV Guide*, 26 February 1994 pp. 10–16.

6 A similar opposition frames male stars who can be roughly divided into those marketed primarily in terms of their physicality, and those marketed primarily in terms of their performance or acting abilities.

7 Jessica Scully, 'Gangster's moll', *Girl About Town*, 12 February 1996.

8 See Tessa Perkins (Gledhill 1990) and Richard Dyer (1979) for a discussion of Jane Fonda's star image. Dyer identifies 'acting' as a key trope in responses to Fonda from the late 1960s onwards.

9 Robin Wood's (1986) analysis of the 'incoherent text' emphasises the ideological contradictions apparent in selected movies of the 1970s. Steve Neale provides a useful summary of contemporary debates in his review article in *Screen* (1976). See also Jim Hillier (1992) and my discussion of new Hollywood in relation to ideas of the 'postmodern' (1996).

10 The groundbreaking feminist film criticism of the 1970s pointed to the deployment of stereotypes, structures of looking and narrative passivity that characterised the representation of women in classical Hollywood. Selected female stars of the period could, by contrast, and in spite of the restrictions of the time, project a strong, emancipated image – partly due to upper-class assertion (Katharine Hepburn) or to working-class determination (Stanwyck, Crawford). Studies enough have identified a process of reading against the grain through which performances by Garbo, Dietrich *et al.* can be

reappropriated. It is possible to argue that the representation of 'masculine' women or lesbian desire is no more (or less) compromised in relation to Sharon Stone or Gina Gershon than those stars of the classic period to whom feminist criticism so often appeals (Bette Davis, Katharine Hepburn, Marlene Dietrich).

Jackie Stacey provides a detailed discussion of *Desert Hearts* in relation to the conventions of romance (Wilton 1995).

11 Hillier (1992) gives several examples of younger film-makers, including Mario Van Peebles, who began their career directing in television.

12 See Jacqueline Bobo and Ellen Seiter (1991).

13 Julie D'Acci (1994) discusses the context within which *Cagney and Lacey* was generated. As discussed in Chapter four, CBS have developed a series on the bi-racial buddy format for women (*Angel Street* with Robin Givens).

14 *Buffalo Girls* does not, however, attempt to tell the story of its sole black female character who is kept to the role of servant.

15 Richard Dyer, paper given at Lesbian and Gay Studies Conference, University of London, June 1992.

1 CROSS-DRESSING, ASPIRATION AND TRANSFORMATION

1 This isn't to say that there aren't some problems with the rubric of 'queer theory' for an analysis of mainstream culture, particularly in terms of the value placed on a transgression which, almost by definition, is rarely associated with the popular. The use of 'queer' as a framework through which to *read* popular texts is, however, ably illustrated by Chris Holmlund in her analysis of *Lock-Up* and *Tango and Cash* (Cohan and Hark 1993).

2 Taken from Chapter six of Beverley Skeggs, *Becoming Respectable: Formations of Class and Gender* (London, Sage 1997). Thanks to Beverley Skeggs for the manuscript of this chapter, a version of which was presented at the AMCCS conference at Sheffield Hallam University in 1996.

3 The movie *Sleepers* (1996), for example, functions entirely in terms of the (romanticised) codes of behaviour amongst the residents of Hells Kitchen which allows the trial of two of its members to be played out as an elaborate scam, a scam facilitated by the Brad Pitt character who has worked his way into the job of Prosecutor (a sort of undercover operation in reverse).

4 These dressing-up sequences pick up on Roberts' evolving star image, alluding to her success in the title role of *Pretty Woman*. The film featured a montage sequence of Vivian/Roberts trying on different outfits and enjoying shopping, set to the title tune. *Sleeping with the Enemy*, which used 'Brown Eyed Girl' for its dressing-up montage, was Roberts' first big movie to follow on from Marshall's comedy, though she starred in two other movies released in the same year (*Hook* and *Dying Young*).

5 In this vein, Carol Clover (1992: 26–8) cites examples from *Psycho* (1960), to *Texas Chainsaw Massacre* (1974) and *The Silence of the Lambs*. Fritz Lang's *While the City Sleeps* (1956) prefigured the device with the pursuit of the 'lipstick killer', a young man styled to look like Elvis Presley (a disconcerting hybrid figure at the time) whose mother, it is revealed, wanted a girl and brought him up accordingly.

6 'That's no dame!' is a line from Billy Wilder's *Some Like it Hot* (1959) of course, a statement that follows the image of Tony Curtis in partial drag kissing Sugar Cane/Marilyn Monroe. The recognition brings with it the threat of death (from the mob) in a fashion that underlines the taboo aspects of the scenario.

7 Bell-Metereau (1985) locates a significant transformation in Hollywood representations of cross-dressing with the possibility of actors playing younger characters (rather than looking to comic effect in the guise of men dressed as older women).

8 See Ed Guererro for a discussion of what he terms the 'bi-racial buddy movie' (Diawara

1993). This sub-genre is also discussed in the final section of Chapter three on contemporary action narratives.

9   Of course, just as we see the existence of two, possibly contradictory, narrative dynamics side by side, cross-dressing is *also* (but not only) a joke in *Tootsie*.

10 This represents a reversal of the typical arguments seen in Hollywood movies over men who have put their careers first. Interestingly this places the 'wife' (Meryl Streep) in a 'masculine' position in a rather different way in *The River Wild* (it is she who has muscles and takes the kids to the great outdoors while it is the husband who is out of place in this environment).

11 It is interesting in this context to note the attention various critics have paid to masculinity as spectacle in the Western genre. Neale singles out the gunfight in Leone's Westerns in which:

> The exchange of aggressive looks marking most Western gun-duels is taken to the point of fetishistic parody through the use of extreme and repetitive close-ups. At which point the look begins to oscillate between voyeurism and fetishism as the narrative starts to freeze and the spectacle takes over.
>
> (Cohan and Hark 1993: 17)

12 Both Lesley Ann Warren and Julie Andrews were nominated for Academy Awards, as was Robert Preston in his role as Toddy.

13 Anzia Yezierska's *Bread Givers*, first published in 1925, describes the struggle of an immigrant woman to gain an education and achieve her independence. She finds herself an outsider within the family and as a college student. Here the figure of the father is more ambivalent, repressive, hated but not finally renounced. The novel ends uncertain of the future: 'It wasn't just my father, but the generations who made my father whose weight was still upon me' (1970: 297).

14 We might contrast, for example, the figuration of husband-director, star-wife in the Julie Andrews/Blake Edwards partnership, not only in *Victor Victoria* but in a series of movies involving themes of performance, showbusiness and male fantasy, including *10* (1979) and *S.O.B.* (1981).

15 Water and bridges, like railroad tracks, are frequently used to inscribe geographical differences of class and race (*Saturday Night Fever* (1977); *Pretty in Pink* (1986)).

16 Philip French, 'Marnie grows up', *Sunday Telegraph*, 2 April 1989, p. 41

17 This, together with Weaver's star image, may explain why Katherine is such an appealing character, despite her manipulations. Suzanne Moore wrote:

> My sympathies were with Katherine. She is so completely set up as a male fantasy of a ball-breaking career bitch – her viciousness in the boardroom matched only by her voraciousness in the bedroom – that it's hard not to fall in love with her.
>
> (*New Statesman and Society*, 7 April 1989 pp. 49–50)

18 There is also an evident reference to the scenario of *A Star is Born*, a tale of which Hollywood is so fond that three versions exist (Fredric March and Janet Gaynor in 1937; Judy Garland and James Mason in 1954; Barbra Streisand and Kris Kristofferson in 1976).

2 COWGIRL TALES

1 Victor Perkins (1996) discusses the film in terms of Crawford's career.

2 See Neale (Cohan and Hark 1993) for a discussion of masculinity in the Western.

3 Ford's *The Man Who Shot Liberty Valence* (1962), Lang's *The Return of Frank James* (1940) or Peckinpah's *Guns in the Afternoon/Ride the High Country* (1962) are obvious examples. Eastwood's *Unforgiven* (1992) features a writer who learns that death in the west lacks the nobility he seeks to attribute to it.

4 Andy Warhol's *Lonesome Cowboys* (1968) has fun with the homoeroticism of the Western. Jackie Stacey (1994) discusses Doris Day in *Calamity Jane*, while Paula Graham writes of the complex lesbian appeal of *Johnny Guitar* (Wilton 1995).

5 Though questions of ethnicity, gender and sexuality are central to the Western, the female gunslingers in recent Westerns are exclusively white. Native-American women are caught up in overdetermined structures of passivity, whilst the clichés of an overdetermining sexuality frame Mexican women in the genre (the stereotypes that frame *Duel in the Sun* (1946), for example). The decision not to subtitle the Chinese woman healer in *Bad Girls* seems all too typical. The contemporary Western, revisionist or otherwise, is not by definition a white woman's game however. The genre has the potential at least to tell a wider range of stories.

6 Advertising culture is quite evidently a source for independent woman imagery in *Bad Girls* – the kind associated in Britain with the Peugeot car 'Thelma and Louise' spoofs and tampon commercials which feature bright, (usually white) young women being athletic.

7 Leslie Felperin, *Sight and Sound*, July 1994: 38. As both Felperin and B Ruby Rich recount, the project lost director Davis (whose cult hit *Guncrazy* (1992) had featured Drew Barrymore) and performer Cynda Williams to become a more mainstream (and all-white) affair. Lizzie Francke cites the movie as an example of the restrictions produced by studio interference (1994: 141).

8 Sexual encounters are often constructed in terms of vulnerability, leaving a hero weak or, in the horror film, couples subject to violence. *Wild Bill* has Bill Hickock caught by Jack McCall as he and Calamity Jane (half-dressed) are having sex on a saloon table.

9 See King-Kok Cheung on Chinese-American masculinities in Hirsch, M. and Keller, E.F., *Conflicts in Feminism* (1990) London, Routledge. I also discuss this in Stecopoulous and Mebel (1997).

10 Schulze's arguments about the television movie (Balio 1990) are discussed in my introduction.

11 In turn these life stories are recycled in such movies as *The Coal Miner's Daughter* (1980) with Sissy Spacek as Loretta Lynn or *Sweet Dreams* (1985) with Jessica Lange as Patsy Cline. Speculation about the loves and lives of country and western performers runs rife: by the time k.d. lang came out as a lesbian performer, she had already been framed in terms of transgression of country codes of dress and performance. Dolly Parton is regularly quizzed about her sexuality (Parton reproduces this as one of the most asked questions at the end of her autobiography), perhaps suggesting the peculiar effect of the 'femininity' she enacts.

12 See Dolly Parton (1994: 309). k.d. lang's *Drag* puns on drag as impersonation and drag as smoking, with a collection of tunes all related to cigarettes in some way. The cover image has lang in drag, hand poised but no cigarette.

13 Victoria Starr, *k.d. lang* (1993: 138).

14 Elvis' other Western was *Love Me Tender* (1956), his feature film debut.

3 ACTION WOMEN: MUSCLES, MOTHERS AND OTHERS

1 Harry is held hostage (briefly) by Payne in a similar way at the beginning of the drama, though on that occasion Payne himself wears the dynamite. As the film progresses the audience no longer needs a visual signal that Payne is liable to explode.

2 I discuss elsewhere (1993) the ambivalent articulation of images of male strength in the context of the narrative suffering undergone by the hero and the insistent display of his body.

3 Barb Wire was originally a comic book character. This stylised articulation of action women is also evident in Brigitte Nielsen's performance in *Red Sonja* (1985) or her villainess in *Beverly Hills Cop 2* (1987) and, even less respectably, in *Chained Heat 2* (in which she plays a lesbian prison warden).

4 The video version invites viewers to keep watching to see 'Pam as you've never seen her before'. The post-credit images offer an extended reprise of the opening sequence.

5 The much touted 'girl power' associated with the Spice Girls is only one variant on this theme, evident in the snarling or expressionless faces of glamour found across fashion spreads (displacing the toothy smiles of the past). Recent No17 cosmetics ads compared lipsticks and mascara to weapons which would mow down boys and get them into shape.

6 Shot in London, the movie uses a cast of well-known, white British performers, with Charles Dance as romantic interest. Yet the black spiritual leader of the group is played by an American, Charles S. Dutton. Hollywood movies have increasingly cast British actors in villainous or troubling roles such as Brian Cox's Lecter, Alan Rickman's Sheriff of Nottingham in *Robin Hood: Prince of Thieves* (1991) or Jeremy Irons' role in *Die Hard with a Vengeance* (1995).

7 See my discussion of homoeroticism and the action film (1993) and essays by Holmlund and Fuchs (Cohan and Hark 1993).

8 Jonathan Romney (1993) takes his cue from the title of *The Last Action Hero* (a box-office failure) to pronounce the demise of the action cinema: 'The action genre is itself worn out, because it has run through all its possibilities' ('Arnold Through the Looking Glass', *Sight and Sound*, 13 (8) pp .7–9).

9 See also Susan Jeffords (Cohan and Hark 1993; Collins et al. 1993).

10 In Britain *True Lies* was cut for video release to gain a 15 certificate.

11 Anxieties expressed around the stability of the body in relation to muscularity increasingly function in relation to technology: possibly in line with the shift from a Vietnam to a Gulf veteran as the currency of ex-military heroism, a shift I discuss in this paragraph. See, for example, Denzel Washington in *Virtuosity* (1995) and in *Courage Under Fire* (1996).

12 See Robin Wood's (1986) discussion of the role of 'the woman' in relation to the male groups/couples found in *Hawks*.

13 Domesticity is similarly entwined with the comedy-action of *Undercover Blues* (1993), a film with far less money evident on screen though equipped with stars Dennis Quaid and Kathleen Turner. The film adopts the tone of the moment at the end of *True Lies* in which Helen and Harry gloat over Simon's distress whilst grinning at each other. Turner reprises the sexy toughness deployed in *V. I. Warshawski* (1991) in the role of Paretsky's heroine.

14 Though here the tomboy's transformation is not through a heterosexual encounter but bound up with the restoration of the family and a regained respect for her father.

15 Although some of the preoccupations found in this film are also evident in other Cameron directed projects, most notably *The Abyss* (1989) but also *Terminator 2*.

16 See Gina Marchetti (1993). Polanski's *Chinatown* (1974) for example, uses the space denoted by the title to suggest the inexplicable and to invoke the inevitability of the triumph of the corrupt and powerful.

17 In contrast it would be difficult to market *True Lies 2* without Schwarzenegger. While Danny Glover took over the Schwarzenegger role in *Predator 2* (1990), the sequel was quite distinct in tone and setting.

18 There is also redemption for the alcoholic Vietnam veteran who claims to have been abducted by aliens and who finally destroys the alien ship by flying into it. An opposition between the two veterans, one associated with the Gulf and one with Vietnam is in line with the shifts discussed in note 11 – the production of Vietnam veteran as abductee adds to a sense of his distance from the mainstream.

19 The first appearance of Reeves' character in *Speed* is a case in point, with the car arriving by leaping onto the screen over one of those San Francisco roads used in any number of car chase scenes, the camera spinning round the car as he and Harry get their gear out of the trunk.

20 'But what is to be gained, for the male viewer' Clover asks:

> by running it through a woman?. . . . Or, to pose the question another way, what difference between the action-film and the horror-film experience might account for the latter's preference for a victim-hero in female form? One answer has to do with horror's greater emphasis on the victim part of the story; for although male action films can indeed wallow in suffering, they also wallow in extended frenzies of sadism of a sort exceptional in horror.
>
> (1992: 18)

Put crudely, Clover opposes a masochistic genre and a sadistic genre from the point of view of the male spectator. The types identified by Clover in relation to the horror film have found a register less in action than in crime/thriller films such as *Copycat* or *The Silence of the Lambs*, discussed in Chapter four. The fantasies at play in the action narrative are more directly concerned with an enactment of empowerment, though to some extent the victim/revenge formulation can be understood as shared.

21 This kind of allusion is also evident in Karen Allen's role in *Raiders of the Lost Ark* (1981). 'Is it', Pauline Kael asks rhetorically of *Star Wars*, 'because the picture is synthesized from the mythology of serials and old comic books that it didn't occur to anybody that *she* could get the Force?' It is later revealed that she has a watered-down, girly version of 'the Force'.

22 *Striking Distance* (1993) features the 'police police' less positively, with Sarah Jessica Parker betraying Bruce Willis' river cop despite their sexual involvement. A suggestion of coldness, of distance from cop camaraderie is evoked by Internal Affairs. The situation of the lesbian character played by Laurie Metcalf as an Internal Affairs officer in *Internal Affairs* (1990) is also suggestive here.

23 Neither the fourth *Alien* film, which features Winona Ryder alongside Signourney Weaver, or the new Demi Moore/Ridley Scott collaboration *G.I. Jane*, varies this significantly. *Set It Off* casts Queen Latifah as a lesbian bank robber, one of a group of four black women who turn to crime in the 'outlaws by default' tradition. Only one of the women escapes alive.

24 Dargis suggests that while, like *Die Hard 3*, the film tries 'to have fun at the expense of his character . . . Jackson makes the humour in each film work for him' (1996: 8).

25 *Driving Miss Daisy* (1989) charts a relationship of antagonism between Jessica Tandy as Miss Daisy and Morgan Freeman as her chauffeur, Hoke Colburn. The former's high-handed affection and the latter's patient loyalty evoke a long history of hierarchical relationships. Both leads were nominated for Academy Awards: Tandy won, as did the picture itself.

4 INVESTIGATING WOMEN: WORK, CRIMINALITY AND SEXUALITY

1 There is a long-standing association between women writers and crime fiction in popular literature, and while writers such as Agatha Christie or Marjorie Allingham may have tended to write around male investigators, female investigative characters (typically amateur) are far from new. It is perhaps indicative of the relative conservatism of the film industry in this regard that movie versions of these characters have been slow to appear. See Munt (1994).

2 See D'Acci (1994) for a detailed discussion of the production of *Cagney and Lacey* and the particular set of factors informing that production. Writing at the end of the 1980s, John Fiske suggested that *Charlie's Angels*:

> Could be said to have an element of radicalism in that it showed three female detectives in roles that were normally confined to men. But the fact that they were cast and photographed to foreground their sexual attractiveness could be seen as a device of incorporation.
> (1987: 38–9)

3 Al Pacino's role as an undercover cop in *Serpico* (1973), *Cruising* (1980) and even *Sea of Love* (1989) are interesting counter examples.

4 Foster's character in *Taxi Driver* stands as yet another acclaimed female performance in the role of prostitute (one for which she was nominated for Best Supporting Actress).

5 Only the pilot of this CBS series, which commenced 15 September 1992, has so far been seen in the UK.

6 At the same time of course, generic hybrids were becoming increasingly common in the cinema. See my discussion of gendered genre (Franklin et al. 1991).

7 *Twin Peaks* also centred around the investigation of a female corpse. The second series of *Murder One* followed three separate cases, thus avoiding the pitfall.

8 Though Joyce Davenport (Veronica Hamel) can also be understood in terms of an independent working woman stereotype. Hamel is regularly cast in campaigning roles in television movies.

9 Heidi Kaye, 'The Truth is Out There/Trust No One: New Age Conspiracy Theory', paper given at Detective Fiction: Nostalgia, Progress and Doubt, University of Liverpool, November 1996

10 Scully's increasing mysticism as the show has gone on has delved into older belief systems, playing up her Catholicism, a faith which seeks to subtly underline her difference from the suits/WASPs of the FBI.

11 Banter and hostility ultimately led to sex/romance (following much speculation) in the 1980s' prime-time hit *Moonlighting*. The convention is continued in such movies as *Lethal Weapon 3* in which Russo moves from comparing scars with Gibson to flooring and bedding him. Likewise in *In the Line of Fire* we can tell Russo and Eastwood are made for each other by the developing exchange of looks and smart remarks. In the case of *The X Files*, whilst producers have insisted that the relationship won't lead anywhere, should ratings fall this assertion might have as much status as Ripley's death at the end of *Alien³*.

12 Consider the David Anspaugh TV movie *In the Company of Darkness* (1993) which stars Helen Hunt and which actually ends with her cop character in therapy crying over her father's rejection. There is a peculiar way in which the undercover scenario permits her to speak about personal experiences whilst in another (criminal) persona. Wired, she speaks to two audiences, the killer she is trying to trap and her cop colleagues who guess that her 'cover' stories of abandonment are actually true.

13 See Maria LaPlace (Gledhill 1987).

14 *Variety*, 11 April 1990.

15 Equally, while role reversal would provide Rita with some female buddies to horse around with in the fictional squadroom, such friendships are few and far between in the cinema.

16 See also Valerie Traub (Epstein and Straub 1991) for a discussion of *Black Widow*.

17 Though I've avoided using the term 'serial killer' to refer to Catherine in *Black Widow*, that is surely what she is.

18 Disguise (even gendered cross-dressing) as a means of exploring hidden territories is a repeated element of detective fiction, reaching back to Conan Doyle's Sherlock Holmes stories.

19 Janet Staiger discusses the movie in Oedipal terms as involving an articulation of two fathers for Starling in the forms of Lecter and Crawford (Collins et al. 1993)

20. The movie here draws partly on the conventions of a rape-revenge narrative with Megan taking the law into her own hands, though the excess of the subway to street shoot-out has different generic roots in horror (the monster that won't die and Curtis' own associations with the hero-victim that began with her movie debut in Carpenter's 1978 *Halloween*).

21 *Sight and Sound* May 1996, p. 52

22 *Hill Street Blues* and *LA Law* used this type, showcased on the big screen by Susan Sarandon in the film of Grisham's *The Client*, now in turn recycled as a television series. This format was also later used by Jonathan Demme in *Philadelphia* wherein the hero-ism of the lawyer in taking on the case and confronting his own prejudices about sexuality is as central as the narrative of the 'victim'/plaintiff.

5 'NEW HOLLYWOOD', NEW *FILM NOIR* AND THE *FEMME FATALE*

1 See Pam Cook (1985) for a discussion of the term. Larry Gross' (1976) brief analysis cites diverse films including *Alphaville* (1965), *Point Blank* (1967), *Performance* (1969) and *The Long Goodbye* (1973).

2 *Time*, 4 August 1981.

3 Noel Carroll also suggests that the film borrows heavily from Robert Bresson's *Pickpocket* (1959), demonstrating that its references are to the European as well as the American cinematic past. A film more regularly cited in this context (and also mentioned by Gross) is *Taxi Driver*.

4 Krutnik (1991) addresses this aspect of 1940s' *film noir* in detail.

5 Of course this random blurring of élite and popular culture is also a characteristic of the postmodern, though Carroll does not mention the term.

6 For critics such as Robin Wood (1986) or Andrew Britton (1986) the *Back to the Future* trajectory of 1980s' cinema indicates the impossibility of speaking directly about the present.

7 The framing indicates the book's concern to explore not only *noir* of the 1940s but a lauded contemporary example through the perspective that the critical act of looking back produces.

8 Sue Harper discusses British movies such as *The Wicked Lady* (1945) in this context (Gledhill 1987). See also Jackie Stacey (1994) for a discussion of Hollywood cinema and wartime audiences in Britain.

9 As discussed in this chapter, the instability of masculinity in relation to the work/sexuality nexus of contemporary *noir* also suggests such a blurring.

10 Brunsdon (1982, 1987) identifies the emergent stereotype of the independent woman. Dyer (1979: 72–98) and Perkins in Gledhill (1990) comment on Jane Fonda's star image in this context.

11 In this movie inevitably draws not only on a tradition of black action heroines, but on a complex history of representation through which, as Bogle (1994) notes, black women have frequently been constituted as nurturing.

12 This is perhaps akin to the way in which Ellen Barkin's enigmatic sexy character in *Sea of Love* works in an upmarket shoe shop. The work of these women confirms their fetishistic status.

13 See Paul Kerr (1986) on the B movie origins of *noir* and Linda Ruth Williams (1993) on the erotic thriller.

14 Madonna's much-hyped book *Sex* came out around the same time (in 1992).

15 *Daily Mirror*, 22 January 1982.

16 See Judith Williamson (1988) for a brief but productive discussion of *Fatal Attraction* and its articulation of ideologies of gender and sexuality.

17 Dyer (1979) discusses Jane Fonda's star image in terms of her Americanness, particularly as it qualified her appearance in European films. On uses of 'Chinatown' see Marchetti (1993).

18 Clover (1992) identifies a more usual process of trickling up than down, in which mainstream films borrow tried and tested formula from less reputable sectors such as straight-to-video. Of course there are limitations and specificities in all arenas of production.

19 Bedelia herself already connotes the figure of the working woman as problematic from her role as John McClane's wife and elusive object in *Die Hard* and its sequel (she is never seen in the third film).

20 The film's release coincided with that of David Mamet's *Oleanna* which also rehearsed issues revolving around sexual harassment.

21 See Pfeil (1995) and Carol Clover (Cook and Dodd 1994) for a discussion of *Falling Down* (1993) in this context.

22 See Paul Burston's analysis of *American Gigolo* (Burston and Richardson 1995). Robin Wood argues that the film not only persistently equates 'gayness with degradation' but that the construction of a black gay man (Leon) as the 'ultimate villain' is indicative of its politics (1986: 59–60).

6 FEMALE FRIENDSHIP: MELODRAMA, ROMANCE, FEMINISM

1 Daniels' monologues to her female therapist, a figure who ultimately is not there when it counts, punctuate the film.

2 As with new *film noir*, the changes associated with developing media pose some interesting questions for an examination of contemporary melodrama: how has the advent of television, with the prime-time soap and the mini-series, affected the expectations of audiences? How have shifting patterns of censorship and contemporary discourses on gender and sexuality impacted on the form? The episodic structure, glamorous settings and cross-cutting of the stories in *Waiting to Exhale* evidently owe a debt to television.

3 Just as queer/gay/homosexual road movies *The Living End* (1992), *Priscilla, Queen of the Desert* (1994) and *To Wong Foo Thanks for Everything, Julie Newmar* function in different ways to reinflect a genre that they nonetheless remain within.

4 The feminist documentary *Rosie the Riveter* (1980) is well known in this context. Feminist historians have also explored the ambivalence of women's response to the circumstances in which they found themselves. Stacey (1994) discusses the awareness of potential loss and danger that framed wartime experiences.

5 British reviews of *Steel Magnolias* on stage and screen varied in their judgement on this double pull. Most identified the ambiguity of the piece, oscillating between witty one-liners and emotional responses to tragedy. For some the comedy undermined the significance of the themes of birth, continuity and death. For others the comedy functioned as counterpoint to emotion. Broadly positive reviews described the play as 'deceptively simple, heart warming comedy' or as a 'tearjerker wedded to a joke programme' (*TES*, 17 March 1989; *Times*, 8 March 1989). By contrast Michael Billington felt the drama offered a little too much 'southern comfort'. Similar uncertainty greeted the film. Under a headline of 'Stale Magnolias', Derek Malcolm comments that the film 'fails to be anything more than a sentimental journey, substituting sympathy for depth and homespun philosophy for real thought' (*The Guardian*, 8 February 1990).

6 Eliane Meyer, 'Bridesmaid Revisited: Lesbian fairy tales and disruption of dominant practices in *Muriel's Wedding*'. Paper given at SERCIA Film Studies Conference, Amiens University, France, September 1996.

7 The limitations of the format are evident in the reproduction of stereotypes around black masculinities for example. See Ed Guerrero (Diawara 1993) and Bogle (1994).

8 *Sight and Sound*, July 1996 pp. 48–9

9 *Ghost* is also a movie where two women do get together, if only momentarily, before Swayze 'replaces' Goldberg whose body he is supposed to be inhabiting. See Z. Isiling Nataf on the possibilities of black lesbian spectatorship in the film (Burston and Richardson 1995: 69–72).

10 Richard Dyer (1993, 1997) discusses an equation between whiteness and death across a range of films. Louise Allen's analysis of *Salmonberries* (1991) suggests a racial mapping of butch/femme identities (Wilton 1995).

11 The novel has Evelyn attend a service at a black church, full of apprehension, but struck with admiration for the beauty of the black women. This episode in part works as Evelyn's encounter with and reflection on the surface liberalism/effective segregation of her life and upbringing, yet her 'new' vision of blackness is equally fantasised.

7 ACTING FUNNY: COMEDY AND AUTHORITY

1 Richard Dyer discusses a related comic articulation of male sexuality, of men represented as uncontrollably led by their desires (Metcalf and Humphries 1983).

2 The first series of *Absolutely Fabulous* was transmitted by the BBC in 1992.

3 Burke's character is a sort of proletarian achiever in the series. She appears in various guises (male and female) in the TV series *Harry Enfield and Friends*.

4 Andy Medhurst has commented on the extent to which comedy is central to British cinema and television, emphasising the particularity of national traditions and regional traditions of comedy, traditions which do not 'travel' well (paper given at Goldsmiths College, University of London, 1995).

5 Jill Marshall, unpublished dissertation, *Fat Women and Problems of Subjectivity* (University of Sunderland, 1996). See also Kathleen Rowe (1990) who discusses Roseanne's refusal of such taboos as a source of comedy.

6 John Lahr, 'Crazy all the way', *The Guardian*, 2 September 1995, pp. 26–34.

7 Ricki Lake's breakthrough role was as Divine's daughter in John Waters' *Hairspray* (1988). Robert Waldron's 1995 biography, *Ricki!* devotes a lot of space to Ricki's size and her comments on it, both in terms of self-image and her experiences in finding work as an actor.

8 Jane Walmsley, *Independent* magazine, 29 January 1994, p. 46.

9 Reggie Nadelson, 'Horrible truth about a whining megastar', *Independent*, 3 April 1990, p. 18.

10 Marshall (1996), see note 5.

11 John Lahr reports that when Roseanne made her television debut on Johnny Carson's *Tonight Show* in 1985, the 'laughs during her monologues were often longer than the jokes' (*op. cit.*: 26).

12 Syal has also appeared on Jo Brand's show and had a recurring role in *Absolutely Fabulous* as one of Patsy's fashion magazine colleagues.

13 CBS broadcast the first series in 1995.

14 Clary was still appearing as the 'Joan Collins Fan Club' at the time.

15 The show, staged and directed by Mike Nichols, opened in 1984.

16 Goldberg first attracted criticism for her part in Spielberg's *The Color Purple*. Her subsequent career has rarely cast her with other black performers, as Andrea Stuart (1993) notes. Donald Bogle describes her revived career in the 1990s in terms of 'incorporation', with her 'work in mainstream cinema' exemplifying 'both the qualified glories and the pitfalls Hollywood proffered African American stars' (1994: 328). In an interview in *The Voice*, Goldberg observed that 'If I hung around waiting for the right roles to come to me, I would never be working' (15 May 1990).

17 Susan Seidelman's other well-known films feature off-the-wall, unconventional heroines: Susan Berman in *Smithereens* (1982), Madonna in *Desperately Seeking Susan* (1985) and Ann Magnuson in *Making Mr Right* (1987). Yet *She-Devil* is atypical in its articulation of a heroine who is far from the trendy young protagonists of those earlier films.

18 *The Sun*, 11 August 1990 p. 13.
19 Joyce Wadler, *New York Times*, 21 February 1983, pp. 36–9.
20 Laura Cottingham is particularly scathing, suggesting that:

> Like Madonna and other women who utilize heterosexuality as a form of economic and social advancement, Bernhard is invested in selling her body for profit. While Madonna markets the suggestion of lesbianism, Bernhard offers some 'actual' lesbianism as a luxury commodity she can put on the market – just as courtesans since Pompeii have graphically advertised their particular sexual specialities.
>
> (1996: 24)

21 Medhurst argues that 'what passes for postmodernism is only heterosexuals catching up with camp' (see also Medhurst 1991; Dyer 1992: 135–47). Yet Medhurst also makes clear that camp is a set of strategies and, to some extent, a politics emerging from an experience of marginality. There is little edge, bitterness or politics in such 'postmodern' movies as *Pulp Fiction* (1994), with its basement leathermen, for example.

8 MUSIC, VIDEO, CINEMA: SINGERS AND MOVIE STARS

1 Kevin Sessums, 'Good Golly, Miss Dolly!', *Vanity Fair*, June 1991.
2 The *Vanity Fair* profile goes on to point out that for all the overt, excessive sexuality deployed in Parton's image, she has yet to film sex scenes, that her 'most famous box-office hits have been in female ensembles, *Nine to Five* and *Steel Magnolias*. Indeed, Dolly Parton has become the billboard for sex without being the product itself'. Larger than life, Parton's image evokes sex in the glitzy, sexless fashion shared by Hollywood and country and western, just as class is evoked in the form of her direct, down-to-earth speech.
3 I discuss this elsewhere in relation to action stars (Tasker 1993: 76). Dyer (1987) emphasises the cultural significance of star images and the possibility of complex identifications of the part of marginalised audiences.
4 See Jim Hillier (1992: 99–121).
5 *Bad Girls* like its evident reference point, *Young Guns* (1988), owes as much to music video as it does to the classic Western.
6 The dynamics between Madonna and the other performers in her show exemplify this. For example a moment in a rendition of 'Why's It So Hard', a hymn to love across boundaries, in which she cradles one of the black women dancers, her gesture simultaneously maternal and paternalistic (*The Girlie Show*, 1993). The film of her 'Blond Ambition' tour, *In Bed with Madonna*, involves her attempt to present herself as matriarch, a view both endorsed and undercut by the film itself.
7 Karen Alexander argues that in *Lady Sings the Blues* 'Ross was primarily a singer delivering a performance, and no actress. Her other films, *The Wiz* and *Mahogany*, confirm this impression' (Gledhill 1990: 52). Ross' film *Mahogany* is discussed by Richard Dyer (Brunsdon 1987). It is interesting to note that, once again, the television movie has provided a more recent success for Ross with her Emmy-nominated role in the 1994 ABC production *Out of Darkness*.
8 Queen Latifah has had supporting roles in a range of films including *House Party 2* (1991). In a *Premiere* interview she defines her choice of role against *The Preacher's Wife* and is described as 'working to get a film about the Empress of the Blues, Bessie Smith, off the ground' ('Women in Hollywood' Special Issue, 1997, p. 83).
9 Again the nomination of Angela Bassett as Tina Turner in *What's Love Got to Do With It*, and Diana Ross as Billie Holiday suggest both the acceptability of such roles and the strength of the performances.

10 Streisand is repeatedly described as talented, striking, an 'imperfect beauty' which centres on her nose as emblem of her Jewishness. The dust jacket to a recent biography of
Midler (Mair 1995) summarises thus: 'she's gone from a not-very-pretty, not-very-lucky
teenager to one of the most sought-after stars in the world today'. Camille Paglia
compares Midler 'growing up in Hawaii' and Sandra Bernhard ('an alien' whose 'creativity springs from . . . cultural conflicts') (1994: 138–9).

11 The movie also features Louis Armstrong. The strategy of using black performers in this
fashion is discussed by Bogle (1994). Karen Alexander cites Lena Horne's late-1940s'
observation that 'I am in Hollywood, but not of Hollywood because I am a Negro. I'd
like to do a good serious role in a mixed-cast movie instead of being confined to café
singer parts' (Gledhill 1990: 50).

12 Wallace suggests that negative responses to 'Bad' on the part of some critics might be
understood in terms of Jackson's challenge to ways of being and performing the 'masculine'. In terms of gender, the reading of Janet Jackson through Michael whose
'trademarks' she has used, as Wallace suggests, produces an equally ambivalent articulation of gender.

13 Jackson's 'Again' (written with James Harris and Terry Lewis) was nominated for an
Academy Award.

14 Both films feature an articulation of failed motherhood. In *Poetic Justice* Lucky removes
their daughter from her mother, calling her unfit, while Justice's mother has committed suicide. See Robyn Weigman on *Boyz N the Hood* (Cohan and Hark 1993).

15 Listing the ten best-paid actresses in Hollywood *Premiere* (1997) puts Whoopi
Goldberg and Houston at fourth and fifth place, both commanding an estimated $10
million a picture.

16 Paul Kerr discusses this in relation to providing an economic account of the *film noir*
style, a need for differentiation, citing a 1938 source on the management of movie the-
atres thus:

> Heavy drama is blended with sparkling comedy. A virile action pic-
> ture is mated with a sophisticated society play. An all-star production
> is matched with a light situation comedy of no star value. An adven-
> ture story is contrasted with a musical production.
>
> (1986: 232)

17 Martha Southgate, 'Survivor', *Premiere*, July 1993, p. 51. In the same feature Doug
Chapion, the film's producer, compares Bassett to Meryl Streep in her pursuit of acting
over stardom.

18 In an interview following the success of her 'Private Dancer' album, Turner said, 'It's
neither rock and roll nor R&B, but it's a bit of both . . . Rhythm and blues, to me, has
always been a bit of a downer . . . in the attitude – in the moan, in the plea. Rock and
roll has always been straight on. You wanna put it on to get you going'. (*Rolling Stone*,
30 April 1984, p. 33).

19 Trish Winter, unpublished dissertation, *An Exercise in Contradiction: Reading the
Aerobics Video* (University of Sunderland, 1994).

20 For Winter, Cher's construction across different fields of performance foregrounds her
physicality:

> As actress, singer and professional 'body', Cher occupies a market
> position which cuts across the film, music and entertainment
> industries. Her star-image centres very much on her body. Like
> [Jane] Fonda, her image carries competing ideologies and dis-
> courses of femininity and is built on motifs of contradiction and
> transformation.

9 PERFORMERS AND PRODUCERS

1 *Premiere*, 'Special Issue' on Women in Hollywood, 1997, p. 26.
2 *Road House* (1989) produced by action movie guru Joel Silver, stars Patrick Swayze as a philosophical bouncer.
3 Nair talks of spending 'nine months of my life doing what I consider the rape and pillage tour – which is the promotion of the film [*Salaam Bombay!*] all over the world. It's good but not very enjoyable. It's very hard work, but mainly I was wanting to do another film' (Cole and Dale 1993: 149). See also their interview with Julie Dash who discusses the process of funding for *Daughters of the Dust*.
4 *Look Who's Talking* (1989), which Heckerling wrote and directed, was a huge commercial success, followed by two sequels in 1990 and 1993 (though Heckerling acted only as co-producer for the latter).
5 Callie Khouri initially worked in music video, as a producer, though Francke quotes her as observing of the industry: 'It was a very distressing experience. It's so obvious, but in pop promos women are little other than objects' (1994: 130). Penelope Spheeris got into the industry via a rock promo company she set up in the 1970s (Cole and Dale 1993: 219).

  Francke also comments on the range of opportunities that television generated for writers, pointing out that *Cagney and Lacey* started out as a film script, but thrived on television (1994: note 4). Film-makers such as Joan Tewkesbury or Donna Deitch who have had successes with theatrical features (as writer or director) have found television (particularly cable) to be an outlet for their work (Cole and Dale 1993).
6 *Vanity Fair*, April 1996.
7 Midler also signed a development deal with Disney and while they had successes with *Beaches* and *Big Business*, Disney/Touchstone refused to back *For the Boys*, a less commercially successful venture (an 'anti-war musical'). In 1993 she spoke with some resignation of the relationship: 'I owe them [Disney] two pictures. And I'm sure they'll be glad to get them. I don't want to sound like I'm quitting – I'm not – but I am annoyed' (Claudia Dreifus, 'The "Gypsy"' in Bette', *TV Guide*, 11 December 1993).
8 Syal co-wrote her first play, 'One of Us', as a student. 'You were categorised very quickly. I wasn't picked for the good parts, she observes (*The Guardian* 6 April 1996).
9 Hillier recounts that Locke regards her understanding of actors, as a performer herself, to be a strength: 'We immediately feel a camaraderie and feel secure together, you can speak their language' (1992: 142). Locke has also subsequently directed for television.
10 *Premiere*, 1997, 'Women in Hollywood', Special Issue. The other women featured as 'uncommon' are performers Queen Latifah, Michelle Khan, Drew Barrymore, Rose McGowan and producer Christine Vachon.
11 See Judith Mayne's careful commentary on the ways in which images of Dorothy Arzner at the time she was working and as reproduced in texts of feminist film criticism and history negotiate her position as a lesbian figure in relation to discourses of gender and costume (1990; 1994).
12 If Streisand used her star power to produce *Serving in Silence*, she has been criticised for producing and starring in *The Mirror Has Two Faces* ahead of *The Normal Heart*. A *Sunday Telegraph* article (21 April 1996) revives the Streisand as 'megalomaniac' line, juxtaposing her supposed political commitment with her failure to push ahead with Kramer's play: 'Kramer sees Streisand's defection from a serious movie that could champion the cause of Aids victims to one about a woman getting a face-lift as not "very decent".' This is in turn linked back to the star's perfectionism and her concern with her appearance ('According to those working on the film, Streisand is worried about how facing up to her age and certain "gravitational forces" is afflicting her face.')

FILMOGRAPHY

Abyss, The US 1989 Dir. James Cameron
Accused, The US 1988 Dir. Jonathan Kaplan
Alien US 1979 Dir. Ridley Scott
Aliens US 1986 Dir. James Cameron
Alien³ US 1992 Dir. David Fincher
All the President's Men US 1976 Dir. Alan J. Pakula
American Gigolo US 1980 Dir. Paul Schrader
Backfield in Motion US 1991 Dir. Richard Michaels (TV movie)
Backstreet Justice 1993 Dir. Chris McIntyre
Bad Boys US 1995 Dir. Michael Bay
Bad Girls US 1994 Dir. Jonathan Kaplan
Bagdad Café US 1988 Dir. Percy Adlon
Ballad of Little Jo, The US 1993 Dir. Maggie Greenwald
Barb Wire US 1996 Dir. David Hogan
Basic Instinct US 1992 Dir. Paul Verhoeven
Beaches US 1988 Dir. Garry Marshall
Bhaji on the Beach UK 1994 Dir. Gurinder Chadha
Birdcage, The US 1996 Dir. Mike Nichols
Black Widow US 1987 Dir. Bob Rafelson
Blade Runner US 1982 Dir. Ridley Scott
Blue Steel US 1990 Dir. Kathryn Bigelow
Bodily Harm US 1995 Dir. James Lemmo
Bodyguard, The US 1992 Dir. Mick Jackson
Body Heat US 1981 Dir. Lawrence Kasdan
Body of Evidence US 1993 Dir. Uli Edel
Bound US 1996 Dir. Warchowski Brothers
Boys on the Side US 1995 Dir. Herbert Ross
Broadcast News US 1987 Dir. James L. Brooks
Broken Arrow US 1996 Dir. John Woo
Buffalo Girls US 1995 Dir. Rod Hardy (TV)
Burglar US 1987 Dir. Hugh Wilson
Cagney and Lacey US 1981 Dir. Ted Post (TV movie)

Calamity Jane US 1953 Dir. David Butler
Casino US 1995 Dir. Martin Scorsese
Chinatown US 1974 Dir. Roman Polanski
Cliffhanger France/US 1993 Dir. Renny Harlin
Clueless US 1995 Dir. Amy Heckerling
Color Purple, The US 1985 Dir. Steven Spielberg
Comes a Horseman US 1978 Dir. Alan J. Pakula
Conversation, The US 1974 Dir. Francis Ford Coppola
Copycat US 1995 Dir. Jon Amiel
Courage Under Fire US 1996 Dir. Edward Zwick
Crying Game, The UK 1992 Dir. Neil Jordan
Cut-Throat Island France/US 1995 Dir. Renny Harlin
Dallas Doll Aus/UK 1993 Dir. Ann Turner
Dead Man Walking US 1995 Dir. Tim Robbins
Demolition Man US 1993 Dir. Marco Brambilla
Devil in a Blue Dress US 1995 Dir. Carl Franklin
Disclosure US 1994 Dir. Barry Levinson
Do the Right Thing US 1989 Dir. Spike Lee
Double Indemnity US 1944 Dir. Billy Wilder
Eddie US 1996 Dir. Steve Rash
Empire Strikes Back, The US 1980 Dir. Irvin Kershner
Eraser US 1996 Dir. Chuck Russell
Executive Decision US 1996 Dir. Stuart Baird
Eye For an Eye US 1995 Dir. John Schlesinger
Fatal Attraction US 1987 Dir. Adrian Lyne
Fatal Beauty US 1987 Dir. Tom Holland
Feds US 1989 Dir. Dan Goldberg
Final Analysis US 1992 Dir. Phil Joanou
First Wives Club, The US 1996 Dir. Hugh Wilson
Fried Green Tomatoes at the Whistle Stop Café US 1991 Dir. Jon Avnet
Godfather, The US 1972 Dir. Francis Ford Coppola
Hard Evidence US 1996 Dir. Michael Paul Girard
I Spit on Your Grave US 1980 Dir. Meir Zarchi
Illusions US 1982 Dir. Julie Dash (Short film)
Impulse US 1990 Dir. Sondra Locke
In Bed with Madonna US 1991 Dir. Alek Keshishian
Indecent Proposal US 1993 Dir. Adrian Lyne
Independence Day US 1996 Dir. Roland Emmerich
In the Line of Fire US 1993 Dir. Wolfgang Peterson
Johnny Guitar US 1954 Dir. Nicholas Ray
Judicial Consent US 1994 Dir. William Bindley
Klute US 1971 Dir. Alan J. Pakula
Last Action Hero, The US 1993 Dir. John McTiernan
Last Boy Scout, The US 1991 Dir. Tony Scott

Last Seduction, The US 1993 Dir. John Dahl
League of Their Own, A US 1992 Dir. Penny Marshall
Leaving Las Vegas US 1995 Dir. Mike Figgis
Leaving Normal US 1992 Dir. Edward Zwick
Lethal Weapon 3 US 1992 Dir. Richard Donner
Long Kiss Goodnight, The US 1996 Dir. Renny Harlin
Manhunter US 1986 Dir. Michael Mann
Maverick US 1994 Dir. Richard Donner
Mermaids US 1990 Dir. Richard Benjamin
Mighty Aphrodite US 1995 Dir. Woody Allen
Mirror Has Two Faces, The US 1996 Dir. Barbra Streisand
Money Train US 1995 Dir. Joseph Ruben
Moonlight and Valentino US 1995 Dir. David Anspaugh
Mortal Thoughts US 1991 Dir. Alan Rudolph
Mrs Doubtfire US 1993 Dir. Chris Columbus
Ms 45/Angel of Vengeance US 1991 Dir. Abel Ferrara
Muriel's Wedding Aus 1994 Dir. P. J. Hogan
Mystic Pizza US 1988 Dir. Donald Petrie
Now and Then US 1995 Dir. Lesli Linka Glatter
Once Upon a Time in the West Italy/US 1968 Dir. Sergio Leone
Outbreak US 1995 Dir. Wolfgang Peterson
Philadelphia US 1993 Dir. Jonathan Demme
Poetic Justice US 1993 Dir. John Singleton
Presumed Innocent US 1990 Dir. Alan J. Pakula
Pret-a-Porter US 1994 Dir. Robert Altman
Pretty Woman US 1990 Dir. Garry Marshall
Psycho US 1960 Dir. Alfred Hitchcock
Quick and the Dead, The US 1995 Dir. Sam Raimi
Raiders of the Lost Ark, The US 1981 Dir. Steven Spielberg
Real McCoy, The US 1993 Dir. Russell Mulcahy
Regarding Henry US 1991 Dir. Mike Nichols
Return of the Jedi, The US 1983 Dir. Richard Marquand
River Wild, The US 1994 Dir. Curtis Hanson
Robin Hood: Prince of Thieves US 1991 Dir. Kevin Reynolds
Sea of Love US 1989 Dir. Harold Becker
Searchers, The US 1956 Dir. John Ford
Serving in Silence: The Margarethe Cammermeyer Story US 1994 Dir. Jeffrey A.
  Bleckner (TV movie)
She-Devil US 1989 Dir. Susan Seidelman
Showgirls US 1995 Dir. Paul Verhoeven
Silence of the Lambs, The US 1991 Dir. Jonathan Demme
Silkwood US 1983 Dir. Mike Nichols
Sister Act US 1992 Dir. Emile Ardolino
Sleeping with the Enemy US 1991 Dir. Joseph Ruben

Some Like it Hot US 1959 Dir. Billy Wilder
Speed US 1994 Dir. Jan de Bont
Star Wars US 1977 Dir. George Lucas
Strange Days US 1995 Dir. Kathryn Bigelow
Steel Magnolias US 1989 Dir. Herbert Ross
Streetfighter US 1995 Dir. Steven E. De Souza
Striptease US 1996 Dir. Andrew Bergman
Taxi Driver US 1976 Dir. Martin Scorsese
Terminator 2 US 1991 Dir. James Cameron
Thelma and Louise US 1991 Dir. Ridley Scott
Tightrope US 1984 Dir. Richard Tuggle
Tootsie US 1982 Dir. Sydney Pollack
Total Recall US 1990 Dir. Paul Verhoeven
To Wong Foo Thanks for Everything, Julie Newmar US 1995 Dir. Beeban Kidron
Trial by Jury US 1994 Dir. Heywood Gould
True Lies US 1994 Dir. James Cameron
Twister US 1996 Dir. Jan de Bont
Undercover Blues US 1993 Dir. Herbert Ross
Unforgiven US 1992 Dir. Clint Eastwood
Up Close and Personal US 1996 Dir. Jon Avnet
Victor Victoria GB 1982 Dir. Blake Edwards
Waiting to Exhale US 1995 Dir. Forest Whitaker
What's Love Got to Do With It US 1993 Dir. Brian Gibson
Wild Bill US 1995 Dir. Walter Hill
Without You I'm Nothing US 1990 Dir. John Boskovich
Working Girl US 1988 Dir. Mike Nichols
Yentl GB/US 1983 Dir. Barbra Streisand

BIBLIOGRAPHY

Acker, Ally (1991) *Reel Women: Pioneers of the Cinema*, Batsford, London.

Arroyo, José (1994) 'Cameron and the Comic', *Sight and Sound* September pp. 26–8.

Balio, Tino (ed.) (1976) *The American Film Industry*, Wisconsin University Press, Madison.

—— (ed.) (1990) H*ollywood in the Age of Television*, Unwin Hyman, London.

Barecca, Rebecca (ed.) (1992) *New Perspectives on Women and Comedy*, Gordon and Breach, Philadelphia.

Bell-Metereau, Rebecca (1985) *Hollywood Androgyny*, Columbia University Press, New York.

Bernhard, Sandra (1993) *Confessions of a Pretty Lady*, Flamingo, London.

Bobo, Jacqueline and Seiter, Ellen (1991) 'Black feminism and media criticism: *The Women of Brewster Place,*' *Screen* 32 (3) pp. 286–302.

Bogle, Donald (1994) *Toms, Coons, Mulattoes, Mammies & Bucks: An Interpretive History of Blacks in American Films* (4th edition) Continuum, New York.

Bordwell, David, Staiger, Janet and Thompson, Kristen (1985) *The Classical Hollywood Cinema*, Routledge, London.

Bristow, Joseph (1989) 'Julian Clary', *Marxism Today*, June p. 48.

Britton, Andrew (1986) 'Blissing Out: The Politics of Reaganite Entertainment', *Movie* 31–2 pp. 1–42.

Brown, Mary Ellen (1990) *Television and Women's Culture: The Politics of the Popular*, Sage, London.

Bruno, Giuliana (1995) 'Streetwalking Around Plato's Cave', in Laura Pietropaolo and Ada Testaferri (eds) *Feminisms in the Cinema*, Indiana University Press, Bloomington.

Brunsdon, Charlotte (1982) 'A Subject for the Seventies', *Screen* 23 (3–4) pp. 20–9.

—— (ed.) (1987) *Films for Women*, BFI, London.

Budge, Belinda and Hamer, Diane (eds) (1994) *The Good and the Gorgeous: Popular Culture's Romance with Lesbianism*, Pandora, London.

Burston, Paul and Richardson, Colin (eds) (1995) *A Queer Romance: Lesbians, Gay Men and Popular Culture*, Routledge, London.

Buscombe, Ed (ed.) (1988) *The BFI Companion to the Western*, BFI, London.

Carroll, Noel (1982) 'The Future of Allusion: Hollywood in the Seventies (and Beyond)', *October* pp. 51–79.

Clover, Carol (1992) *Men, Women and Chainsaws: Gender in the Modern Horror Film*, BFI, London.

Cohan, Steve and Hark, Ina Rae (1993) *Screening the Male: Exploring Masculinities in Hollywood Cinema*, Routledge, London.

Cole, Janis and Dale, Holly (1993) *Calling the Shots: Profiles of Women Filmmakers*, Quarry Press, Ontario.

Collins, Jim, Radner, Hilary and Preacher Collins, Ava (eds) (1993) *Film Theory Goes to the Movies*, Routledge, London.

Cook, Pam (ed.) (1985) *The Cinema Book*, BFI, London.

—— and Dodd, Philip (ed.) (1994) *Women and Film: A Sight and Sound Reader*, Scarlet Press, London.

Cottingham, Laura (1996) *lesbians are so chic . . . that we are not really lesbians at all*, Cassell, London.

Creed, Barbara (1987) 'From Here to Modernity: Feminism and Postmodernism', *Screen* 28 (2) pp. 47–68.

—— (1993) *The Monstrous-Feminine: Film, Feminism, Psychoanalysis*, Routledge, London.

—— (1995) 'Lesbian Bodies: Tribades, tomboys and tarts', in E. Grosz and E. Probyn (eds) *Sexy Bodies: The strange carnalities of feminism*, Routledge, London.

Curti, Lidia (1988) 'Genre and Gender', *Cultural Studies* 2(2).

D'Acci, Julie (1994) *Defining Women: Television and the Case of 'Cagney and Lacey'*, University of North Carolina Press.

Dargis, Manohla (1996) 'A Man for All Seasons', *Sight and Sound*, December pp. 7–8.

Diawara, Manthia (ed.) (1993) *Black American Cinema*, Routledge, London.

Doane, Mary Ann (1991) *Femme Fatales: Feminism, Film Theory, Psychoanalysis*, Routledge, London.

Dyer, Richard (1977) 'Entertainment and Utopia' in R. Altman (ed.) (1981) *Genre: The Musical*, RKP, London.

—— (1979) *Stars*, BFI, London.

—— (1982) 'Don't Look Now', *Screen*, 23(3/4) pp. 61–73.

—— (1987) *Heavenly Bodies: Film Stars and Society*, BFI, London.

—— (1992) *Only Entertainment*, Routledge, London.

—— (1993) *The Matter of Images: Essays on Representation*, Routledge, London.

—— (1994) 'Action!', *Sight and Sound*, October pp. 7–10.

Epstein, Julia and Straub, Kristina (eds) (1991) *Body Guards: The Cultural Politics of Gender Ambiguity*, Routledge, London.

Ferris, Lesley (ed.) (1993) *Crossing the Stage: Controversies on Cross–Dressing*, Routledge, London.

Fiske, John (1987) *Television Culture*, Methuen, London.

Flagg, Fannie (1987) *Fried Green Tomatoes at the Whistle Stop Café*, Vintage, London.

Francke, Lizzie (1994) *Script Girls: Women Screenwriting in Hollywood*, Routledge, London.

Franklin, Sarah, Lury, Celia and Stacey, Jackie (eds) (1991) *Off–centre: Feminism and Cultural Studies*, HarperCollins, London.

Friedberg, Anne (1993) *Window Shopping: Cinema and the Postmodern*, Routledge, London.

Gaines, Jane and Herzog, Charlotte (eds) (1990) *Fabrications: Costume and the Female Body*, Routledge, London.

Garber, Marjorie (1992) *Vested Interests: Cross–Dressing and Cultural Anxiety*, Routledge, London.

Gledhill, Christine (ed.) (1987) *Home is Where the Heart Is: Studies in Melodrama and the Woman's Film*, BFI, London.

—— (ed.) (1990) *Stardom: Industry of Desire*, Routledge, London.

Gross, Larry (1976) 'Film Apres Noir', *Film Comment*, July/August pp. 44–5.

Guerrero, Ed (1996) 'Devil in a Blue Dress', *Cineaste*, April pp. 38–41.

Halberstein, Judith (1991) 'Skinflick: Posthuman Gender in Jonathan Demme's *The Silence of the Lambs*', *Camera Obscura*, 27 pp. 37–52.

Hallam, Julia (1993) '*Working Girl*: A Woman's Film for the Eighties', in Sara Mills (ed.) *Gendering the Reader*, Harvester Wheatsheaf, London.

Hamilton, Mary (1996) *The Queen of Camp: Mae West, sex and popular culture*, Pandora, London.

Harling, Robert (1987) *Steel Magnolias*, Samuel French, London.

Hillier, Jim (1992) *The New Hollywood*, Studio Vista, London.

Hirsch, M. and Keller, E.F. (1990) *Conflicts in Feminism*, Routledge, London.

Holmlund, Christine (1991) 'When Is a Lesbian Not a Lesbian?: The Lesbian Continuum and the Mainstream Femme Film', *Camera Obscura*, 25/6 pp. 145–78.

Hussain, Humayun (1992) '*Bhaji on the Beach*', *Artrage*, December p. 24.

Jameson, Fredric (1984) 'Postmodernism and Consumer Society', in Hal Foster (ed.) *Postmodern Culture*, Pluto, London.

Jones, Amelia (1991) '"She Was Bad News": Male Paranoia and the Contemporary New Woman', *Camera Obscura*, 25/26 pp. 297–320.

Kamins, Toni and Lucia, Cynthia (1991) 'Should we go along for the ride? A Critical Symposium on *Thelma and Louise*', *Cineaste*, December pp. 28–36.

Kaplan, E. Ann (ed.) (1980) *Women in Film Noir*, BFI, London.

—— (1987) *Rocking Around the Clock: Music Television, Postmodernism, and Consumer Culture*, Routledge, London.

Karnick, Kristine Brunovska and Jenkins, Henry (eds) (1995) *Classical Hollywood Comedy*, Routledge/AFI, London.

Kerr, Paul (ed.) (1986) *The Hollywood Film Industry*, RKP/BFI, London.

Kirkham, Pat and Thumin, Janet (eds) (1995) *Me Jane: Masculinity, Movies and Women*, Lawrence & Wishart, London.

Krutnik, Frank (1991) *In a Lonely Street: film noir, genre, masculinity*, Routledge, London.

Kuhn, Annette (1985) *The Power of the Image: Essays on Representation and Sexuality*, Routledge, London.

Lebow, Alisa (1993) 'Lesbians Make Movies', *Cineaste*, December pp. 18–23.

Low, Gail Ching–Liang (1989) 'White Skins/Black Masks: The Pleasures and Politics of Imperialism', *New Formations*, 9 Winter pp. 83–103.

—— (1996) *White Skins/Black Masks: Representation and Colonialism*, Routledge, London.

Lury, Celia (1996) *Consumer Culture*, Polity, Oxford.

Maddison, Stephen (1992) 'On *not* being manly', *Gay Times*, November pp. 62–3.

Mair, George (1995) *Bette*, Birch Lane, New York.

Marchetti, Gina (1993) *Romance and the Yellow Peril: Race, Sex and Discursive Strategies in Hollywood Fiction*, California University Press, Berkeley.

Mayne, Judith (1990) *The Woman at the Keyhole: Feminism and Women's Cinema*, Indiana University Press, Bloomington.

—— (1993) *Cinema and Spectatorship*, Routledge, London.

—— (1994) *Directed by Dorothy Arzner*, Indiana University Press, Bloomington,

Medhurst, Andy (1990) 'Pitching Camp', *City Limits*, 10–17 May p. 19.

—— (1991) 'That special thrill: *Brief Encounter*, homosexuality and authorship', *Screen*, 32(3) pp. 197–208.

—— (1996) 'Review: *The First Wives Club*' *Sight and Sound*, December p. 46.

Metcalf, Andy and Humphries, Martin (eds) (1983) *The Sexuality of Men*, Pluto, London.

Mosley, Walter (1996) *The Walter Mosley Omnibus*, Picador, London.

Munt, Sally (1994) *Murder by the Book: Feminism and the crime novel*, Routledge, London.

Murphy, Kathleen (1991) 'Only Angels Have Wings', *Film Comment* 24(4) pp. 26–9.

Neale, Steve (1976) 'New Hollywood Cinema', *Screen*, 17(2) pp. 117–22.

—— and Krutnik, Frank (1990) *Popular Film and Television Comedy*, Routledge, London.

Noel, Pamela (1985) 'Who is Whoopi Goldberg and what is she doing on Broadway?', *Ebony*, March pp. 27–34.

Paglia, Camille (1994) *Vamps and Tramps*, Penguin, Harmondsworth.

Parton, Dolly (1994) *Dolly: My Life and Other Unfinished Business*, HarperCollins, New York.

Perkins, Victor (1996) 'Johnny Guitar', in I. Cameron and D. Pye (eds) *The Movie Book of the Western*, Studio Vista, London.

Pfeil, Fred (1995) *White Guys: Studies in Postmodern Domination and Difference*, Verso, London.

Powell, Anna (1994) 'Blood on the borders – *Near Dark* and *Blue Steel*', Screen 35(2) pp. 136–56.

Quart, Barbara Keonig (1988) *Women Directors: The Emergence of a New Cinema*, Praeger, New York.

Rich, B Ruby (1993) 'At Home on the Range', *Sight and Sound*, October pp. 19–22.

Rowe, Kathleen (1990) 'Roseanne: Unruly Woman as Domestic Goddess', *Screen*, 31(4) pp. 408–19.

Sabratnam, Shirani (1994) Interview with Meera Syal, *Artrage*, Feb/March.

Schatz, Thomas (1993) in J. Collins, H. Radner and A. Preacher Collins (eds) (1993) *Film Theory Goes to the Movies*, Routledge, London.

Schrader, Paul (1972) 'Notes on Film Noir', *Film Comment* 8 (1).

Shadoian, Jack (1979) 'Yuh Got Pecos! Doggone Belle, Yuh're as good as two men!', *Journal of Popular Culture*, 12(4) pp. 721–36.

Sobchack, Vivian (1987) *Screening Space: The American Science Fiction Film* (2nd edition), Ungar, New York.

Stacey, Jackie (1987) 'Desperately Seeking Difference', *Screen*, 28(1) pp. 48–61.

—— (1994) *Star Gazing: Hollywood cinema and female spectatorship*, Routledge, London.

Starr, Victoria (1994) *k.d. lang*, St Martin's Press, New York.

Stecopoulous, Harry and Uebel, Michael (eds) (1997) *Race and the Subject of Masculinities*, Duke University Press.

Stuart, Andrea (1993) 'Making Whoopi', *Sight and Sound* February pp. 12–13.

—— (1994) 'Blackpool Illumination', *Sight and Sound* February pp. 26–7.

Tasker, Yvonne (1993) *Spectacular Bodies: Gender, Genre and the Action Cinema*, Routledge, London.

—— (1996) 'Approaches to the New Hollywood', in James Curran, David Morley and Valerie Walkderine (eds) *Cultural Studies and Communication*, Edward Arnold, London.

Taylor, Lisa (1995) 'From psychoanalytic feminism to popular feminism', in Mark Jancovich and Joanne Hollows (eds) *Approaches to Popular Film*, Manchester University Press.

Thornham, Sue (1997) *Passionate Detachments: An Introduction to Feminist Film Theory*, Edward Arnold, London.

Waldron, Robert (1995) *Ricki!*, Warner Books, London.

Wallace, Michele (1990) *Invisibility Blues: From Pop to Theory*, Verso, London.

Weiss, Andrea (1992) *Vampires and Violets: Lesbians in the Cinema*, Jonathan Cape, London.

Williams, Linda (1988) 'Feminist Film Theory: *Mildred Pierce* and the Second World War' in E.D. Pribram (ed.) *Female Spectators*, Verso, London.

Williams, Linda Ruth (1993) 'Erotic Thrillers and Rude Women', *Sight and Sound* July pp. 12–14.

Williamson, Judith (1988) Review of *Fatal Attraction, New Statesman*, 15 January.

Wilton, Tamsin (ed.) (1995) *Immortal, Invisible: Lesbians and the moving image*, Routledge, London.

Winter, Patricia (1995) 'An Exercise in Contradiction: Reading the Aerobics Video', in *Border Tensions: Dance and Discourse*, proceedings of the Fifth Study of Dance conference, University of Surrey.

Wood, Robin (1986) *Hollywood from Vietnam to Reagan*, Columbia University Press, New York.

Yezierska, Anzia (1970) *Bread Givers*, Women's Press, London (orig. 1925).

Young, Elizabeth (1991) '*The Silence of the Lambs* and the Flaying of Feminist Theory', *Camera Obscura*, 27 pp. 5–35.

INDEX